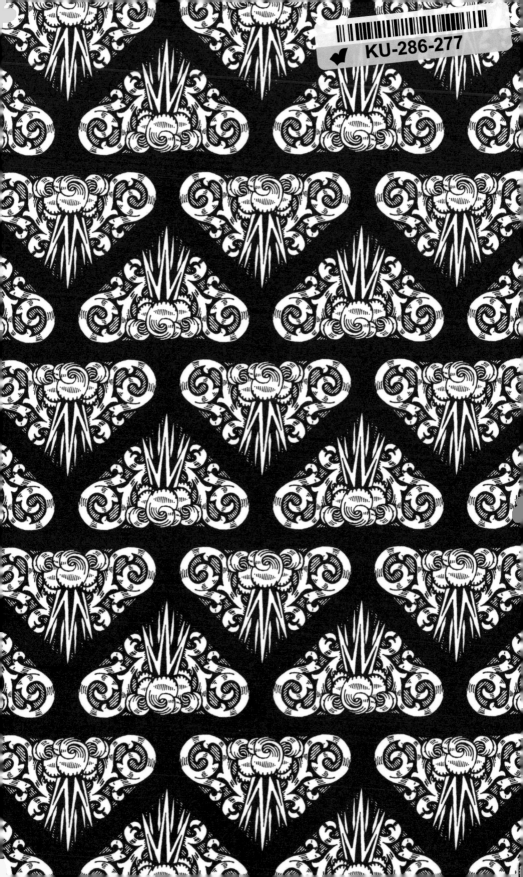

Witchcraft

Witchcraft

A History in Thirteen Trials

MARION GIBSON

**SIMON &
SCHUSTER**

London · New York · Sydney · Toronto · New Delhi

First published in Great Britain by Simon & Schuster UK Ltd, 2023

Copyright © Marion Gibson, 2023

The right of Marion Gibson to be identified as the author of this work has been
asserted in accordance with the Copyright, Designs and Patents Act, 1988.

3 5 7 9 10 8 6 4 2

Simon & Schuster UK Ltd
1st Floor
222 Gray's Inn Road
London WC1X 8HB

www.simonandschuster.co.uk
www.simonandschuster.com.au
www.simonandschuster.co.in

Simon & Schuster Australia, Sydney
Simon & Schuster India, New Delhi

The author and publishers have made all reasonable efforts to contact
copyright-holders for permission, and apologise for any omissions or errors in
the form of credits given. Corrections may be made to future printings.

A CIP catalogue record for this book is available from the British Library.

Hardback ISBN: 978-1-3985-0850-7
Trade Paperback ISBN: 978-1-3985-0851-4
eBook ISBN: 978-1-3985-0852-1

Typeset in Sabon by Palimpsest Book Production Ltd, Falkirk, Stirlingshire

Printed and Bound in the UK using 100% Renewable
Electricity at CPI Group (UK) Ltd

MIX
Paper | Supporting
responsible forestry
FSC
www.fsc.org
FSC® C171272

Contents

PART THREE: TRANSFORMATIONS

Acknowledgements

This book could not have been written without the help of many people and organisations, who generously shared their expertise, creativity and resources. Thanks to Cambridge University Library; the African Studies Library, University of Cambridge; the British Library; UK National Archives; Booth Family Centre for Special Collections, Georgetown University; Gloucestershire Archives; Bristol Archives; University of Exeter Special Collections; Essex Record Office; Suffolk Archives; Nottingham Roman Catholic Diocesan Archives; *The Antigonish Review*; Ancestry.com; FindMyPast.com; and to Liv Helene Willumsen, Peter Sanders, Malcolm Gaskill, Jamie Hampson, Anya Bergman, Mita Choudhury, Victoria Bates, Christopher S. Mackay, Jonathan Barry, Peter Elmer, Tom Killingbeck, Neil Wiffen, Scott Taylor, Annie-Rose Grant, Jennifer Skinner, Harry Bennett, Joanna Swainson, Fran Jessop, Kat Ailes, Sarah Levitt, Sally Howe, Kerri Sharp and everyone who has encouraged me on the journey.

Introduction: What is a Witch?

What is a witch? To answer that question, we have to start with another: What is magic, the force witches use? That answer depends on time and place. In early history, magic was considered to be a power innate in healers, shamans and religious leaders across multiple cultures. It allowed them to go beyond natural abilities, to change the world in inexplicable ways. Communities would have several such magical workers, combining medical and priestly roles. There was no clear line between their magical healing and harming, since good and bad magic were two aspects of the same force. On Monday a user of magic might bless you, on Thursday they might curse you – that was just how things were. If you felt a magically gifted person was using that force to do harm, you might vilify them as a 'witch' – a user of evil magic – and you might hold a local trial and mandate repentance. You might banish or kill the witch if their crimes were unacceptable. But witchcraft accusations would not spread widely, and, on the whole, you would not begin to believe all magic was evil. Some societies were concerned about this possibility – the ancient Greeks and Romans feared magic was inherently ungodly – but most retained a blurry notion that magic could be a force for good.

This changed in Europe during the medieval period, when a new theological science was established: the study of devils or demons, appropriately called 'demonology'. By the 1400s, the Christian clergymen who developed demonology had convincingly claimed a unique insight into the workings of the cosmos and God's will. Now, demonologists argued, witchcraft was not just good magic gone bad; it was envisioned as a career committed to wickedness, setting itself against the church. The imaginative world of the fifteenth to eighteenth centuries was crammed with curses and blessings, angels, devils, ghosts, spirits that could invade bodies, fairies, elves and, ruling over it all, a benevolent God. Demonologists did not perceive the Christian God's supernatural ability as part of that wider magical universe, however. Their deity's powers, and the miracle-working of his priests, were not classed as magic. Instead they were thought of as springing from religious truth, a special class of power reserved for Christian clergymen. Therefore, all the other supernatural powers swirling about in the world must be lesser, and they came to be seen as evil witchcraft.

The either/or thinking that shaped demonology developed partly because the Christian Church was splitting internally. What began as a series of arguments over church doctrine soon escalated into violence, part of a culture war called, with bland understatement, the 'Reformation'. The Reformation's disagreements forced people to choose between Catholic (traditional) and Protestant (reformed) sects. This religious conflict began with good intentions when pious Catholics challenged their church's leaders to be better Christians. The pope, cardinals and bishops were no longer humble preachers, reformers argued, but palace-dwelling oligarchs condoning the sins of rich donors. Mystics like Caterina of Siena, scholars like Jan Hus and translators like John Wycliffe began to claim alternative sources of Christian wisdom: visions from God, reinterpretations of ancient texts. Some reformers were embraced by the church, but others were cast out. In the sixteenth century hundreds of thousands left the main body of the church to form their own sect, Protestantism.

As hatred between the two sides grew, it became permissible to kill fellow Christians, now branded as demonic opponents; something that Christians had been inflicting upon Jews and Muslims for many centuries but had now turned on each other.[1] Catholics and Protestants came to regard each other as heretics: misbelievers, haters of the true church and therefore, in binary thinking, Satan's people. The punishment for heresy was to be burned alive.

In such a violently divided culture, suspicion bred suspicion; leaders of both sects soon began to investigate whether Satan had other agents within their congregations. Before the fifteenth century, most churchmen regarded the healers and diviners in their communities as ineffective fantasists – mild sinners trafficking in charms and curses who couldn't do much harm. But as Reformation either/or logic sunk in, the fear grew that these magical practitioners had an evil source of power: Satan. If the force they used wasn't obviously Christian, it must be evil. That would make them witches, and it was a short step from burning heretics to burning witches; although not identical, both were enemies of God. The magic deployed by the career witch was simply a maximally dangerous type of heresy.[2]

Who were the people accused of witchcraft? Most witches were thought to be female. Although healers and shamans could be of either sex, as magic became associated with evil, so it also moved towards association with women; Christian priests were all male. While many churchmen were good Christians, true to their gospel of love, others were obsessed with the regulation of women: their sexuality, conduct and thought. There were female saints in Catholic theology and Christ's mother, Mary, was a venerated figure – such female role models were deemed acceptable – but clergymen brooded over Eve, the first woman. Eve had lived peaceably with her husband Adam until she succumbed to Satan's temptation to eat a fruit symbolising knowledge. She fell into sin, persuaded Adam to join her and condemned their descendants to damnation unless they led repentant lives. Churchmen educated on the Eve myth – often celibate as part of their religious commitment – therefore tended to distrust women as dangerous rebels, rather like heretics. Women's

minds were clearly easily confused by demonic lies, and what was
worse, their tongues then talked men into sin, these churchmen
wrote. If a demonologist was looking for Satan's people, it was
logical he would start with women.

Just as Eve had been corrupted by Satan, so fifteenth-century
women were also seen as open to his suggestions. These were not
just mental temptations but were imagined as physical appearances
by the devil offering practical help. By the 1480s, demonologists
thought if a woman was poor, Satan could appear offering money
or goods and actually enrich her. If she resented obeying men, he
could free her. If she wanted companionship, the devil could visit
as a lover or a pet. If she wanted revenge, he could crush her
enemies. Satan might appear in human or animal form as a
'familiar', a supposedly friendly spirit. But if he offered you his
services, his fee would be your soul, your link to God and your
hope of a place in heaven. Once you accepted this pact – donating
your soul in exchange for assistance – Satan would mark you with
a blemish or growth, showing you belonged to him. And then he
would lend you the power you'd wanted, and you would become
a witch.

A witch could make her enemy's wife sick, steal his cows' milk,
harm his goods, crops or health, or kill him, demonologists
explained. And once the deal was done, the witch was damned.
She would join Satan's church, an evil-twin opposite of Christianity.
Its congregations would perform obscene rites at meetings called
'Sabbaths', a word echoing the name given to the Christian holy
day. At these meetings – to which they were sometimes thought to
fly on animals or broomsticks – witches worshipped the devil and
sought new recruits to give their souls to Satan. The devil, demonologists decided, was not just a tempter and facilitator of evil; their
new science concluded he had become the witches' god, a worker
of wonders served with murder and mayhem. Their either/or
inverted thinking – God/devil, devout/heretical, Christian/witch –
prompted mass witch trials. After all, if witches were totally evil,
enemies of God and humanity, the only possible response was to

put them on trial, convict and kill them. Hundreds of witches were tried by churches and states – executed, imprisoned or exiled as enemies of God and humanity.

Of course, that was demonological theory, rather than reality. It was impossible to prove that magic actually caused illness and death; no physical evidence of Satanic Sabbaths was found and verbal accounts of them varied widely. So if we don't believe that the people accused of witchcraft really did kill their enemies with curses or worship at a Satanic church, then how do we explain their accusation? Misogyny plays a crucial part here, underlying the accusers' fear, hatred and discrimination. Most accused witches were poorer women, some with unusual beliefs about religion or an assertive manner that worried their neighbours. Some were comparatively wealthy, but still attracted their community's dislike. Some were older women, widows living alone. But many were younger women: with or without children, some married, others not, some working, others begging. They were often women who their communities perceived had been hurt, bullied, jilted, refused charity or a job. Their neighbours sometimes heard them spitting out sharp words.

Then something happened to a person who had offended the suspected witch: their cow died, their child had visions, their ship sank. People began to think a witch had caused the harm. Perhaps in reality the accused had attempted magic. They were often individuals without much power in their societies, and the idea that a disempowered person could use magic did offer hope – which was in actuality limited by gender, economic status or differences of belief and opportunity. But sometimes there was no compelling evidence that suspects had done anything magical at all.

Either way, when the accused people were arrested and dragged to the minister or magistrate, it would not be unusual for them to confess to witchcraft, or at least admit to a belief in magic. An accused witch would have her own folk beliefs about witches and magic, often differing from her interrogators' fears. Left to herself, she was more likely to imagine performing healing charms than curses, say she had interacted with ill-defined spirits rather than devils, and invent folkloric stories about bargains with fairies or ghosts instead of formal Satanic worship. But under pressure, her story would likely come to align with her accusers' to the extent that conviction was plausible.[3]

In some jurisdictions, suspects were tortured – torture using specially designed apparatus was legal across much of Europe. A tortured person might confess anything: mass witch-meetings, devil-worship, orgies, grave-robbing, baby-killing, flying, cannibalism. The interrogators' own anxieties regarding what was evil, forbidden or taboo would influence what they asked suspects and, therefore, what was confessed. And even in jurisdictions where torture was banned, a witchcraft suspect would be intimidated by the officials who questioned her – churchmen and magistrates, lords and kings. Normally these men paid little attention to women like her, so she told them what they wanted to hear. She might be bullied, lied to, threatened. In some places sleep deprivation – not understood to be torture – was permitted.[4] Under this assault she might dredge from her memory some charms she had used – angry thoughts she'd had about trader Peter; spiteful words she'd spat at farmer Anna.

Even if she had done nothing wrong and confessed nothing under interrogation, the accused person would be sent to the court that judged suspected witches in her locality. Medieval and Reformation Europe was full of jurisdictional confusion. Where Catholicism was the official faith (broadly, across middle, southern and eastern Europe), church officials known as inquisitors often led witch trials, although bishops, parliaments, secular rulers and local magistrates also had their own jurisdictions. In Protestant areas (largely the north and west) state authorities replaced religious courts. Increasingly, as demonology moved west to America, a witch trial might be prompted by ordinary people, low-level officials or amateur investigators. In state courts, there was no inquisitor. Instead, multiple accusers would give evidence to a panel of judges or jury of citizens, who would decide the verdict. At the trial, the suspected witch might be exonerated and freed. But she might be sentenced to penance, imprisonment, exile or death by hanging or burning. It depended on the laws of her church or state whether she was shamed, banished or killed as an enemy of her people. Because that, by the late fifteenth century, was the answer to the question: 'What is a witch?' Witches were the representation of everything evil. They were the enemy.

In telling this seven-century story, *Witchcraft: A History in Thirteen Trials* shows how the demonological idea of the witch originated and grew, changed over time but did not die. Instead, it was repurposed so that witches continue to be put on trial globally. The image of the witch as the devil-aligned enemy spread across the Christian world – which is the focus of this book – from the fifteenth to the eighteenth century. In Part One, the book tells six stories of witch trials, moving from those conducted directly by high officials of church and state to others run by more autonomous citizens who had absorbed the ideas of demonologists.

All the 'witches' of Part One are women. This is because, as we've seen, a particular focus of anxiety at fifteenth- to eighteenth-century witch trials was female knowledge, with Eve as the model. Throughout history women have had little access to training in theology, law, medicine and other professions. But they have possessed expert knowledge of the female body and domestic sciences. In medieval and early modern Europe people often believed magic was essential to that knowledge. Most places had female magical practitioners – nurses, charmers, advisors, midwives – sometimes earning money from their unofficial wisdom. Some of the witches of Part One are this kind of woman.

To help a sick baby such women might chant prayers and spells, advise on feeding and care, correctly or not. To bless faulty brewing or dairying, they might throw a hot iron object into a beer vat or milk pan. They might touch a patient to transmit healing, or prescribe a herbal drink. They might sell blessing charms: seeds in a cloth bag, a dried animal's foot, a written prayer. Women who were not magical practitioners, just ordinary housewives or gentle-women, also used such prayers, tips and charms, and so did some men. But church and state authorities came to dislike these signs of power. Sometimes, not unfairly, they judged the remedies useless, but they also thought them demonic: if they didn't work naturally and were unsanctioned by the church, maybe the devil operated them. Patients and clients for whom magic had not worked well might come to agree. Because of these suspicions and the associa-tion of women with sin, female magical practitioners were often accused at witch trials.

But they were accused alongside other women, some of whom had used their services, some of whom were suspected of witch-craft for other reasons. Among the other reasons to think that women were witches were suspicions of heresy and a reputation for promiscuity. Some of the witches of Part One were seen as misbelievers, members of the 'wrong' Christian sect or actively opposed to Christian power. Some were indigenous people, who had their own religion. Other women accused of witchcraft in Part One were thought to have extramarital lovers or they had given birth to illegitimate children, both of which marked them out as transgressors against Christian morality. Their unregulated sexual activities and their lone child-bearing troubled their accusers, and were thought to be linked to special female knowl-edges about sex and fertility.

In many jurisdictions, women made up 75–90 per cent of the accused, a huge overrepresentation. Men were also tried and, in a few places, were in a majority among suspects. But overwhelmingly witchcraft was a female crime. Some historians have interpreted witch trials as a gendered persecution, sex-related if not sex-specific, but most have examined economic, social and political factors in accusations. One persuasive insight has been that poorer people were disproportionately more likely to be accused than richer people. People who stood out because of their character, beliefs, behaviour or unpopular life choices were also likely suspects. Religious and political strife bred witch trials, setting communities against each other. Once the period of European colonisation began globally in the fifteenth century, it's also clear that indigenous peoples were often selected for accusation because of their religious and racial differences from colonists. All these insights are important and are discussed in this book. But surprisingly often the preponderance of female suspects is overlooked or minimised by scholars, as if it were too obvious to mention or was secondary to another explanation.[5] This book foregrounds the fact that women of all kinds were overwhelmingly the victims of witch trials, and that misogyny still haunts global cultures. If we miss this fact, we fail to understand the persecution carried out under the name of 'witchcraft', and cannot account fully for the continuing weaponisation of the concept today.

Once the demonological idea of the witch had been created, it did not matter when the world changed and an 'Enlightenment' brought deeper interest in scientific experimentation and greater religious tolerance. By the mid-eighteenth century, the Christian world no longer needed mass trials of practising witches; it was a subtler, more nuanced place. Minds and laws began to change. Explanations of misfortune altered, often through increased understanding and knowledge of the natural world and medicine. For some people the either/or habit of mind weakened, replaced by exploring complexity: the puzzles of biology, philosophy, economics. Demonology declined and conspiracy theories grew after the French Revolution, with a new enemy in the form of secret societies: Freemasons, Jesuits, Illuminati. This extended to other marginalised groups; Jewish people were often targeted, as they had been throughout history.[6] By the late nineteenth century the supposed enemies might be spiritualists, anarchists, communists, suffragists, homosexual people, and, in the twentieth century, civil rights campaigners and anti-colonial nationalists joined the list.

These enemies were no longer called witches, and the perceived threat they posed to the established order would vary, but often, and tellingly, attacks on them were called 'witch-hunts' by opponents. Indeed, suspects were treated in ways echoing the witch trials of earlier centuries. This new type of witch trial is the focus of Part Two: post-demonological but still based on the binary thinking of demonology. Old habits die surprisingly hard, and the idea of the enemy within remained. People still demanded scapegoats and politicians still needed enemies. These metaphorical witches of Part Two carried right on being women of all kinds, poorer women and men, those who were noticeable for their religious or cultural politics, race, non-conforming sexuality or unorthodox religion. Where once they imagined a Satanic church, people now feared a new 'evil'.

However, many people, then and now, believed and believe in the literal existence of witches. Not everyone in the Christian world experienced secularisation, revolutionary changes in political structures or the belief that modern citizens should care more about society than religion. Christianity expanded globally during the colonial era of the late eighteenth to twentieth centuries, and its missionaries and worshippers took with them the demonological image of the witch, whether they meant to or not. They met believers in many other kinds of witchcraft and magic across all continents, cultures and religions, and changed them as they encountered them, often adding demonology to indigenous beliefs. There is no global consensus, therefore, that witches have ceased to exist.

Part Three of the book concludes the story of witchcraft in history by exploring the meaning of real and metaphorical witches and witch trials today across two continents, Africa and North America. In some parts of the world, even today, the practice of vigorously persecuting a neighbour who is viewed as demonic or suspected of practising witchcraft is distressingly common; exiling, imprisoning or killing them after official or unofficial witch trials that are absolutely real. Meanwhile others joyfully claim the identity 'witch' because they are followers of modern pagan religions, believing magic to be real – sometimes as an effective tool against political enemies, often as a personally empowering faith. These people can also be subject to persecution.

*

The witch in all these forms has long been the subject of fascination for historians, but often, 'witches' appears in scholarly studies merely to illustrate a theory about the selection of suspects. The circumstances and life stories of those individuals as people – just like you and me – have often been ignored. So this book aims to tell the accused witches' stories largely from their own perspective, adding newly researched information about their backgrounds and families, beliefs, hopes and fears, *their* history rather than the history of their persecutors. We'll see what happened to them in their social, political and economic context but the focus will be on what their experience felt like to them. Witch trials are intended to exercise power over others – to hurt, silence, judge and kill. If we don't feel that pain and the resentment it should spark, we can't understand the illegitimacy, the sheer wrongness, of persecution. If we don't feel it, how can we fight it? So, where I can, I get close to the accused, call them by the names they called themselves, imagine what they would have seen, heard, smelled, thought. Women's history in particular is sometimes thought irrecoverable. But this is not always the case. There are gaps in our knowledge of women's experience, largely due to the fact that court records were written by men whose society conditioned them to misogynistic beliefs and who were not much interested in the lives of those they condemned. But some of those gaps can be filled by further research or creative thinking. This is not a history of speculation; its sources, including original records and expert studies, appear in the notes. Armed with this research, the book's aim is to give back identities other than 'witch' to the accused, allowing you to discover and know them yourself.[7]

Witches continue to be the products of people's fears, the embodiment of the other, and the witch trial remains a useful mechanism for those in power. As some marginalised groups have gained more leverage over the last three centuries, the image of the witch continues to be a helpful tool for their suppression – and it is becoming more common to hear of witch trials, not less. By the end of the book, I hope you'll know how to recognise a witch and take their side against the accuser, the inquisitor, the trial judge and the witch-hunter. An understanding of the history and habits of persecution is of vital importance today, once we see that witches are still on trial.

PART ONE

Origins

CHAPTER ONE

The Trial of Helena Scheuberin:
A Demonologist Hammers Witches

In Innsbruck, Austria, stands a house with golden tiles that sparkle in the crisp Alpine sunshine. The house is on Innsbruck's main square, and its golden roof shelters a balcony looking over the market. In the 1480s the house belonged to Innsbruck's rulers: Archduke Sigismund of Austria and his wife Katharina. Sigismund was a mini-emperor, one of Europe's richest Catholic princes. From his windows, he observed stalls selling Venetian glass, silks and spices from China and Indonesia, Alpine salt and silverware, German wurst and wines. Innsbruck made its money – kreutzers and, later, the silver thalers that became the dollar – from the German and Italian trade routes that met in the city. Its citizens eagerly displayed their fortunes in fancy goods and indeed golden roof tiles. Sigismund's wealth-creating merchants lived around the market and bridge over the River Inn, the 'Inn's *brücke*' giving the city its name. Festivals, pageants and religious dramas took place there on feast days. African dancers and Polish musicians entertained crowds wolfing down strudel pastries and pale Tyrolean beer. The square also housed Innsbruck's governmental buildings, and on the morning of Saturday 29 October 1485, onlookers saw dignitaries converging on the town hall. Many were long-robed priests, wrapped in black wool against the winter chill. Clerks scurried about with books and papers. They had assembled these records for a witch trial.

Innsbruck's town hall was the heart of municipal life. Councillors met to do business, there were shops on the ground floor, and above the meeting rooms and public offices soared a huge watch-tower, 180 feet high. From the tower, guards surveyed city life and the countryside beyond the walls. They watched for fires, invaders and disturbers of the peace, whom they could arrest and hold in a prison within the town hall. In these cells, in October 1485, seven witchcraft suspects waited to be called into court. All were women: Helena Scheuberin, Barbara Selachin, Barbara Hüfeysen, Agnes Schneiderin, Barbara Pflieglin, Rosina Hochwartin and Rosina's mother, also called Barbara. They had already been questioned in the building's council hall, to which they would return for their trial, and all had been imprisoned for several weeks. Now they were to be charged with witchcraft in a trial planned by their judge, the inquisitor Heinrich Kramer. Inquisitors were the top Catholic officials who investigated heresies – beliefs contravening church teachings. By the late fifteenth century, some churchmen thought witchcraft was a heresy whose supporters worshipped the devil. Heinrich Kramer was one of these new-generation thinkers, a demonologist. He wanted a show trial to demonstrate demono-logical theory.

The story of the witch trial that gripped Innsbruck in 1485 starts with Heinrich's obsession with witches, which was part of his obsession with silencing dissent. He'd been born in about 1430 at Schlettstadt in Alsatia at a time when Reformers were attacking the Catholic Church's hierarchy in the region. Young Heinrich had the intellect necessary to provide a defence for the church; he became a monk, a big step up, since he was from a shopkeeping family, and rose fast in his profession. By 1474 Heinrich was an inquisitor, investigating all kinds of heresy, but it was witchcraft that fascinated him. In the 1480s, most churchmen still held quite traditional views of witches, thinking them ineffective dreamers, dabblers in curses and charms. But over the last half century an

influential minority, Heinrich among them, had come to believe
that witches were devil-worshippers who had given their souls to
Satan, who prayed to the devil, who killed animals and people,
and performed every evil they could imagine. Or rather, that
Heinrich could imagine.[1] As a celibate monk, Heinrich knew little
of the women he suspected. He imagined them shallow, vain creatures, seductive, untrustworthy, obsessed with sex and power. Like
the incel culture that has grown up in our digital age, some medieval churchmen sought a way to blame women for their sexuality
while simultaneously expressing their own fascination with it.
Heinrich's brooding in that subject convinced him that, since the
devil was male, witches would have sex with him as part of their
Satanic deal. Then, just like Eve, they would use their power to
deceive men. It seems astonishing that churchmen could invent and
spread such beliefs, but this new thinking, demonology, caught on
in scholarly circles.

Heinrich had perfected his personal demonological theory and
method of witch-hunting the year before, in Ravensburg, about a
hundred miles west of Innsbruck. He had arrived in the town in
1484 bearing a letter from the local overlord, which, as in Innsbruck,
was Archduke Sigismund, the man with the golden roof who ruled
much of Austria along with parts of Germany, Hungary and Italy.
Working with the town's authorities, Heinrich then interrogated
women under torture as was, unfortunately, his right as an Austrian
inquisitor. In Ravensburg, he focused on two, Anna of Mindelheim
and Agnes Baderin. Under his questioning, which planted ideas in
their terrified minds, both women confessed. They confirmed
Heinrich's theories: yes, they had killed horses, caused storms and
worshipped the devil. Anna and Agnes also confessed to having
sex with devils and even causing a man's penis to disappear. Why?
Because Heinrich hypothesised that female witches hated men and
wanted to castrate them. It was a ludicrous hypothesis, one that
could only have occurred in a male-dominated society, but bizarre
as Heinrich's particular brand of demonology was, Anna and Agnes
were burned alive because of it.[2]

In August 1485 Heinrich Kramer arrived in Innsbruck. After the Ravensburg executions, he had reported his witch-hunting success to Archduke Sigismund. As a churchman he was in theory independent of Sigismund's secular control, but for practical, political reasons, if Heinrich wanted to continue his investigations, then Sigismund would need to agree. Heinrich had also reported back to the pope, however, and was able to show Sigismund papal decrees authorising his demonological work and telling the archduke to cooperate. So, if he wanted to keep the pope's favour, Sigismund had to help. He had no desire to see heretics or witches flourishing in his archduchy, surely, and, according to Heinrich, this was the case. But although he went along with Heinrich's witch-hunt, Sigismund was irritated by the church's power. Here was an inquisitor sweeping in, telling the archduke what to do. What if Heinrich disrupted communities that were peaceably getting on, making money for their secular ruler? And so, Sigismund's support was not unconditional; he wasn't going to shelter witches under his golden roof, but nor did he want the flow of merchants' money that had funded it to dry up.

Heinrich met similar ambivalence from the Bishop of Brixen, whose diocese was part of Sigismund's archduchy. Bishop Georg Golser had been recently confirmed in post after decades of political conflict between the archduke, the pope and Georg's predecessor as bishop, who had fought constantly over control of lands, religious institutions, courts and taxes. Bishop Georg had no desire to damage relations with Sigismund, so recently repaired. He thought Heinrich a good scholar, was in awe of his letters from the pope and had no reason to be suspicious of his motives, but, acting on advice from Sigismund, he wrote to several trusted colleagues asking them to observe the inquisitor's proceedings – under the guise of assisting him, of course. Like Sigismund, Georg was right to be worried that events would get out of control. But what neither could have foreseen was the pivotal part to be played by a woman: someone with no role in church or state, no trading empire, no reputation as a theologian or politician and who was expected to sit quietly while men were talking about spiritual matters. This woman was the first to be investigated as a witch in Innsbruck and her name was Helena Scheuberin.

Helena was born and brought up in Innsbruck. Eight years before Heinrich's arrival, she'd married the merchant Sebastian Scheuber. As was conventional, her surname 'Scheuberin' was Sebastian's surname with the suffix '-in' to indicate her femininity, so we don't know her own family name. When she married in 1477, Helena was a good catch, and as well as Sebastian she had had another admirer, the archduke's cook – no humble pot-stirrer but manager of the archduke's kitchens. He couldn't win Helena and instead married a Bavarian woman. Then, in 1485, when Helena was probably in her thirties, this man and his wife walked from Sigismund's court to meet Heinrich Kramer and accuse Helena of witchcraft. The cook told Heinrich that he and Helena had been lovers before her marriage and that she 'would have been glad' to marry him. When they split up, he claimed, they had remained friends. She had married Sebastian Scheuber, and then attended her ex-boyfriend's wedding. But who really dumped whom? If Helena was so smitten by this man, why did she marry before he did? It was at his wedding that the rumours began. The cook – not named in the evidence because he was allowed to make anonymous accusations – said that at the reception Helena told his bride, 'You shall not have many good and healthy days here.'[3] Maybe she meant something innocuous by this, or perhaps she never said it at all – or maybe her remark really was hostile. Either way, the bride thought she heard a threat to bewitch her. In her evidence to Heinrich on 18 October 1485, she reported only one healthy month since her wedding seven years earlier.

Meanwhile, since her own marriage, Helena had remained attractive. According to her neighbours, she had had 'an intimate friendship' with a knight, Jörg Spiess, and he had wanted more,[4] but Helena had rejected his advances. Jörg had been devastated and died suddenly in spring 1485. On 15 October, the Spiess family responded to Heinrich's public invitation to witch-accusers – given in church during the sermon – and alleged that Helena had murdered Jörg. His brother Hans said that the day Jörg died he had eaten with Helena. He had been ill before this meal but afterwards he seemed panicky, hunched over, talking wildly about poison. 'I have eaten something I can't get over,' he said, and 'the reason why I'm dying is that that woman killed me!' Jörg sent his servant to buy a supposedly universal antidote and called a doctor whom he'd been consulting. This physician had told Jörg he should 'not approach' Helena anymore, but he hadn't listened.[5] Now, as the doctor tried to console him, Jörg fell down and died. Jörg's brother Hans told Heinrich, 'These events were known to the whole population.' Helena was a celebrity in her little city with a population of just five thousand – a pretty, rich young woman whom people liked to gossip about. And just like today's celebrities, with that gossip came criticism.

The evidence presented to Heinrich shows Helena had been suspected of witchcraft for at least seven years by this point, with the allegation she'd killed Jörg Spiess added recently. Unfortunately, Hans Spiess was well placed to spread rumours about her; like the cook who told the earlier story about Helena, and several others who informed against her, he worked at Archduke Sigismund's court. Hans was also a relative of Sigismund's mistress Anna Spiess.[6] In and out of the archduke's palaces and townhouses, Hans hobnobbed with princes and priests. He even controlled access to the archduke, and in his later evidence against another two suspects, Rosina Hochwartin and her mother, he explained that he was able to stop lobbyists bothering Sigismund. One woman had offered him a bribe of ten gold florins – several hundred dollars in modern terms – to present a petition, he said, such was his influence. Was it Hans who suggested to Sigismund that he allow an investigation of witches in Innsbruck? At least two other accusers worked in Sigismund's household and these people together may have swayed the archduke into facilitating Heinrich's visit; presumably they hoped to end the witch-craft threat by getting an expert to remove their enemies.[7]

If so, they reckoned without Helena Scheuberin. As well as being good-looking and rich, she had a strong personality and opinions. Historians often present Helena as causing trouble by confronting Heinrich in August 1485, but Helena knew that his witch-hunt was wrong and did not see why she should pretend otherwise. She seems to have been less interested in self-protection than in justice. No sooner had Heinrich arrived than Helena began to attack his witch-hunting mission, although she had not yet been accused herself. Later Heinrich wrote to the bishop, Georg Golser, that 'not only did she harass me with constant rebukes from the start (I had scarcely been in town for three days)' but 'one time when I passed her and did not acknowledge her, she spat on the ground, publicly uttering these words: "Pah – you! You lousy monk! I hope you get the falling sickness!"' It sounds as though Helena was cursing Heinrich with a reference to epilepsy: probably not a literal curse, but capable of being understood as one. 'For this reason,' Heinrich primly says to Georg, 'I had to investigate her name and life for the first time.'[8] Luckily for him, there were several people who were more than happy to accuse her of witchcraft.

Heinrich had felt secure coming to Innsbruck and was genuinely surprised by Helena's challenge. 'When I was preaching,' he continued in his letter to Georg, 'first every day for fifteen days and then on individual holy days over the course of two months, she not only didn't attend the sermons at all, but even held others back as much as she could.'[9] Helena was disgusted by the content of Heinrich's preaching. Maybe she knew his reputation before he came to Innsbruck, but if not, she quickly decided his views were dangerous nonsense. She told friends his demonology was 'heretical', adding, 'When the devil leads a monk astray, he spouts nothing but heresy. I hope the falling sickness knocks him on the head!' There are several versions of Helena's words in the witch-trial records. One account says she shouted at Heinrich, 'When will the devil take you away?!' When Heinrich questioned Helena about why she was badmouthing him, she said simply it was because he 'had preached nothing except against witches'.[10] And she was right:

the events in Ravensburg the previous year show that Heinrich had
a grotesque obsession with witchcraft and was itching to stage
another witch trial.

Imagine the fear his sermons must have caused! He rode into
town in August, nailed up his papal credentials on church doors,
and every day for two weeks spelled out his theory that murderous
witches were everywhere. He called for anyone who knew about
witchcraft in Innsbruck to come forward. For the town's women
there was no escape. As he bellowed out his sermons, Heinrich
surveyed the burghers' wives grouped in front of him. Each knew
she was being assessed: was she listening attentively, responding
when prompted? Was she dressed modestly: her linen headdress
clean, her neckline high? How much jewellery was she wearing –
enough to look like a proud Jezebel? Heinrich wanted women
– even smugly wealthy, matronly women in silks and furs – to
submit to him, attend to his words. Controlling the congregation's
daily movements to and from church by summoning them to
sermons, orchestrating their subjection under his eye, he established
his authority on witchcraft matters. Now he intended to have a
number of his congregation killed. No wonder Helena was angry.

Helena has been underestimated by history: pitied as a victim
or rebuked as a shrew. Few people have read her actual words.
When we do, we can see her bravery: she shouts insults at the
persecutor of women; she warns others away from his sermons.
She was not overreacting, nor was she ignorant of the risk – the
lives of women in her town were in danger, so she spoke up. Far
from being a witch she was an intelligent, engaged Christian. She
knew enough theology to argue with Heinrich when she was questioned in October. In one of his August sermons, Helena accused
Heinrich, saying he had spoken heretically. He had described 'the
method of striking a milk jug for finding out about a witch who
has taken milk from the cows'. Heinrich was nettled. He was
quoting this belief from evidence given to him, he fumed. An accuser
had told him someone was stealing her cows' milk by witchcraft
and that to identify the milk-thief she would hang a jug of milk

over her fire and smash it, saying she did it in the devil's name. The thief would come running, drawn by a magical connection to the milk as it hit the flames.[11] Nonsense, Helena snorted: good clergymen thought it was demonic to perform rituals in the devil's name. If Heinrich wasn't endorsing that, why mention it? Scornfully, she told him she would continue to skip his sermons. Now who was the heretic?[12]

Helena's attack on the inquisitor suggests she endorsed some reforming ideas of the 1480s. She surely knew of the Czech reformer Jan Hus. In the early 1400s, Hus founded a movement criticising a number of Catholic practices. Hussism flourished in Bohemia and Moravia (the Czech Republic), Germany, Austria and Switzerland where it influenced other groups who met secretly for Bible-study and debate. Many Hussites thought monks corrupt, arguing monastic foundations should be abolished. They criticised sexual hypocrisy in church institutions, and clergy who took multiple paid roles they didn't perform. Anti-monastic feeling might flavour Helena's words to Heinrich: 'you lousy monk'. Another translation is 'you criminal monk', strengthening her condemnation. If she did have Hussite sympathies, Helena would have been appalled by Heinrich's views on heresy and his personal morality. Accusations of bullying and corruption had soured his career; he'd been investigated in 1474 and 1475 for slandering colleagues and in 1482 for embezzlement. These scandals no doubt became known in Innsbruck.[13] Even Heinrich's official work would have offended a reformer. One of his sources of income was selling indulgences: documents granting benefits to wealthy Christians, buying them out of afterlife punishments for sins committed on earth. Hussites thought indulgences a money-making racket, condoning sin. They also disliked church violence as inherently unchristian. Burning heretics or witches offended them and Helena opposed it just as they did.

Heinrich had been investigating Hussites since the 1460s and thought Helena showed signs of reformism as well as witchcraft.[14] As he drew up her trial documents, he wrote he suspected her of 'double heresy, namely a heresy of the Faith and the Heresy of Witches'.[15] Of course, she was also female. Heinrich carefully omitted his misogyny from the trial paperwork, but afterwards, during 1486–7, he wrote a demonological book called *Malleus Maleficarum*, the 'hammer of witches'. Hammers were used to torture accused witches, driving wedges into iron boots so the victim's legs were pulped. In his weaponised book, Heinrich explained 'every evil is small compared to the evil of a woman'. Women are 'defective in all the powers of both soul and body', he noted, and an evil woman is 'more carnal than a man', 'lying in speech' and 'unwilling to be ruled'.[16] These claims echo the accusations he and others made against Helena: she was promiscuous, untrustworthy, independent. In a letter to Bishop Georg Golser, Heinrich describes her as 'deceitful, spirited and pushy'. He explains her guilt must be assumed: she must be questioned under torture and tried 'cautiously and with cleverness'.[17] Elsewhere he calls her 'a lax and promiscuous woman' and alleges that as well as Jörg Spiess and the archduke's cook she had many other lovers. They were harsh claims even for their time and place. Heinrich even stated: 'More than one hundred men would have made depositions against the persons under detention, particularly Scheuberin, but they were kept back . . . because of the fear of the names of the deponents being made public.'[18] He believed these men had been silenced by Helena; having seduced them she now threatened exposure and bewitchment.

As well as Helena, other Innsbruck women who made their own decisions about sex and religion caught Heinrich's attention. Two were from the Judaic community of bankers and foreign traders' agents, although both had converted to Christianity. Such conversions, whether real or forced, helped Jews minimise the persecution they suffered. Jews were massacred in the 1420s across Austria, and the survivors deported before being allowed to return fifty years later. They were banned from many professions and regarded as outcasts unless they converted. Yet despite her conversion Ennel Notterin was accused of performing a heretical

magical rite, whipping an image of Christ while chanting blasphemies – a classic anti-Semitic slander. The other Jewish woman, Elsa
Böhmennin, supposedly bewitched her own sister out of jealousy.
An undercurrent of anti-Semitism runs through several of the other
Innsbruck accusations: one alleges a suspected witch sent her servant
to the Jewish quarter to gather excrement as a magical ingredient. As
well as from the Jewish quarter, the accused women came from all
over Innsbruck and – as the witch-hunt sucked in suspects beyond
the original seven – from surrounding villages.

Some, like Elsa Heiligkrutzin, a priest's sister, belonged to pious
families. Some, like Rosina Hochwartin, were connected to the
archduke: Rosina's husband had been Sigismund's gun-maker until
the archduke fired him. Barbara Hüfeysen, a friend of Helena's,
was named for practising magical medicine but her patient, Barbara
Pflieglin, was also accused for commissioning the cure. Such remedies – prayers, amulets – were common. They were the magic
ordinary people did, and, before demonology was invented, they
were usually seen as harmless. But as well as healing, Barbara
Hüfeysen's magic was thought deadly. She fasted for three Sundays,
a practice thought to kill an enemy, and instructed young women
'how demons are to be invoked for love or the infliction of illnesses',
it was said. Some women were accused of promiscuity combined
with magic: Agnes Schneiderin had supposedly cursed her lover.[19]
Accusers were male and female, housemaids and courtiers, which
was normal: anyone who was ill, bereaved or faced financial loss
might believe it was caused by magic. Barbara Pflieglin and Rosina
Hochwartin were charged by their servants, others by rivals in
business or love. Two of the wider group of accused were midwives,
one a nurse; such women were common targets because of the
power they held. Several female accusers described how during
sickness or childbirth they found hidden in their homes charms
made of cloth, seeds and stones. These might have been placed
there by magical healers. But in the context of a witch-hunt, they
were interpreted as signs of attack.

Other accusations were more bizarre: Rosina Hochwartin had

supposedly smeared a shirt with magical paste to cause illness in its wearer, boiled the head of a dead man and used a dead mouse as a charm to get the archduke to favour her. Barbara Pflieglin had caused diarrhoea by holding a reed in the current of the River Inn. The grotesque and disgusting ingredients and outcomes of magical rites suggest that Innsbruckers saw witches as dirty pests, polluting their community. Helena Scheuberin was regarded by Heinrich and others as leading this swarm of witches. Her accusers suggested that Jörg Spiess's obsession with her was because of a love spell, and Jörg's sister thought that instead of using poison to kill him, Helena had used a piece of child's flesh. This accusation links her to the other women accused alongside her, some of whom were thought to use dead babies' bones in charms. Witches were often seen as unwomanly women: child-haters, anti-mothers, anti-housewives. It was an inversion of the knowledge that underpinned women's traditional professions of childminding, nursing, midwifery and the giving of domestic advice – instead of helping, people came to suspect these women had murdered babies and children. Instead of cooking wholesome food they brewed poison or boiled human flesh for magical potions – an idea echoed in local mid-European folktales like *Hansel and Gretel*.[20]

By the time Heinrich had finished his investigation, sixty-three people had been accused, although only the original seven were formally charged, having been dragged from their homes and imprisoned. Sixty-one of the accused were women, with two men. One was the husband of an accused woman. The other was an unnamed potter, accused of performing magic to discover who had bewitched a woman named Gertrud Rötin. He told Gertrud to dig under the threshold of her house. There she found a wax figure of herself stuck through with pins, pieces of cloth and ashes, wood from a gallows, thread from an altar cloth and bones – supposedly of unbaptised children. Gertrud said the potter had known they were there because he was the lover of Barbara Selachin, who had put them there.[21] The potter was a healer and diviner, and found himself accused because his supposedly good magic was reinterpreted as bad, something that happened often during a witch-hunt. But he was also suspected because he was linked to an accused woman. It's an inescapable conclusion that Heinrich Kramer was looking almost exclusively for female witches, more fanatically so than other inquisitors of his time. Only women were eventually charged.

When they were questioned by the inquisitor in private preliminary hearings, all seven denied they were witches. At this stage, no one was tortured, but now they would be tried to determine whether there was a case to answer and whether torture was necessary to discover the 'truth'. So, on Saturday 29 October, Heinrich and his clerks processed across the marketplace to Innsbruck's town hall to hold their witch trial under the eye of the bishop's and archduke's officials. It was a church court, authorised by the pope but organised by the local bishop and overshadowed by Archduke Sigismund's power. Heinrich would be the judge, although he was an accuser of at least one of the women, Helena, and had already made his belief in her guilt clear. But this was how the Inquisition had run its courts since its twelfth-century beginnings: accusations, investigations and judgment were given by the same people. Nevertheless, Heinrich's conduct seems particularly tainted with unfairness. He used regular Inquisition procedure to stage a test case for his new demonological theory. He allowed personal dislike and misogyny to influence his choice of suspects. He pushed for torture. And he made his primary target obvious in his schedule for the trial's first day: Helena Scheuberin was the first to be called into court.

By nine o'clock the dignitaries had settled in the council hall, scraping chairs and shuffling papers, hitching up their furs against the chill. As well as Heinrich, attendees included Christian Turner, an observer representing Bishop Georg Golser. Other observers were Sigismund Sämer, parish priest of nearby Axams, and Dr Paul Wann, a churchman from Passau and another friend of the bishop's. Bishop Georg was ill and unable to attend, but he had ensured he had eyes on Heinrich. A city notary took minutes, and behind them all was the archduke's authority. Although he was not present, the court was yards from his golden-roofed house and the trial only went ahead with his approval. Heinrich told the usher to summon Helena from the cells under the town hall where she had been since early October. Their first exchanges were spiky. Helena quibbled about taking an oath, binding her to speak honestly, which might be further indication of her reformist leanings since some reformers rejected oath-taking involving holy objects. Eventually 'after many words were put to her by the Inquisitor', the minute-taker sums up: 'She finally swore by the four gospels of God to tell the truth.' She would now be questioned and then, if the court agreed it necessary, she would be tortured. At that point she would probably confess and be condemned to death.

First, she had to respond to Heinrich's questions.[22] These started innocuously: 'Tell me where you were born and brought up.' 'In Innsbruck,' said Helena, minimally. 'You are a married woman?' 'Yes.' 'How long have you been married?' 'For eight years.' The minute-taker added, 'Husband: Sebastian Scheuber', suggesting Helena spoke his name – a respected one in Innsbruck. Sebastian was not allowed to attend court to defend his wife, but his name mattered. A frisson ran through the courtroom as people recalled the gossip: had Helena been faithful to Sebastian? Hadn't Jörg Spiess fancied her as his mistress? Heinrich knew this was a weak point in Helena's reputation and clawed at it. 'Are you of a good way of life?' he began, and when she said she was he asked her, harshly and quickly, 'Were you a virgin at the time of your marriage?' There was a sharp sucking-in of breath from the assembled officials. Surely no one asked *that* question of a respectable Innsbruck wife! And the question that was meant to shame and trap the suspect empowered her. Helena refused to answer. Into the shocked silence cut the voice of the bishop's official, Christian Turner, asking Heinrich what need he could possibly have for such information.

Primed by Bishop Georg, Christian knew that some of the accusations were unsavoury. He needed no further excuse to intervene. Although the trial was set up under the authority of the bishop and archduke, both of them had had doubts. Was it wise to let an outsider disturb their community and harass its merchants? Was this inquisitor, for all his papal authority, a dangerous crank? The archducal, city and diocesan authorities had cooperated with the inquiry so far: the pope could hardly doubt their good faith. But now Heinrich had shown how low he personally was prepared to go, and Christian pounced. The sex lives of Innsbruck's leading citizens were, he said, 'secret matters that hardly concern the case'. The notary recorded that Christian was therefore 'unwilling to take part in these matters because it was irrelevant', and asked Heinrich to move on. Christian spoke for the local church, so Heinrich complied. But as he began a further question, Christian again interrupted. Why, he asked, had Heinrich not produced written 'articles' – charges to be investigated by the court – in advance of the hearing? Shouldn't he do so now? Disconcerted, Heinrich agreed to suspend the court until eleven o'clock, write the articles and bring them back to the courtroom. Helena was ushered back to the cells.

However, she did not go quietly. We don't know the exact chain of events, but when she reappeared at eleven o'clock, Helena was not alone. With her was Johann Merwart of Wemding – a town near Munich, 200 miles north. Johann was a university-trained specialist in church law. Suddenly everything changed: Helena had an expensive, expert advocate and Heinrich was in trouble. Without revealing exactly how or when he had arrived, Johann explained he would act 'in the capacity of legal representative for the said Helena Scheuberin and the other women in detention'. He had no official mandate as yet, he said, but he wished to have their appointment of him noted. And so 'at twelve o'clock, Helena Scheuberin, Rosina Hochwartin, her mother Barbara, Barbara Pflieglin, Barbara Hüfeysen, Barbara Selachin, and Agnes Schneiderin, being present in person, all together and each apart, jointly and separately, appointed as their legal representative in these matters the said Lord Johann of Wemding to plead and defend their cause'.[23] Helena and her fellow accused had got themselves a hot-shot lawyer.

Where Christian had been circumspect, Johann tore into Heinrich. He challenged the choice of notary, citing a conflict between the pope's letters authorising Heinrich to set up a court, and legal conventions by which notaries were appointed by the bishop. He joined Christian Turner in deriding Heinrich's questions, arguing that 'he conducted the inquisition regarding hidden sins' when instead 'he should have examined the women regarding articles of bad reputation, which he . . . did not do because he had not yet drawn up articles of this kind'. Clearly, Johann scoffed, Heinrich had 'just seized the women before he instituted the proceedings in the proper set-up'. Heinrich writhed with irritation, but worse was to come. 'With these and many other things having been set out verbally,' wrote the clerk, Johann 'rejects the Lord Inquisitor as being a suspect judge in this cause.' Finally, unthinkably, Johann 'asked the Lord Commissary, in place of the Lord Bishop of Brixen, to take the Lord Inquisitor into custody'. Suddenly it was Heinrich who was going to jail. Meanwhile, Johann 'enjoined Scheuberin (who was present) and the other women, jointly and separately, not to give the Lord Inquisitor any responses to his questions because he was no longer their judge'.[24]

It was a sensational fightback. Johann's case wasn't completely watertight, and aspects of it remain unclear. He must have drafted arguments hastily between the court's suspension and its resumption at noon. But the details didn't matter: the plan worked. Heinrich protested – still in the judge's chair but gripping the arms tightly – that in his opinion 'he was a competent judge in this case'. Fine, said Johann breezily, I'll appeal the matter to the pope. At which point, the bishop's official, Christian Turner, stepped in again as if in the role of mediator. What we should do, he suggested, is take a moment to reflect – say, until Monday? Yes, Monday. And on Monday, he said, he would give his judgement as the bishop's representative about whether Heinrich was to be the judge. After all, it was the bishop's diocese, wasn't it? Heinrich, scrabbling for the final word, squeaked that he too would give himself until Monday to make a similar decision because, after all, he was the judge on the pope's authority. But the pope's powerbase in Rome was a long way from Innsbruck. And so the court was adjourned.[25] It had taken just over three hours for Helena, her friends and their legal team to smash Heinrich's case like a milk jug over a fire.

Two days later, on the last Monday in October, the court reconvened. It was the evening before the festival of All Saints, in modern times known as Halloween, when witches were thought to party. It was certainly a happy Halloween for Helena. Her trial had been moved from the town hall to the house of a gentleman named Conrad Gunther, and Innsbruck's authorities, its archduke and bishop, were moving to smother the case in a closed hearing. In Conrad's private room, Johann Merwart asked Christian Turner for his decision. Were the protocols in order? Surely the proceedings were nullified by Heinrich's conduct of them – arresting suspects without written charges, and so on? Christian concluded that 'this trial was instituted in violation of the legal system'. Accordingly, 'the women in detention on account of this are to be released'. Paul Wann, the visiting dignitary, chipped in, revealing he had spoken with representatives of Archduke Sigismund over the weekend. The archduke ('most illustrious prince and lord') had paid all the women's prison bills, as well as the expenses Heinrich had claimed in Innsbruck. He didn't have to, but he had. Now, Paul suggested forcefully, Heinrich could go home. No doubt Heinrich protested, but his protestations were not recorded. He was completely silenced. Sigismund had spoken, and the witch trial was over.

Sigismund was a clever politician. Attempts were made to offer Heinrich a face-saving exit, making sure the pope did not take offence. Each woman was made to swear to Christian Turner they would not flee from any further trial, and would abide by church law, unless they wished to be judged guilty. Each provided signatures from several male guarantors who, in effect, posted bail for them. The guarantors swore to pay a large fine if the women fled and 'that the women, jointly or separately, by themselves or through other persons, will not inflict, or cause to be inflicted, any insult or harm on the Lord Inquisitor'. Heinrich would have nothing to fear from either magical or legal revenge and would be allowed to bravely run away. On Thursday 3 November in Innsbruck's council hall – once again in full view of the market traders and the burghers in the fine houses – Sebastian Scheuber guaranteed Helena's compliance with the court's decision, while various other men stepped forward to similarly back her co-accused.²⁶ Helena Scheuberin walked out of that courtroom feeling like a million thalers. Her witch trial was never resumed.

Helena and her fellow suspects had needed all the courage they could muster to face down Heinrich, under threat of torture and execution. But they could not have won alone. They were women: they could not study or practise law, hold church office, or post their own bail. Bishop Georg and his officials had tried to ensure a fair hearing. Johann Merwart worked fast to build a case. Archduke Sigismund withdrew his favour from Heinrich and transferred it to the accused witches: who knows exactly how or why. His accusatory courtiers – Hans Spiess and the archduke's cook – swallowed their words. The women's husbands, sons and male friends stood by them. These allies saved the women, who could not otherwise have saved themselves. But their own agency was crucial nonetheless. It was Helena's refusal to answer Heinrich's question about her virginity that tipped the trial. Schooled in submission, she and her co-accused had to speak up and know when to refuse to speak. They had to take the initiative, engage and brief Johann Merwart. They had to accept their way out when it was offered: not complete vindication, but an exit allowing everyone to go home.

Heinrich was slow to go home, however. He lingered in Innsbruck, waiting for the trial to resume. Bishop Georg wrote increasingly hostile letters to him throughout 1485 and 1486, urging him to leave. In November, politely addressing Heinrich as 'your Paternity', he advised him 'to leave this place in light of present circumstances' since 'many people are irritated, and they think that the procedure of your Paternity is unusual or take it badly'. 'I wish your Paternity farewell,' he concluded pointedly. But Heinrich did not go, and by February 1486 the bishop was writing to his cathedral choirmaster that 'I am altogether sick of the monk being in the bishopric'. He had decided, he said, that Heinrich was demented: 'childish' because of age, perhaps, or simply insane. 'He really seems to me to be crazy,' Georg fretted. 'He would perhaps still be happy to proceed in the matter of the women, but I will not let him get involved, so much has he erred previously in his procedure . . . he presupposed many things that were not proven.' He wrote to Heinrich on the same day: 'I am very astonished that you remain in my diocese.' This time his letter ends bluntly: 'I actually thought that you had long since left. Goodbye.'[27] Eventually, Heinrich did leave, stubborn, self-righteous and graceless to the last.

There the matter should have ended. And as far as this particular courtroom drama went, it did. We don't know any more about Helena and her co-accused, although one day archives might show us how they went back to their lives. But the consequences of the Innsbruck witch trial sadly went further. The inbuilt advantages that centuries of male and clerical privilege had bestowed upon Heinrich included access to the printing press. As he licked his wounds in Germany after Helena's victory, Heinrich wrote his demonological textbook *Malleus Maleficarum* as a manual for future witch-hunters. He may have finalised the book with a university colleague, Jakob Sprenger, but most likely he drafted it alone; later, university theologians condemned it as encouraging injustice. The book is a compendium of false logic, cruelty and misogyny. Heinrich presents women as becoming witches because they are 'like children', 'foolish', full of 'irregular desires and passions' and obsessed with 'filthy carnal acts'. The first woman, Eve, was 'twisted and contrary, so to speak, to man', he asserted. Accordingly, women are 'lying in speech', 'bitter and dangerous' to men and 'governed by carnal lusting, which is insatiable in them'.

So it was 'unsurprising that more women than men are found

to be tainted with the Heresy of Sorceresses', he said. Indeed, God had 'preserved the male kind from such disgraceful behaviour'. Unlike godly men, witch-women spent their time poisoning husbands and suitors, turning men into animals, having sex with devils and sacrificing babies. *Malleus Maleficarum* went on in this way for hundreds of pages. It linked women and witchcraft in the minds of its readers – fellow clergy and secular magistrates – and urged them to bring witches to trial. The scars of Helena's victory caused Heinrich to argue there was no need early on in a witch trial for 'the screeching and posturing of a courtroom' or lawyers who were 'fussy about legal niceties'. Instead, soon after their arrest, suspects should be tortured by being hung up so their joints cracked and their muscles tore. Indeed, he explained earnestly, only 'the lightest torture (being raised barely an inch off the ground)' by their arms tied behind their backs would be enough to get them to confess.

Although many scholars dismissed *Malleus Maleficarum* as unsound, and historians know other demonologies were also influential – Johannes Nider's *Formicarius* and Jean Bodin's *Daemonomanie*, for example – the book put down an important marker. It stated witches were real, must be killed and almost all of them were women. The book's misogyny is not an aberration: it was unusually comprehensive, but its principles were widely shared.[28] The phenomenon of the witch-hunt gathered pace across Europe, fuelled by demonology.

Undeterred by his failure in Innsbruck, Heinrich went on to conduct further inquisitions in Germany, Bohemia and Moravia. He was delighted by his success and that of men who thought like him. In 1486 he boasted that an Italian inquisitor had condemned forty-one women to be burned for witchcraft. Others, he regretted, had escaped by 'taking flight to the dominion of Sigismund, the Archduke of Austria', who was now a confirmed enemy of his. The golden roof did indeed come to shelter witches, thanks to the turning point provided by Helena Scheuberin's witch trial.

Heinrich related the stories of Helena and the other Innsbruck suspects in *Malleus Maleficarum*, anonymised. He wasn't, he protested, relating these stories 'to disgrace the most illustrious Archduke, but to praise and glorify him'. Sigismund 'has made no small efforts in the extermination of sorceresses, with the assistance of the Most Reverend Bishop of Brixen'. It was just such a pity that they had failed, lied *Malleus Maleficarum*. In future, these and other authorities would be properly prepared and Heinrich's demonological book, among others, would help them conduct better witch trials.[29] Unfortunately, for all Helena's bravery, Heinrich was right.

CHAPTER TWO

The Trial of the North Berwick Witches: A King Delights in Demonology

Books like *Malleus Maleficarum* spread demonological ideas that sparked an explosion in witch trials. Sold from bookstalls in university and cathedral towns, they reached a network of readers: not just churchmen but nobles, queens and kings. By 1600 demonology was essential knowledge for national rulers, with around forty-five demonologies in print across western Europe. As it gained traction, witch trials became more common.[1] They were a matter both of correct belief and of correct governmental action – passing laws, tasking officials with investigation – which was hard to get right in a time of religious change. Attacks by Protestants on the Catholic Church had strengthened, and as conflict intensified so did interest in identifying heretical, Satanic opponents of true religion (whichever one that was thought to be). Ironically, Catholic and Protestant communities held very similar witch trials, despite other religious differences, because both sects shared the either/or thinking that powered demonology. The main difference was that in Protestant areas there were no monks, and therefore no monastic inquisitors – there was no one to play the Heinrich Kramer role. Instead, state authorities – kings, dukes, electors – worked with royal officials. The young Protestant King James VI of Scotland was no exception to this interest in state witch-hunting, and in the late 1580s his education in demonology spilled off his library shelves and into real life.

In summer 1589 a marriage was brokered between James, King of Scotland, and Anna, daughter of the Danish–Norwegian King Frederick II (Denmark–Norway was then a single kingdom). Scotland had been in turmoil since before James's accession to the throne as a baby, with feuding nobles kidnapping and trying to kill their young prince. By age twenty-three, James's intense attachments to male friends, avoidance of women and lack of an heir was encouraging his enemies to speculate that he might die childless. He was, in modern terms, gay, but marriage was a must to produce royal children.[2] The unified kingdom of Denmark–Norway was a natural location for him to seek a wife, as it was a Protestant polity like Scotland, and Scots and Danes had a shared history. Danish possessions ringed Scotland, from Orkney and Greenland through Iceland down the Norwegian coast to Schleswig-Holstein. Stavanger in Norway is closer to Edinburgh than London is, and there was a substantial trade between the nations, although the trip involved a hazardous sea journey. James had not made plans for a voyage to Denmark–Norway, however. Anna would be married to him by proxy, and only then sail to Scotland. But, as things turned out, James would be forced to brave the North Sea to fetch his bride, and his new Danish family believed they knew who was to blame for this unforeseen emergency: witches.

Witch-hunting was well established in the southern section of Denmark–Norway (Denmark today) by 1589. The first documented witch executions were in 1540. In Denmark, just as in Austria, the impetus to prosecute witches had gained ground as demonology spread: godly people should 'hunt [witches] down like wolves', as the Danish bishop Peder Palladius wrote in the 1530s. Denmark–Norway had recently converted to Protestantism, abandoning Catholicism, and this change in religious practice might have been expected to lead to a lessening in the witch-hunts, but it did not come, and instead the Christian sects turned the trials on each other. After the break with Catholicism the Danish demonologist

Niels Hemmingsen used the terms 'idolatry', 'heresy', 'apostasy', 'sacrilege' and 'Catholicism' all to describe witchcraft. Any type of non-Protestant belief might, he thought, be a sign that a person was a witch. It was not just Danish churchmen who were tasked with hunting witches, however; royal officials led the way. Peder Palladius warned witches that the king's courtiers would pretend to employ them for their magical abilities – as healers or diviners, like some of the people who troubled Archduke Sigismund's court in Innsbruck – and then 'immediately seize you, to bring you to the gallows to be burned to glowing ashes with skin and bones, flesh and body'.[3]

It was to this witch-hunting country that James VI sailed in 1589 to collect his bride. He had to fetch Anna because in travelling to her new home in Scotland, the queen's fleet was driven off course. Six attempts to leave Denmark's Skagerrak strait failed, and her ship began to leak. The royal party retreated to the nearest city, Oslo in southern Norway, and Anna wrote to James as firmly as she could manage – she was only fourteen – that she would spend the winter there. James had been preparing for his wife's arrival for months; he was alarmed at the embarrassing delay. So, he made a surprise announcement: he would take a ship immediately to collect Anna. It meant leaving his kingdom in political and possibly even military danger from feuding courtiers. He had to appoint caretaker officials to run day-to-day affairs, including his cousin Francis Stewart, Earl of Bothwell, whose chief skill hitherto had been killing other courtiers in duels. He had to scribble a humiliating note to the English ambassador explaining the purpose of his trip, in case Elizabeth I of England should mistake his little convoy for an offensive war fleet.[4] But the prize of his sudden departure was a cultural one: an enhanced reputation for courage and decisiveness, a submissive wife and silenced critics.

James sailed to Flekkefjord, near Stavanger, and then travelled overland to Oslo, where he and Anna were married in person in November 1589. The couple then spent Christmas at Helsingør at the court of Anna's brother King Christian IV, where courtiers and admirals were already arguing over whether witches had attacked the royal family, specifically Anna's ships. This would lead to the trial in summer 1590 of Anna Koldings, Karen Weuffers, Maren Matts Bryggers, Maren Mogensis and at least eight other unnamed people in Copenhagen. These women, alleged the king's finance minister Christoffer Valkendorff, had caused the sea storms that afflicted Anna's fleet. It was thought they had done it by sending demons floating out to the ships in barrels, who attacked the hulls.[5] James's Scottish party therefore prudently remained on land during the storm season; Anna won her argument for staying in Norway, and the newlyweds sailed home in May. But this ocean crossing too was disrupted by foul weather. Both royal households were now convinced that witches were trying to murder them. So, in 1590, a parallel series of witch trials began in Scotland and Denmark with James himself leading the investigations in his capital city, Edinburgh.

King James VI was unlike most previous witch-hunters. Heinrich Kramer was a Catholic monk, cloistered and elderly. James was a flamboyant Protestant princeling in his twenties. One of the best ways to get to know him is to visit the Banqueting House in Whitehall, London, and gaze up at him. On the ceiling is a giant canvas by Peter Paul Rubens representing James's reception into heaven. Although it was commissioned by James's son Charles, it completed a design begun by James himself and it tells us about his conception of himself as a king and a man. Looking up is important: James believed that kings were divinely appointed, closer to God than most humans. He wrote two treatises making this argument: *The True Lawe of Free Monarchies* and *Basilikon Doron*, in the 1590s. 'Monarchy', he stated, 'is the true pattern of divinity' and kings 'sit upon God his throne in the earth'. A king is 'the minister of God', 'over-lord of the whole land' and 'master over every person that inhabiteth the same . . . the king is above the law'. So, James is shown in the Banqueting House painting with his feet resting on an imperial eagle and a globe: the world – like the witches that he persecuted – rightly beneath him.

James's notion of royal merit went deeper than earthly entitlement. Instead of grovelling at the feet of Christian angels, in his
portrait James is lifted into heaven by a classical figure, Justice,
and he looks rather like a flying Greek or Roman god himself.
Churchmen like Heinrich Kramer and many of the pastors of
James's own kingdom would have disapproved. For them, sinful
human beings were granted salvation only by God's generosity. It
was to be received with self-abasement, not smug celebration.
Although supposedly he believed the same thing, in practice James
was not humble. He would go to heaven because he was worth it.
Justice was a particularly important attribute of kingship to him:
in *The True Lawe of Free Monarchies* he listed the administration
of 'justice and judgement' among his foremost duties.[6] James
thought himself a just king, and so in his giant portrait on the
ceiling of the Banqueting House, God is depicted as equally justly
rewarding him for that. And the Banqueting House's related murals
depict the other kingly attributes that he thought entitled him to
salvation: Heroic Virtue, Wisdom, Temperance and Liberality,
Religion, Scriptural Truth and Victory.

We know a lot about James, more than we know about Heinrich
Kramer. In his portrait, James deliberately displays himself to us,
flying triumphant above all the 'broiling spirits' that he said wanted
to 'stir up rebellion' in his kingdom.[7] He looks invulnerable from
the neck down. But not every trace of humanity is gone. The king's
face stands out because despite his salvation his brow is furrowed,
his mouth opening to utter the tremulous gasp of a worried man.
In other depictions he also looks bleak, nervous, ill at ease.
Sometimes he looks positively dangerous, as in Adrian Vanson's
1595 portrait. Here his grey eyes are flat, angry, defensive, with
tired shadows beneath, and the little mouth tightens under a wispy
moustache. Portraits of his wife Anna show much more assurance.
She also looks haughty, with a Mona Lisa smile. We remember
her winning the argument about overwintering in Norway. Anna
looks like she's in charge. James looks like he's waiting to mug old
ladies, which of course is one way of looking at a witch trial. In

this sulky hostility, despite all their differences of religion, age and lifestyle, James is akin to Heinrich Kramer.

If, like Heinrich, James had concerns about female power, then such an insecurity would have plausible causes. When he was a year old in 1567, James's mother Mary, Queen of Scots, was forced from her throne accused of complicity in murdering her husband, James's father Lord Darnley. She had then married the chief suspect, so the allegations may have been true. Baby James was crowned and committed to foster parents. A regent was appointed to govern Scotland. But in 1568 Mary rebelled. James's foster-father, the Earl of Mar, was poisoned. The Earl of Morton, who succeeded him as regent, was executed. He was then succeeded by the Earl of Lennox, but in 1582 Lennox was accused of seducing the sixteen-year-old king. James was then kidnapped by Lennox's opponents, while his regent, friend and possibly lover was exiled. In 1588 James's mother Mary was executed by Elizabeth I of England – and that brings us to 1589, the year of James's marriage and his trouble with witches. James had a militant, possibly murderous, mother, a strong queen-consort and an even stronger queen as his English neighbour. He was a young, anxious king pressured by dominant women. Was it coincidence that he took on an unusual role for royalty by leading a witch trial in person?

James drew on the Danish model of witch-hunting. Peder Palladius's connection between Danish courtiers and magical practitioners had caught his attention. As he returned home with Anna, James became worried that enemies at his own court were employing witches to depose him. Depressingly, he suspected one of the plotters was his cousin, the man he had left in charge when he went to Denmark–Norway: Francis Stewart, Earl of Bothwell. The idea of treasonous witchcraft was not wholly new to Scotland. Several witches had been burned in the fifteenth century and the Scottish state had enforced modern laws against witchcraft since 1563 – a parliamentary act that banned any type of witchcraft, without defining exactly what that meant. The law was introduced partly because witches were conflated with Catholic heretics filled with 'abominable superstition'. In 1568 Sir William Stewart was executed for using magic to predict the future of the monarchy and kill the regent, so James knew how magical treason might work.[8] But the 1590–91 'North Berwick' trials (as they were soon known) were new in their focus on theories of royal power and their identification of subversive Satanic witchcraft as its direct opposite. Where Heinrich Kramer had stressed the opposition between God's church and the devil's witches, what James imagined had happened in Denmark, and was now happening in Scotland, was an international conspiracy of hundreds of witches, toe-to-toe with kings. It was a royally focused version of the demonology that had caused so much trouble in Innsbruck.

It began with suspicions about two women on the periphery of the royal court and their relationship with Francis Stewart, Earl of Bothwell. The two women were magical healers, Geillis Duncan and Agnes Sampson. Geillis – known as Gillie – was a maidservant of David Seton, the baillie or state magistrate of the town of Tranent in Lothian. Tranent is ten miles from Edinburgh and was home to the Lords Seton, David's important cousins. David served as chamberlain to his Lordship, and along with his father – also named David – owned multiple properties including Foulstruther Castle in Edinburgh and a house in Tranent known as the Royal George. Here Gillie laboured for the David Setons: making beds and beating carpets or chopping vegetables and boiling stews. But she also had her own life. Sometimes she was out all night. Although she was young, Gillie had a reputation as a healer, someone who could 'help all such as were troubled or grieved with any kind of sickness or infirmity'. We don't know any of the cures she used, but from her 'confession', in which she describes a walk to Dalkeith, up a hill from the 'king's ford' on the sleepy River Esk to 'gather a broad-leaved grass', we can assume she knew something about plants. Maybe it was for use in a herbal medicine or a woven charm? Gillie also played a 'Jew's trump', a metal instrument held between the teeth that makes a zingy, hypnotic tune.[9] She was an asset to her community, all this implies; talented and interested in helping others.

But although some saw Gillie as a skilled friend, her employer did not. David thought Gillie was using ungodly magic in her healing: she 'did not those things by natural and lawful ways', he said. As a woman, she was not a medically qualified professional, yet some of her supposed cures were described as 'most miraculous'.[10] This was a word associated not just with magic but with Catholicism. 'Miracles' such as hers were fine in the Bible when performed by Jesus Christ, but in modern times pious people thought them either fake or demonic, and certainly not to be worked by women. Even her Catholic employer thought some of Gillie's remedies were too effective or too strange to be holy. So, David Seton questioned her and tortured her unofficially and illegally with thumbscrews. Gillie confessed to witchcraft and investigations began locally to find out who she had been working with. One of the names she mentioned was Agnes Sampson.

Agnes – also known as Anny – came from Nether Keith, near Haddington, seven miles beyond Tranent. She was suspected by local magistrates and churchmen, both of whom questioned her, probing experimentally to see if their demonological preoccupations were echoed in her activities. Anny seems to have been seen as more dangerous than Gillie, because her influential 'patients' included the 'lady of Kilbaberton', 'Lady Littledean', 'Lady Roslin', 'the laird of Reidshill's son', the wife of the sheriff of Haddington and 'Laird Parkie's lass'. In particular, Anny was suspected because she had tried to help the wife and daughters of the wealthy gentleman Patrick Edmiston. These women had reported attack by a supernatural black dog. The dog was also referred to as 'the devil', making him sound like a demonic spirit that Anny was expected to drive away – perhaps he represented anxiety or depression, or was thought to be the familiar of another, hostile, witch. Witches were sometimes believed to work with devils in animal form, an idea stemming from folk beliefs about magical animals. Such images merge with demonological fears when suspects are forced to confess. When questioned, Anny said she commanded the devil-dog to reveal whether her patients would live or die. She was told Euphan, dowager Lady

Edmiston, would die but at least two of her daughters would survive. Later, Anny says, she stopped one daughter – Elizabeth Pringle, Lady Torsonce – from drowning herself, frustrating the devil's plan. Anny did all this healing by the power of 'prayer', she said, and had learned her skills from her father.[11] But her description of contact with a spirit was easily perceived as wicked witchcraft by questioners influenced by demonology.

Anny most likely didn't think of her work that way. Her healing method was traditional, trusted and impressive, passed down through her family. It was, to her thinking, wholly Christian. Yes, she dealt with animal spirits and magical charms, but she was on the side of good and she helped people. How could this be Satanic witchcraft? Many of her patients would have agreed. Imagine you're sick: sick with fear and sadness about your life, perhaps, as well as having a strange pain in your hips or your belly or your feet. You can't get on with your usual work – tending your crops, minding the children, slogging through your mercantile accounts. You're so *weary*. It's winter, and each day it's dark for far longer than it's light. Is God punishing you? Is the devil snapping at your heels? And you start to worry about being bewitched. There was that threadbare old woman you met by the bridge, the one with the angry black dog. She looked at you with such hatred, you thought, and you weren't sure why. The world is a terrifying place, and you want nothing more than to hide from it and its crazy folk. So, one day you just go back to your warm, soft bed in the afternoon, and you stay there. After a bit you stop talking to your family, and friends who visit are shocked by your mute, vacant stare. At that point they send a child or a servant to call Anny Sampson.

And Anny does an amazing thing. She comes to your bedside, and she grips you tightly by the arm. She gazes hard into your tired eyes. 'I prayed for you,' she says. 'I said my special prayer that my father taught me.' And she tells you the prayer. You recognise it: it's the Apostles' Creed, a verse that you all recite in church. But it's different. Some of it's in dialect, some of it doesn't make much sense, but it's beautiful:

I trow in almighty God that wrought
Both heaven and earth and all of nought;
Into his dear son, Christ Jesu,
Into that anaplie lord I trow;
Was gotten of the Holy Ghost,
Born of the Virgin Mary,
Stoppit to heaven that all well then
And sits at his Father's right hand.
He bade us come and there to doom
Both quick and dead, as he thought convene.
I trow also in the Holy Ghost;
In Holy Kirk my hope is most,
That holy ship where hallowars wins
To ask forgiveness of my sins;
And syne to rise in flesh and bone
The life that never more has gane.
Thou sayest, Lord – loved mocht ye be! –
That formed and made mankind of me,
Thou cost me on the holy cross
And lent me body, soul and voice,
And ordained me to heaven's bliss,
Wherefore I thank thee, Lord, of this.
And all your hallowaris loved be
To pray to them to pray to me
And keep me from that felon fee
And from the sin that soul would slay.
Thou, Lord, for thy bitter passion
To keep me from sin and worldly shame
And endless damnation
Grant me the joy never will be gane.
Sweet Jesus Christus. Amen.

Anny tells you how the prayer works when she says it. If it had
been 'stopped' while she was chanting – perhaps by a knock at the
door, by a fault of memory or stumbling over a word – she would

have known you would die. But it was not stopped. Anny knew that you would live, that everything would be alright. So here she is to see you.

And she has brought her special charms. If that woman by the bridge did bewitch you, Anny will fight for your life. She puts something under your pillow and something else under the foot of your bed. And then she grips you again, hard and tight, and she says:

> All kinds of ills that ever may be,
> In Christ's name I conjure thee.
> I conjure thee, both more and less,
> With all the virtues of the Mass;
> And right so by the nails sore
> That nailed Jesus and no more;
> And right so by the same blood
> That reeked over the ruthful rood.
> Forth of the flesh and of the bone
> And in the earth and in the stone.
> I conjure thee in the Lord's name.

Anny breathes in with her eyes closed, arching backward from you until she lets out a moan of such anguish that tears come to your eyes. It's your anguish, your pain that she's taking into her. Anny calls this 'taking off the pain and sickness'. She groans and wails. And then she lets go your arm and slumps down on the floor. Her daughter, waiting on the threshold with big eyes, helps her up. They stagger from your house, and later someone tells you that Anny spent the whole of that night squirming in her bed with 'great groanings and torment'. The next morning, she got up, threw your sickness out of her window onto a passing dog, and slowly you began to get better.

Anny's method was common among magical healers – both at the time and since, in different communities across the world. Something like it was probably practised in Innsbruck and later we'll see it done elsewhere, including in places as far apart as Pennsylvania and Portsmouth and as late as the 1940s. Like these later healers, Anny called on the Christian deity for help, and because she was a sixteenth-century Scot she referred to the Catholic services, personnel and artefacts that she would have learned from her father, who used the charm before the state's conversion to Protestantism. These Catholic references were the Mass, the 'hallowaris' or saints and the 'rood' or cross. Anny also used the Latin prayer 'Ave Maria'.[12] In her father's day, these were holy words, but now that Scotland was Protestant they were suspect; particularly in a woman's mouth they signalled danger. Anny was feared as a potent speaker of such words. Later on, another suspected witch, Janet Kennedy, said that she had once been summoned to meet Anny and when she refused the messenger had 'threatened her in Agnes Sampson's name' and said Anny would 'compel' her to come. Anny was a spiritual celebrity, just like Helena Scheuberin had been a social celebrity in fifteenth-century Innsbruck. She was a bit too visible. When she and Gillie Duncan were questioned, both admitted Anny had interfered in royal affairs. Collaborating with witches from Denmark's capital Copenhagen they had worked towards 'staying [stopping] of the queen's coming home'.[13] Perhaps it was a fantasy or a real memory of trying to influence politics by magic, but either way it was a fatal confession, moving from discussion of folk-magic towards admitting a Satanic conspiracy against the Scottish state.

The women's statements to their local authorities in May 1590 snagged King James's attention. He had suspected witches were attacking him and now they had been found. So, he told royal officials the women should be tried in Edinburgh, in his own home: the rambling gothic palace Holyroodhouse. He would attend with his inner council and together they would question and judge the suspects, with a token jury of local gentry. It was an exceptional decision. In the late sixteenth century, Scotland did not have a whole-state justice system with predictable outcomes in neatly layered courts. Instead, the administration of justice was often devolved to local landowners or royal appointees. Now James's decision to try the witches himself transformed what had been local hearings into a national show trial, an experiment in applied demonology. As with later witch trials, like the ones at Salem, flexing normal court processes in response to a powerful authority can lead to mass injustice – and that happened in Edinburgh in 1590. As Anny and Gillie were questioned, they named more suspects. Meanwhile, the king stood 'undaunted': 'so long as God is with him, he feareth not who is against him', an observer wrote. Some suspects confirmed that 'the king needs to be feared of nothing under God'. Here is an early version of James's self-image as God's own monarch. To do him justice he was intellectually curious: the witch trial was a chance to examine the workings of the universe. But he focused chillingly on his own special place within it. James 'took great delight to be present at the [witches'] examinations', said one attendee. 'Delight' is not a word that sits well with witch trials, and it has haunted James's reputation.[14]

In the autumn and winter of 1590, however, James was not thinking about how history would record his actions. He wanted to know how these healers, Gillie and Anny, had meddled in his affairs and threatened his kingdom, so they were tortured on his authority to find out. What happened to Anny – on an unspecified date sometime late in 1590 – is detailed in a printed account of the witches called *Newes from Scotland*. All the hair was shaved off Anny's body by state jailers so that she could be examined for demonic marks – the spots or warts supposedly made by Satan to show a witch belonged to him – and then 'her head [was] thrawn with a rope'. It was wrapped around her temples and twisted to agonising tightness. Anny was a strong woman. She held out for an hour without confession, but when her 'privities' or genitals were searched and a mark supposedly found, her resistance crumbled. And of course, her torture and sexual assault, and the tortures of other suspects once they were arrested, led to false confessions. After the trial was over, several of the 'witches' withdrew their admissions of guilt and other statements. Donald Robson and Janet

Stratton, for example, said that they had given 'false and feigned' evidence because they were in fear of their lives and in 'torment'.[15] We know hardly anything else about them, but we know they were tortured into confessing.

All the suspects told James what he wanted to hear. In her evidence, Gillie explained that Anny had been working to thwart the king's marriage plans since at least autumn 1589. She gave no reason that she and Anny might be enemies of the state, simply stating they had conspired just as James feared. We don't know if the women actually knew each other before their trial, but now Gillie said they did. In November 1589, she explained, Anny had said threateningly to her, 'Now the king is going to fetch his wife, but I shall be there before them.' Instead of contradicting this accusation, when she gave her evidence to the court in late 1590 Anny agreed: she said that during James's time abroad 'the devil said to her the king should hardly come home, but that the queen should never come except he fetched her with him'. Significantly, Anny told James that she had asked the devil 'if the king should have any bairns' and added she had been present by magical means on his wedding night in Norway. To prove it, she whispered into James's ear the very words that the king had said to his new wife – phrases that in reality were likely overheard and repeated by servants.[16] But to James, Anny's words seemed like magic. Everything confirmed his suspicions and established for him the correctness of his demonological understanding of witchcraft.

Anny and Gillie were both poor, uneducated people, like many of the other suspects who were drawn into the trial. They were used to agreeing with powerful men who deigned to speak to them and that is their main difference from Helena Scheuberin a hundred years before. Helena had courage but that was partly because she had wealth, family support and religious education. Anny and Gillie could not defy their persecutors in the same way. When Anny was asked 'how she began to serve the devil' she accepted the premise of the question, revealing her isolation and poverty. The devil came to her when she was widowed, she said, offering her money to accept him as her 'master'. She was among the poorest women in her society: a widow who lived in an overcrowded, cold hovel, sharing a bed with her younger children, one on each side for warmth. Gillie reinforced Anny's account of deprivation. She said the witches had worked for the Earl of Bothwell and others to earn 'gold and silver and victual to help Anny Sampson and her bairns'. After her trial, Gillie said that she had 'slandered' her co-accused because 'she was caused and persuaded so to do by the two David Setons in Tranent and others'. 'It was all but leasings, of the which she craved God forgiveness,' she confessed, using the dialect term for lies. Unlike Helena Scheuberin, when Gillie and Anny were intimidated by powerful men, they could not afford lawyers to defend them. What else could they do but confess?

Both women told wilder and wilder stories as the witch trial went on into 1591. In particular they confessed to creating a sea storm, the one that had afflicted James and Anna in 1589, through a Danish–Scottish witch alliance. As part of forming this international alliance in 1589, the Copenhagen group had supposedly given Gillie a witch-name, baptising her into their Satanic faith. The group had then sent a black dog to swim under and damage the royal ships, Anny and Gillie claimed, and at Leith a christened cat had been thrown into the sea with the limbs of dead men robbed from graves. All the anti-Christian horror imagined by demonologists spilled out in the women's confessions. In order to plot this harm, witches had met at 'conventions' across Scotland, they said. Here, the devil explained to them how to harm the king. Satan promised that if Anny moulded a wax 'picture' or image of the king – like the one found by Gertrud Rötin under her threshold in Innsbruck – he would work evil upon it and then deliver it back to his followers to melt, dissolving away the king's life. Satan also instructed his team to kill and roast a toad, hanging it up to let its poisons drip out. They should gather an adder's skin, some stale urine, and an oyster shell to catch the toad-juice. This mixture could then be dropped onto the king or be smeared on his cast-off clothing to transmit its poison to him magically.[17]

Finally, the Scottish branch of the supposed witch-cult met again at North Berwick, Anny explained. This last convention – or 'Sabbath', as witches' meetings were known – was the biggest. It had over a hundred delegates, six men and the rest women. Sensationally, Anny said it took place inside North Berwick church, twenty miles north of Keith where she had lived. Sabbaths were thought to parody church services, inverting Christian rites to worship the devil, but it was a bold step to hold one inside a Christian church. Anny said that one evening she was walking in fields near Keith when the devil appeared to her. He instructed her to go to North Berwick church next day. At first, she said that her son-in-law John Couper took her there on his horse, although she later also said the witches had sailed to the church – which stood on a headland – in sieves. Sieves are, of course, as full of holes as Anny's terrified confession (although later William Shakespeare would use this detail from Anny's story in *Macbeth* (c.1606), the most famous witch story of all time). However, they arrived at North Berwick, and once there the witches danced a 'reel', or folk-dance, through the churchyard, all of them singing. Gillie played her Jew's trump. The dancers broke into the church by magic and there was the devil, in the form of a Black man wearing a black gown and hat. He looked like the minister who would normally have been there. Anny was imagining the most breath-taking opposite of normality she or her questioners could think of: a devil in church instead of a preacher; a black-skinned leader instead of a white one; dancing instead of praying. This was exactly how demonologists wanted suspects to describe witchcraft: the binary opposite of everything good.

Satan creaked up the wooden steps to the pulpit and draped himself cynically on the lectern. Anny said that a local schoolmaster – John Fian, who also stood accused of witchcraft – took a register of attendance. Satan called out names and everyone answered 'Here, master!' The devil then demanded a report of harm done since the last meeting, and awarded a divisive promotion to another accused man, Robert Grierson. The published account of Anny's evidence also claims the devil 'did greatly inveigh against the king' in an impromptu sermon and when the witches asked 'why he did bear such hatred to the king', he replied, 'Because the king is the greatest enemy he hath in the world.'[18] If Anny did say this, then it was music to James's ears. If she didn't, then this Satanic endorsement was so good it had to be invented. Finally, the devil turned his back on his congregation and pulled up his gown. Titillated, the worshippers expected something sexual, but instead Satan heaved himself up onto the pulpit rail and told the witches: 'Kiss my arse!' So they did. Then they dug up bodies from the churchyard. Anny grabbed a winding sheet and two joints to grind into magic powder. Unfortunately, she lost these trophies before her interrogation, which is often the way with physical evidence that never existed. After her confession of everything that was expected of her, Anny was hustled back to prison at Holyroodhouse, along with Gillie and a mounting number of new suspects.

By Christmas 1590, the outline of a magical conspiracy was evident. But James and his officials were so transfixed that their witch trial dragged on throughout 1591. As the list of accused grew, some efforts were made to check the status of demonological elements in confessions. The court planned confrontations between accusers and suspects to compare their stories, resolve contradictions and detect 'leasings'. But it was not exacting enough, likely because they did not really want to bring their theories crashing down. For example, there were repeated descriptions of how at one Sabbath a circle of witches passed round the wax image of the king. It went 'widdershins', right to left, and finally it was handed to Satan. Anny said, 'Take there the picture of James Stewart, prince of Scotland', and she called the devil 'Mahoun', an abbreviated, Islamophobic version of 'Mohammed', coined because medieval western Christians had assumed the Prophet was a devil. This was all fascinating, but no one apparently cared that the coven personnel varied from one confession to another, and the person who passed the parcel to Satan varied too. All they noticed was that the witches had been hoping 'to have drowned her Majesty and her company' by their 'treasonable magic', and that although this hadn't happened, 'the queen was put back by storm'.[19]

As questioning dragged on, Gillie named many new suspects. Accusations moved across the map from Keith and Tranent to Edinburgh and up the social scale to women previously 'reputed for as civil, honest women as any that dwelled within the city'. A gentlewoman, Barbara Napier, was accused of using Anny's magic to help her husband and gain favour with courtiers. She had bought from Anny an anti-morning-sickness charm for Lady Angus, and an enchanted ring, and had killed the Earl of Angus, it was said, using a wax image. A noblewoman, Euphan McCalzean, known as Effie, was accused of bewitching her own husband and father-in-law, and consulting with witches including Anny about her family's health. Anny had eased Effie's labour pains by scattering charms round her bed: a stone with a hole in it, a written charm – magic items the women of Innsbruck also used. Anny supposedly helped Effie seduce a local laird; like Helena Scheuberin, Effie was the subject of gossip about an extramarital affair. Both Effie and Barbara Napier were put on trial. Desperately, Anny fitted them into her story of the witch-conspiracy: these 'great women', she said, were employed in 'winning of great lords' and ladies' favours to put this turn in execution against the king'. Although Effie's family employed lawyers, it was too late. They couldn't stop the trial because the king was running it; there was no higher authority. Even wealthy, confident, educated women – the Helena Scheuberins of Edinburgh – couldn't save themselves from state persecution.[20]

At the end of her trial on 27 January 1591, Anny was found guilty. Whether the jury would have convicted her without the king's insistence on traitorous conspiracy we don't know. As it was, demonology had blended with folk beliefs to – apparently – prove her guilty of Satanic witchcraft against the state. Anny was taken to Edinburgh Castle and imprisoned until a stake and a pyre of dry wood could be built. By the stake, she was strangled, and her dead body was dumped onto the pyre and burned to ashes; this was the usual punishment for witchcraft. Gossiping in the shopping streets or shuttered inside their homes, people smelled the smoke drifting over the city on the east wind.

When Gillie Duncan was (still) being questioned in December 1591 the woman being tried alongside her was Bessie Thompson, Anny Sampson's daughter, implicating two generations of that family. The Tranent schoolmaster, John Fian, was charged alongside his neighbour Gillie. John was said to have officiated with Satan at the North Berwick church convention, keeping his register and – as one of the few literate people in his community – taking notes. He was also accused of doing magic tricks and telling fortunes. Perhaps as a learned young man John had knowledge of casting horoscopes. His punishment was horrifying torture with hammers and metal leggings before he was executed.[21] Many other ordinary villagers from Keith, Tranent and the surrounding hamlets – Marion Ranking, Meggie Thompson, Alexander Whitelaw, Janet Campbell, Ritchie Graham, Janet Fairlie, Kate Gray, Isobel Lauder, Helen White, Marion Paterson, Janet Nicolson and many more – were named as conspiring to tip the king off his throne and put Francis Stewart, Earl of Bothwell, there instead. It was unclear why they would care who was king.

Gillie Duncan and Bessie Thompson were executed side-by-side on Castle Hill on 4 December 1591.[22] Barbara Napier was acquitted by her jury, but the king then put the jurymen on trial, forcing them to reverse the verdict. Barbara escaped immediate execution because she was pregnant, and then she disappears from history. Effie McCalzean was burned alive on 15 June 1591, an exceptional punishment because she was an 'undutiful' wife, a witch who had tried to murder her husband and father-in-law and magically seduced another man. In Scotland these anti-patriarchal crimes were called 'petty treason', the rebellion of a wife against her lawful sovereign: her husband. The national treason supposedly committed by Anny and Gillie was echoed in Effie's domestic crime, showing demonologists were correct: witches were a subversive threat at every level of society from the marital bed to the palace. In 1597

King James wrote a demonology himself, called simply *Daemonologie*, making this point.[23]

The Earl of Bothwell, who had been named as the instigator of the witches' attack on the king and queen, had prudently fled Scotland in 1591. Once the political climate had eased several years later, he returned and was formally tried in 1593 in order to bring the case to a close. The earl was accused of consulting witches – Anny and some of the others – about his political fortunes, buying a charm to make the king love him and asking how to 'cut away' the king, killing him by wax image, shipwreck or poison or detaining him abroad.

We catch our last glimpse of Anny, Gillie, Effie and the others in the documents from the earl's trial; they are described as 'umwhile', a dialect term meaning 'deceased'. Their own trials were long in the past – they had paid the penalty for the witchcraft they had supposedly performed for the earl, and which they had confessed under torture. They had been dead for two years by the time he followed them into court to answer for the crimes that they had all committed together. Surely he too would be convicted and subjected to terrible punishment. But the Earl of Bothwell was a man, a nobleman, the king's courtier; he had legal advice and the backing of fellow nobles. With James's consolidation of his power the political mood had also changed. So the Earl of Bothwell was acquitted.[24]

CHAPTER THREE

The Trial of the Vardø Witches: Demonology at Europe's Colonial Edge

Thirty years after the executions of Anny, Gillie, Effie and the others in Edinburgh, Scots were emigrating to the American colonies, the Caribbean islands and anywhere else with a 'new world' to explore. 'New worlds' lay not just to the west, but north and south of Europe as well, even stretching deep into the ominous vastness of the Arctic Circle. By the seventeenth century colonists from further south – Norwegians, Danes, Germans, Dutch, Faroese and Scots – had settled in these icy regions, in what is now northern Norway and Sweden. They expanded medieval trading posts, farmed smallholdings, founded fishing and fur-shipping businesses and built forts, but there were still less than three thousand people spread over nearly twenty thousand square miles. The northern Scandinavian coast was tundra, mountain and fjord, the end of firm-footed safety and the beginning of a vast cold sea, where icebergs moaned in the wintry dark under skies that flamed inexplicably with red and green lights. No wonder the far north haunted settlers' imaginations. It was not empty, however, although incomers chose to think so. In the early seventeenth century, about half the population were indigenous Sámi people and the other half southern incomers.[1] The Arctic Circle had long been home to nomadic peoples, herders and hunters, a place mapped in their stories in ways colonists could not understand. While for colonists, islets such as at Vardø and Vadsø were dots on a map with miles of nothing between them, the indigenous peoples saw tracks, campsites and landmarks where settlers saw only blank wilderness.

Travelling in the wake of those colonists, you can fly to Vardø in a small plane that lands at Svartnes, the black headland. Svartnes is in the Finnmark og Troms region of Norway, a county bordering Finland and Russia as well as the Atlantic and Barents Sea. From Svartnes, take a taxi through an undersea tunnel to Vardø island. The driver will likely drop you by the harbour, and from there head south-west, past the red and orange clapboard houses hemmed with sullen gulls, towards the spire of the old chapel. As you skirt past its graveyard down a dirt track, an astonishing structure rises from the sea's edge. You can't look away: what is it? A long, sharp-edged shape, something like a bridge, something like a sail, or a scaffold or a knife. A plank walkway slopes invitingly into its interior. At its far end lurks a smoked-glass box, mysteriously opaque. Scattered in the scrub by the beach are waist-high poles and your growing sense of surrealism will deepen as you realise that atop each one is a bright orange, stiletto-heeled shoe. The buildings are the Steilneset Memorial: a tribute to the Finnmark witches, around ninety of whom were executed between 1600 and 1700.

Eventually, a staggering 4.5 per cent of the population of Finnmark would be accused of witchcraft between those dates.[2] The monument, designed by Louise Bourgeois and Peter Zumthor, and with exhibition texts written by Liv Helene Willumsen, stands at one of the many sites of execution, commemorating those who were killed. The slate-blue sea rattles over grey pebbles and crows swagger fatly along the strandline. Nothing so terrible should have happened on this lonely, lovely shore.

The first well-documented witch accusation of the Vardø area was in 1620 and began a series of interlinked trials lasting into 1621. It was a continuation of the efforts of Christian IV – James VI's brother-in-law – to eliminate witches from Denmark–Norway.

Christian's witch-hunt echoed the North Berwick trials of 1590–91, since it was overseen by a Scotsman – John Cunningham, governor of Finnmark – a courtier of King James VI and Queen Anna. The Danish king Christian made John first a captain, then admiral of a fleet sent to Greenland in 1605 and 1606. There, John's shipmates named Mount Cunningham (already named Qaqatsiac) after him. John was 'honest and resolute', but a frightening leader. When his crew contemplated mutiny because of icebergs, 'islands of ice . . . like huge mountains', he forced them forward. Two sailors accused of a crime were abandoned on the Greenland shore. John also killed or captured several Greenlanders in conflict. In 1606 his expedition kidnapped another five. Back in Denmark, he captained a warship during the Kalmar War of 1611–13, fought by Denmark–Norway against Sweden. By 1619, his harsh personality, naval and colonial leadership and life experience – he was in his forties by then – made him ideal for the Finnmark governorship. It was a district where the Danish government wanted the local populace, a mixture of indigenous people and settlers fishing and working small farms, crushed into Protestant conformity, tax-paying and military rule.[3]

The royal officials of northern Norway were often foreign nationals like John Cunningham. They were welcomed because, notionally, they brought good practice from their home countries: new trades, mercantile knowledge, legal or military experience. In Vardø, John Cunningham helped to enforce Christian IV's new anti-witchcraft law. In 1601 the death of Finnmark's previous governor had been blamed on Sámi witchcraft, and since then Christian IV had become increasingly concerned about this supposed threat.[4] In 1617 he issued a decree, 'About Witches and Their Accomplices', which redefined witchcraft. Christian's decree stated that it was every responsible Dane's and Norwegian's duty to report anyone thought to be a witch. Failure would mean they themselves could be punished as 'accomplices' to witchcraft. But what *was* 'witchcraft' by 1617? The decree explained that some witchcraft was diabolic, involving a pact with the devil, while some involved using charms. These definitions recall both Austrian and Scottish developments in demonology during the fifteenth and sixteenth centuries. In its new law, Denmark–Norway was codifying demonological theory in the style of Heinrich Kramer, linking witchcraft with heresy, devil-worship and healing folk-magic. The spread of demonology continued, now often led by royal officials, with witch trials bubbling up in its wake. And from 1617 onwards all witchcraft and magic in Denmark–Norway would be punishable by death, or, for lesser offences, exile.

This new demonological definition reached the extreme northern edge of the European continent in Norway in 1620. One of the people who carried it there was John Cunningham. As well as all the available reading on the subject, John had direct experience in his youth of Scottish witch trials. His birthplace, Crail in Fife, was just twelve miles from North Berwick where Anny Sampson and Gillie Duncan supposedly met the devil in 1590. In 1597, when John was in his early twenties, there had been further witch trials around Crail itself. So he brought to Finnmark both broad demonological theory and detailed knowledge of what Scottish witches had confessed – ideas which hadn't featured in previous Norwegian trials.[5]

Christian IV's 1617 decree had made a wave of witch trials likely, but John Cunningham turned this into a certainty. In 1620 he began to oversee witch trials as governor of Finnmark, often holding them at the Vardøhus fortress at Vardø. Vardøhus still stands, rebuilt, its stone walls topped by turf banks bristling with cannon. The fort was a defence against external enemies but also a prison. Suspected witches were held in its small, damp cells, tight in the grip of state power and awaiting a trial by jury presided over by a local magistrate. Some witchcraft suspects were Sámi, and the authorities believed Sámi had special powers of attack – ones that might overwhelm even the strongest guards. This was, of course, untrue, and most of the Sámi people who lived in Finnmark were only interested in herding their animals and fishing their seas. Yet still they were feared.

Sámi were familiar to the southern incomers both as year-round neighbours and nomads passing through. Some Sámi lived permanently in fjord villages while others trekked annually into the mountains. The nomads herded semi-domesticated reindeer or caribou, which migrated (then, as now) between their winter lichen-grazing inland and their summer grass-grazing by the sea. Reindeer can travel fifteen or twenty miles a day, so the Sámi moved quickly across the landscape with them, arriving on the coast in March or April and leaving after harvest time in September. Their migration coincided with the last and first snowfalls of the year. In Finnmark, snow lay on the ground for up to six months and the Sámi's reindeer pulled sleds over it. The deer were a source of meat and dairy products, housing and clothing materials, tools and musical instruments. Their hide made pole-supported tents, *lavvu*, similar to a Native American Lakota tipi but domed and flatter. Hide also clothed the Sámi. It made stout boots with curled toes, belts and distinctive waterproof hats, and these were padded and finished with the fur of reindeer and other creatures: seal, hare or fox. Many Sámi would have been dressed head to foot in skilfully tailored and decorated animal skin.

Sámi communities did not resist Norwegian settlers – in fact they traded with them while continuing their traditional way of life. In the vast Arctic landscape, contact between the groups was limited, however, and there was no organised missionary effort before the eighteenth century despite settler anxieties about Sámi paganism. For the incomers, migrating Sámi were an impressive sight: small, powerful leather-clad herders, women and men together, striding or skiing confidently through blizzard and dark, sun and rain. Early observers referred to them as 'striding Finns', and the medieval chronicler Adam of Bremen said they could move faster than wild animals.[6] In the seventeenth century, Sámi were referred to as Finns and Lapps – people from 'Finnland' and 'Lappland' – but their own word for themselves was Sámi, meaning people belonging to the land they called 'Sapmi'. Their ability to live successfully in the far north, blending into the landscape and flexing with the weather, was the envy of incomers. Although there were years of hunger and exceptional cold, Sámi bore them stoically. They seldom caught southern European diseases like plague, and they were hardy in ways settlers could only admire. They were set apart from the incomers by culture and language too: different groups of Sámi spoke their own varied but related languages, with roots in the Ural Mountains to the east. For example, the people around Vardø were from the Northern Sámi language group. Famously, some Sámi languages have over two hundred words for different types of snow, and their speech and its thought-world was difficult for settlers to understand.

As part of this projected strangeness, magical powers were attributed to the Sámi, which was why Christian IV thought they had murdered his previous Finnmark governor. These powers were thought to derive from their religion: animist, with animal spirits, ancestors and nature deities important in their cosmology. Such spirits were connected with humans by shamanistic 'noaide', men who beat ceremonial hide drums. The drumbeat helped a noaidi to attain his trance state and divine, using a bone pointer moving by vibration across symbols on the drum's skin. Symbols included storms, sun, reindeer and – as the Sámi absorbed Christian vocabulary during the later sixteenth and seventeenth centuries – God or gods, angels and demons. A noaidi would 'play for' neighbours requiring divination, and if the pointer stopped near a dangerous symbol, harm would follow. Unfortunately, this divination could also be interpreted as *causing* the harm: divining a storm could be mistaken for raising it. Sámi seers were thus thought to cast evil spells or 'gand'. Gand took the form of arrows, balls of hair and moss-like organic bullets, or demonic flies that the Sámi supposedly kept in leather pouches and sent to bite their enemies. Alternatively, a Sámi witch might summon a hawk or owl that would 'spew out these gand flies from its beak', while others would 'shake out of the bird's feathers and wings'. No wonder the defenders of Vardøhus fortress were scared of gand. It was beliefs like this that led sixteenth- and seventeenth-century ethnographers like Olaus Magnus and

Peder Claussøn Friis to study the Sámi people. Peder Claussøn Friis described them as evil-tempered, dangerous enemies, steeped in demonic paganism and witchcraft.[7]

It's no surprise, then, that the first person to be tried as a witch after John Cunningham's arrival in Finnmark was a Sámi woman, living at the tiny settlement of Omgang, along the coast from Vardø. There had been a few earlier trials in 1601, 1610, 1612 and 1617, but almost all of their documentation is lost. The first well-documented trial was of 'Find-Karri', or 'Kari the Finn', in 1620. By then, Sámi people were using some Norwegian names: 'Kari' may be a version of 'Karen', although it might also be a Sámi name. Official records refer to Kari as Karen Edisdatter, 'Karen daughter of Edis', and Edis is a male Sámi name. Kari therefore had a complex identity between and as part of two cultures. Because she stood out among her neighbours, she was believed to have magical abilities linked to her indigenous heritage. Kari was accused of witchcraft and tried on 13 May 1620 by a ten-man jury at the court of the magistrate, His Majesty's Bailiff Søffren Nielsen, who worked with John Cunningham enforcing local law. Kari, her neighbours said in court, was responsible for two separate drownings in the fjords that frayed the edge of the plateau of northern Finnmark, and for other crimes against Anders Rasmussen and his wife. First of all, at Båtsfjord, Abraham Nilsen, from the hamlet of Hop, had fallen overboard when he went to his ship's rail to relieve himself. And a man known simply as Henrik, who had lived at both Hop and Omgang, had then drowned too. Abraham's death seemed the more significant of the two because of his convoluted previous history with Kari and his connection with Finnmark's new governor, John Cunningham.

Abraham was a moderately wealthy trader who employed at least one servant, Ingeborgh. Just before his death, Ingeborgh told Abraham she was pregnant. Abraham blamed Johannis Oelsen, saying he was the father of her child. But whether or not Johannis was Ingeborgh's seducer, he was certainly Kari Edisdatter's lover. Kari's neighbours said she and Johannis 'have had each other in wedlock' in a 'licentious relationship', awkward phrases suggesting a sexual relationship like a marriage but not sanctioned by the Christian church. So, Kari was drawn into Johannis's trouble. Abraham, angry and resentful, first approached Johannis with a request that he support Ingeborgh materially. 'Since my maid is with child by you,' he said bluntly, 'make sure she is fed.' Johannis did not deny that he was the father of the child. But he answered Abraham in a shuffling, offhand way that infuriated him. 'If I can get hold of anything I shall give it to her,' Johannis said, and Abraham clenched his fist and took a swing at him. Unfortunately for Kari, she was watching the confrontation. She stepped between her lover Johannis and Abraham, shouting, 'If you hit him, the devil will be set loose!' Perhaps it was a threat, perhaps she meant that violence was unchristian, or was sure to escalate. Whatever her intention, Abraham resented Kari's outspoken words. They were recorded for use against her and would come back to haunt her in court.[8]

A few days later, Abraham sailed along the coast on official business along with Johannis. We don't know their relationship, but they both played some role in this trip. Abraham was in one of two ships that made up the convoy, a boat belonging to John Cunningham himself. And it was from John's boat that Abraham fell to his death on the voyage home. John and Abraham's boat had been parted from the leading boat at Båtsfjord, with Johannis on the first one. As soon as he stepped onto the jetty, Kari asked him some suspicious-seeming questions. 'Where is the other boat?' she queried. 'Oh,' said Johannis, 'it was left behind at Båtsfjord.' Kari thought for a moment and began sighing. 'Alas, alas,' she said, as if there were some tragedy at hand. 'What does it matter to you?' Johannis queried, but she did not reply. When the second boat of the two docked at Omgang the next day, and news spread that Abraham Nilsen had been lost overboard from it, Kari said simply, 'I knew that already.' Perhaps she regarded herself as a seer, or she had consulted a diviner about Abraham's attack on Johannis. Perhaps she did curse Abraham for his assault on her lover or she just had a feeling about that delayed boat. Whatever

the truth, people later remembered her remark, and Johannis treach-
erously reminded them of it.

Johannis looks like a weak man in his evidence at Kari's trial.
Not only did he accuse her of cursing Abraham, but he had also
apparently cheated on her and then abandoned his other girlfriend,
a pregnant maidservant. When he was questioned about his 'licentious relationship' with Kari, he squirmed. Kari, he said, had forced
him to love and have sex with her: he dared not resist her 'for fear
that she might harm him', he alleged. She had said, 'If I cannot
have you, you shall not have anybody in all of Finnmark.' Yet the
story suggests Kari had done all she could to help him. When she
was questioned about Abraham Nilsen's accusation of Johannis,
she turned to a boy known as Jacob N, and said instead of Johannis
it was Jacob who had fathered Ingeborgh's baby. Jacob denied it,
but then injured his back – so badly he told the court it was 'broken'
– and blamed Kari's witchcraft. Even in defending Johannis, she
was trapped. The evidence of their relationship and her apparent
revenge on Abraham and Jacob looked bad to her trial jurors. It
was the old story of the lustful, untrustworthy witch, like the
accusations made against Helena Scheuberin and Effie McCalzean.
The evidence against Kari was, however, stronger: no one disputed
her intimacy with her accuser.

The accompanying charges about Henrik's drowning added to
suspicion: Kari had quarrelled with Henrik during movements from
Hop to Omgang and Gamvik. Evidently, she travelled the coast
and the sandy valley of the Tana River, perhaps migrating season-
ally for herding or trade. She was paid for small sewing tasks, but
we know little more about her. Yet in 1620 everyone knew the
distinctive 'Find-Karri' and her feud with Henrik. Recently they
had seemed more friendly, until Kari visited Henrik at Omgang
and asked him to give her a small container. When Henrik refused,
it was over this petty pot that Kari finally lost her patience. His
drowning seemed to be the result.

When people fell out with Kari, the jury must have felt, something bad happened to them afterwards. Maybe it was gand! The

evidence also looked compelling in the case of Anders Rasmussen and his unnamed wife. Anders's wife had given Kari some work to do on two scarves that she wanted repaired, and one day she went to collect them from Kari, expecting to be able to pay later. However, Kari wisely insisted on immediate payment before she parted with the repaired garments. When Anders's wife refused, Anders said at Kari's trial, she fell ill. She became so lame that she had to walk with crutches, stumping painfully and unsteadily through the icy mud. Anders was furious when he thought of it: his dear wife pestered for payment by this suspicious 'Finn' who seemed to have made her sick. He went to see Kari himself and threatened her, and Kari insisted that his wife should come and see her, bringing the money that she owed. Once she had visited Kari and paid the debt, immediately Anders's wife recovered, so much so that she didn't need to use her crutches on the walk back from Kari's house. It seemed a stark example of the harm witches could do with the devil's help, how easily they could manipulate others and why they were a danger not just to their neighbours but to the government. If John Cunningham's associate Abraham Nilsen could be thrown out of the governor's own boat by witchcraft, no one was safe. And in the evidence of Anders and Johannis, the state, represented by the bailiff, was presented with a clear case against Kari.

However, to help the jurors – an all-male, settler panel – decide their verdict, Bailiff Søffren Nielsen decreed Kari would be 'swum' in the harbour. This meant, shockingly, that she would be thrown into the icy sea to see if she sank or floated. It was a regular test of witches in Finnmark – an ancient 'ordeal' trial supplementing questioning of the accused. It was also practised in several other northern European countries: there are instances in Scotland, although there is no record of the test in the cases of those tried in the North Berwick trials. The ordeal was based on folk belief that those who sank were innocent, whereas those who floated were guilty. If a person floated, the God-created water had rejected them, people thought. After all, sensible, modest women did not go sea-bathing, so most of them did not know the skills of buoyancy. Floating was unnatural and what was unnatural might be demonic.

Kari floated, thrashing desperately to drag herself from the bitterly cold sea. Half-drowned, she was then convicted of witchcraft by the jury. But her misery was not over. In Norway, unlike Scotland, torture happened after conviction in order to get the guilty person to name accomplices and cleanse their soul ready for death. It focused on the rack, a machine for stretching the victim's body agonisingly, particularly their joints, which were often dislocated. The rack was also used in Austria and was what would have been used on Helena Scheuberin and her co-accused if they had not had a good lawyer. Kari had no representation, unlike Helena, so she was tortured. We see a glimpse of the vicious, cold-blooded assault when her trial record notes that her confession occurred 'at the height of her distress'.[9]

During the torture, Kari confessed whatever her pitiless questioners wanted, just as Anny Sampson and Gillie Duncan had done thirty years before. She said she had become a witch as a young girl. Tired by herding animals, she had fallen into a state neither sleeping nor waking. A 'ghost' in the shape of a headless man had come to her in this trance and offered her a bunch of keys. 'If you accept these keys,' the spirit tempted, 'all you wish to do in the world will come to pass.' But Kari was a Sámi – perhaps she lived in a *lavvu* tent with only a few possessions. What use did she have for keys? Instead, she said she noticed the ghost was carrying a pretty ribbon, probably the kind of decoration that Sámi people sewed into their clothing. 'Give me that ribbon,' she said to the ghost, adding, 'I do not know how to use the keys.' And the ghost agreed. Of course, when she was questioned by Christians during her torture, Kari was forced to say that this 'ghost' was in fact the devil and in accepting his gift she had become a witch. Heartbreakingly, she also told her questioners that this devil had tortured her into madness by 'stretching her limbs' when she later refused to do his bidding, hurting her until she bled from her nose and mouth. But it was not the devil who put Kari on the rack – it was Søffren Nielsen, acting for the governor and the king by enforcing their new anti-witchcraft law. At the end of her trial, the innocent Sámi herder Kari Edisdatter was burned to death as a witch.[10]

After Kari's execution, stories continued to circulate that led to a continuation of the witch-hunt with several related trials. Suspicions focused on Kari's stepsister, whom she had named as an accomplice: Lisbet Nilsdatter, married to Rasmus Joensen of Omgang. Also suspected was a woman known as 'Morten Nilsen's Anne from Langefjord', who might also have been a stepsister of Kari's, although naming conventions leave this unclear. Seventeenth-century Finnmarkers were often known by descriptive names rather than modern-style surnames: for their second name, children took on the forename of their father plus 'sen' (son) or 'datter' (daughter) and wives were often referred to by their husband's names and placenames, like Anne, who was married to Morten Nilsen of Langefjord. So, despite their different namings, Lisbet and Kari were stepsisters and the stories about them suggest that Anne may have been another sister. Lisbet Nilsdatter was tried on 28 April 1621: she 'knew witchcraft', the court was told, 'was able to extort whatever she wanted from people' and 'had no second thoughts about killing a man or two'. Like her stepsister, she was tried by swimming, after which she confessed. Lisbet said she had learned magic from Kari five years earlier when Kari came to the goat-shed on her small farm, accompanied by Satan in the form of a grey buck goat. Goats were new to nomadic Sámi, who had previously milked reindeer. In the shape of this magical goat Satan supposedly made a pact with Lisbet, during which she renounced her baptism and promised to serve the devil.[11]

Then, Lisbet said, Kari taught her something useful. What should it be but milk-theft – exactly the same trick attributed to Innsbruck witches a century before. Kari and Lisbet's method was to hold a goat's horn under the belly of any animal they fancied milking; the horn would fill with milk. Lisbet explained in desperate excitement that she could magic up 'a whole bucketful . . . as often as she wanted to in the course of a day'. This imagined luxury was wonderful while it lasted. But, sadly, Lisbet told the court that her supposed power left her when her stepsister was executed. And, of course, Kari had died accusing Lisbet, a wretched legacy. Trapped, Lisbet admitted complicity in the murders Kari said she had helped with: drowning Abraham and Henrik. She added that the witches had also met in the summer of 1619 for a Sabbath, just like the meetings of the North Berwick witches. Here they had danced and drunk into the long light night of Arctic Circle July. Lisbet named several other women who had been at the Sabbath, one of whom was Anne from Langefjord, who was also present in the courtroom among the crowd of fascinated villagers and 'furiously' denied it. We don't know what happened to Anne. Did her angry denial save her? Or is she the 'Ane Larsdatter' or 'Ane Edisdatter' who were tried later, in 1621 and 1624 respectively? Miserably, like her stepsister Kari, Lisbet was burned for witchcraft.[12]

The killing of Abraham and Henrik, two prominent fishermen-traders, and the execution of their supposed murderers got the Finnmark community talking. Of most interest was the belief that witches could summon storms. In both Denmark and Scotland witchcraft was blamed for ship-wrecking tempests, and both Norwegians and Sámi also believed that storm winds could be created, sold and bought. An artificial breeze could be caught in a tie-neck gand bag or in knots in a length of string, and it could be activated by untying. This was useful for becalmed sailors, but dangerous if an enemy let loose a killer gale. Such deadly storms were a frequent occurrence off the Finnmark coast, so much so that Sámi divining drums featured a storm symbol. And in the same year that Christian IV's witchcraft decree was published, on 24 December 1617 a violent storm had whirled into Vardø. It filled the bays along the east coast from Kiberg in the south to Vesterbarvika in the north, whipping up huge waves whose spray clouded the sky. 'The sea rose like ashes,' said someone who saw it. More than forty men from the Finnmark fishing fleet were out that day in their distinctive boats, the nordlanders. They were (and are) strong, light, narrow craft like the Viking longships from which they're descended. Nordlanders were ballasted by rocks, but they had a shallow profile, with only a short keel digging down into the sea. If a storm came up when nets were over their sides, they were vulnerable to flipping over. This was exactly what happened on Christmas Eve 1617.

The storm that day should not have caused a disaster. Many Norwegian fishermen were skilled sailors, as generations of their Norse ancestors had been. They could read clouds and tides, predict rain and gales. Even if all their experience failed them and they went into the water, they were better protected against the cold than almost anyone else on earth. They often wore leather overalls that formed a waterproof bag around their bodies. Underneath was a thick multi-layered coat of woollen insulation. Yet none of this saved the men of Vardø and its surrounding settlements. Forty of them drowned that day in 1617 and their womenfolk and children were left to mourn uncomprehendingly in half-empty villages. But during the trials of Kari Edisdatter and Lisbet Nilsdatter, a new possibility emerged that might account for the terrible death toll. Perhaps it could be explained retrospectively by witchcraft? Suspicion settled on eleven more women: Mari Jorgensdatter, Siri and Else Knudsdatter, Kirsten Sørensdatter, Marrite Olsdatter, Guri Olsdatter from Lille Ekkerøy, Guri Olsdatter from Store Ekkerøy, Ane Larsdatter, Kari Olufsdatter, Ragnhilde Olusfdatter and Mette Thorgiersdatter. Although some of the records of their trials are lost, we still have transcripts of several of them including the trial of the most important 'witch' of 1621: Kirsten Sørensdatter.[13]

Kirsten was sometimes known as Kirsti and she lived at Kiberg, a tiny village seven miles from Vardø, where she was the wife of Anders Johansen. Kirsti had come to Finnmark with him in 1597 shortly after their marriage. She had been born near Helsingør in Denmark, over a thousand miles to the south, had worked as a

servant and lived in the big mid-Norwegian town of Bergen. The
couple's ambitious relocation to the far north must have seemed a
promising new start. It was a migration offering new opportunities
for trading and prosperity – like the ones other settlers were under-
taking at the same time to America. By 1620 Kirsti was fifty-seven
years old, a capable, well-travelled Danish woman. But in 1617 she
found herself suspected of a witchcraft offence: killing four cows
– a charge that doesn't seem to have been brought to trial until
1621, when she was charged with leading the group who caused
the tempest that killed the forty fishermen. This accusation was
made because Kirsti had quarrelled with one of the victims, Anders
Blom, shortly before his death. Her accusers alleged that the other
suspected women – especially Else Knudsdatter and the two Guri
Olsdatters – had offered to help Kirsti get her revenge. Anders Blom,
Kirsti's neighbours said, had assaulted her over a petty quarrel and
then he had drowned; thus, she had killed him, just as Kari had
killed Abraham Nilsen. Kirsti had also later argued with another
man, Henrik Meyer, and like Anders he had died. From this grew
the allegation that she and some of her fellow witches had killed
all the men who had drowned on Christmas Eve 1617.

Why was it not until four years after the loss of the fishermen
that Kirsti Sørensdatter and her friends were accused of killing
them? The answer, in part, has to be John Cunningham. We can
see his distinctive preoccupations, drawn from the North Berwick
witch trial and others and transported with him to Finnmark, all
over the evidence he extracted from Kirsti. Unlike the trials of Kari
and Lisbet – where he had oversight as governor but was not
present in person – Cunningham attended all of Kirsti's trial.
Through him, the upper echelons of the Danish–Norwegian state
took direct control of this key trial focused on the supposed mass
murder of seafarers, ensuring the verdict that was needed and firmly
establishing demonology as the basis of future Finnmark witch
trials, just as the 1617 decree required.

Kirsti's trial took place in the Vardøhus fortress on 26 and 28
April 1621. Taking his seat in the crowded courtroom, John

Cunningham was deferred to by all present – he's described in the records as 'the illustrious Hans Køning' (as a foreigner, he was also known by variants of his name such as Hanns Køningham and Hans Cunninghiemb).[14] Despite the formal role of the presiding bailiff, John-Hans shaped the evidence, just as James VI had shaped the trial of Anny and Gillie with his omnipotent authority. Kirsti must have been intimidated to see the governor himself sitting with the bailiff and jury. At first, she 'fiercely denied' all the allegations, exclaiming her accusers 'had slandered her cruelly'. It was a good strategy, but meant the court threatened her with the swimming ordeal. And Kirsti could not face it. It was April, and the sea temperature was about three degrees centigrade. Kirsti had spent her life by and upon the ocean. She knew what happened to people who succumbed to its numbing hug so far north. Intimidated, exhausted by her imprisonment and alone, her resistance collapsed, and, like all the others, she wretchedly confirmed for her questioner exactly what he needed to hear in order to enforce his king's new law.

First, Kirsti told John a story about how she had learned witchcraft, probably in answer to a question. She was trained as a sixteen-year-old in Helsingør, she said, when she worked as a maid and farmhand for an old woman there. One day, when she was herding the farmer's geese home, Satan appeared to her in the form of a dog, rather like the devil-dog or familiar spirit who bothered Anny Sampson's clients. The dog proposed a deal to Kirsti, just as any demonologist would expect: 'If you agree to learn witchcraft, all that you do in this world will succeed,' he said. What Kirsti had to do was renounce her baptism and serve the devil, just like the North Berwick witches, just like Kari. Kirsti was not sure what to do, so she asked for advice. Her employer told her to agree to the devil's demand. In fact, the farmer revealed, she was already a witch herself, so Kirsti could join her witch-conspiracy. Kirsti's employer then offered her knowledge, just like Eve. It involved book-learning, an exciting prospect for a servant girl. The farmer read to Kirsti, teaching her witchcraft, and even set her an exam: could she make a ball of wool float on water? Kirsti could. She enjoyed blowing on the wool, watching it move across the surface. Of course, this was all, in various ways, nonsense tied to the fear of female knowledge. Perhaps what Kirsti's employer actually taught her was a little literacy, some tips to heal geese or a charm to find a good husband. Kirsti tried to exit from her confession by saying that she had not used her witchcraft for ten years after her initiation. But the court would not let her go.[15]

She was forced to tell the story of the rest of her life: her next job as a servant in Bergen, her marriage in 1597 – the year John Cunningham was learning more about witch trials back home in Crail – and the bold colonial move to Finnmark with her husband. Thinking about that hard sea journey into the day-long dark seemed to remind her that she was in a witch-haunted place, one that was believed by everyone in the hushed courtroom to be besieged by gand and the devil. Kirsti was supposed to be confessing, and no doubt John Cunningham reminded her of that. Prompted, she crumbled and said that in Finnmark she had once again used her magical skill and turned it on her neighbours. Yes, she had attended Sabbaths. She and her fellow witches had sailed there across the sea or flown through the air. Yes, she had killed people too.

The court remanded her until 28 April. It is likely Kirsti was then tortured, and John Cunningham may have been present during her racking, asking questions as she wept and screamed. It's hard not to flinch away from her pain – pain endured for no purpose but to extract a magically transformed story of Kirsti's life, her reality bleeding out of her and clotting into crazy demonological tales. Back in court on 28 April, bruised, aching and broken, she confessed to further acts of witchcraft. Yes, she had worked with Else Knudsdatter to 'raise a bit of weather for Anders Blom's and Anders Rasmussen's people so that they drown'. Yes, they did this by tying knots in a piece of fishing line and blowing upon it 'so that the weather turned foul and the many men perished'.[16] The state had found what it wanted: an explanation for the Christmas Eve shipwreck of 1617.

*

Why can we infer that John Cunningham steered the events of Kirsti's trial? Because knowledge of previous witch trials, especially Scottish ones, shapes her confession, and it is very likely that demonological knowledge is John's. There are broad similarities with the Scottish cases but there are also detailed likenesses, and there are references to John's own life experiences. Kirsti's story appears to be partly John's story, just as Anny Sampson's was partly the story of James VI. It looks as if Anny's story also shapes Kirsti's because John likely knew Anny's story, perhaps from the printed trial report *Newes from Scotland*. Demonology spread in print, remember, as well as by experience and word of mouth.

Certainly, Kirsti's account of the Finnmark witches is very like that of the North Berwick witches. The idea that witches caused storms was common in Danish–Norwegian trials like the one in 1589, but there are other details that echo the North Berwick case. Both sets of witches sail to their Sabbath. Both involve a devil-dog or familiar. One of the crimes Kirsti was charged with was being the 'master and admiral' of the witch fleet and the word 'admiral' was used about one of Anny's group too. 'Admiral' also precisely describes John Cunningham's own role in his naval career, on those expeditions to Greenland.[17] His importation of Scottish demonological ideas, drawing on his own experience, shows how they spread so that one witch trial spawned others.

Some of the details of the Sabbaths said to have been attended by both Scottish and Finnmark witches are also exactly the same. In her confession, Kirsti said that the witches 'drank and danced and played' at these parties, like the North Berwick witches. In addition, she explained that a man named Bertil Henriksen 'wrote for them'. Meanwhile, Ane Larsdatter stated that Kirsti 'led' the witches 'with flute and drum'. These seem to be echoes of the roles of John Fian and Gillie Duncan at the North Berwick Sabbaths: John Fian was the witches' scribe, keeping a register of attendance, and Gillie Duncan led the witches' dances by playing on a Jew's trump. Neither of these details – the writing or the music – is elaborated by Kirsti or Ane; they feel like ideas inserted into their

minds by a questioner, perhaps like the word 'admiral'. Maybe as
the women shuddered in fear and pain, John Cunningham drew
on his demonological knowledge to ask: 'Did someone write notes
for you at the Sabbath?' To which they replied, 'Yes, Bertil did.'
Or he might have said, 'Did someone play music for you?' To
which Ane replied, 'Yes, Kirsti did that on a flute and drum.' While
the details could have occurred spontaneously in both cases – and
witches were accused of similar activities in some other trials – the
list of similarities feels too long to be coincidence.[18] These similarities did not arise because Kirsti, Ane and the North Berwick accused
were all members of the same pagan cult; it is far more likely they
occur because the accused women were being asked to confirm
elements of a conspiracy theory suggested to them by elite agents
of the Christian state, men whose demonological ideas had travelled
with them internationally.

Like Kari and Lisbet, Kirsti Sørensdatter was burned. Her name
and theirs now grace the witch trial memorial by Vardø's beach.

In Kirsti's trial we saw local, popular understandings of witchcraft
meet with internationally imported demonological ideas in a toxic
mix, just as they did in Scotland thirty years before. The mention of
a drum in the evidence against Kirsti, for example, differs from the
Jew's trump played by Gillie Duncan, and that part of the evidence
sounds authentically local because it suggests Sámi divining drums.
In later trials Sámi drums were even confiscated as Satanic artefacts. This happened to the drums of Quiwe Baarsen and Anders
Poulsen, two Sámi noaide, or shamans, accused of witchcraft later
in the seventeenth century. Tried in 1627, Quiwe described his 'rune
drum which is made of a pine root over which strong hide from
a reindeer bull is stretched, or buckskin'. It was decorated with
the claws of every type of animal and symbols for 'their God' (as
his trial record puts it), sun, moon and animals.[19] Tried in 1692,
Anders Poulsen echoed Quiwe's description, adding Christ, God, the
church, the Holy Spirit, St Anne and the Virgin Mary, indicating
that by 1692 the ancient Sámi symbols had been part-Christianised.

But Anders's piety did not protect him. While Quiwe Baarsen was burned, Anders was murdered by an anti-witchcraft vigilante while in custody. The killer explained he had 'heard that the said Sámi had cast spells on a large number of people and boats that had disappeared', and that was why he had killed him.[20] Once again, international demonology and local people's folk beliefs about witchcraft had met in seventeenth-century Finnmark, this time in stories that merged Satanic conspiracy with witch-drums, Danish and Norwegian magical charms and Sámi gand; and as a result, Anders had been murdered. 'Witches' like him were still being suspected of sinking ships nearly eighty years after the trials of Kari, Lisbet, Kirsti and the others in 1620–21.

In response to the witch trials of 1620–21 and after, as well as other colonial aggression, the Sámi gradually moved away from the settlers. They were driven north by the arrival of more traders and Christian ministers who increasingly wanted to stop them practising their own religion. Their permanent migration north freed up their more southern lands for the colonists. Witch trials were not just misogynist festivals of torture and hatred, they also directly facilitated the building of empire. Although most of the accused witches in Norway were settler women, the colonial dimension of witchcraft stories recurs in many witch trials. The Sámi encountered the same kind of religious prejudices that Native American peoples would be subjected to by the colonists who, in the years of the first Finnmark witch trial, were sailing across the Atlantic to another 'new world'. There too, Native peoples would be demonised and driven from their lands, and some would be accused of witchcraft in trials that would frequently grow to include settlers, but where often the first accused was an indigenous person. Demonology spread like a virus across the globe, meeting local beliefs as it went. In each new location Satan's agents were discovered and subjected to witch trials.

CHAPTER FOUR

The Trial of Joan Wright:
Practical Magic and America's First Witch

A century and a half after Kari Edisdatter and Kirsti Sørensdatter's deaths, the future American president Thomas Jefferson was shuffling through papers in coffee houses and courtrooms in Williamsburg, Virginia. Peering through his self-designed eyeglasses in uncertain candlelight, he was looking for documents from the earliest European colony in the 'new world' – Virginia, settled in 1607. As a lawyer, Thomas was well connected at the establishments where Virginian civic leaders drank, and as a historian he knew where to look for old records. He found treasures. One of them was from the library of the Williamsburg Courthouse. The courthouse had kept the earliest records of the Virginia colony, their crinkly, fragile pages often 'in such a state of decay that the leaf falls to pieces on being turned over', as Thomas wrote to a friend. By the 1770s, there were one hundred and fifty years of volumes in the Williamsburg Courthouse library or scattered beyond it. Many of Virginia's oldest records had been sold or discarded. Some were being used as wastepaper – scraps on which Williamsburg clerks and merchants could make notes when they met at Henry Wetherburn's Raleigh Tavern, Jane Vobe's King's Arms or John Marot's English Coffee House.

It's not clear where Thomas found his volume of court records.

Perhaps by the card tables at the Apollo where he had danced with his college crush Rebecca Burwell, or in the conference room at the Raleigh, where he helped design an intelligence agency for the American colonies in the 1770s. But it was an important discovery: a record of cases in Virginia's General Court in the 1620s. The General Court lived up to its name, hearing all legal disputes in the new territory. Its judges were the colony's top officials, members of the company that had financed Virginia as a plantation for luxury commodities like tobacco and wine. Their court heard cases about land rights, trade, debts and moral crimes, and also granted new land to settlers arriving from England. Because it dealt with everything, its records were a valuable source of information about America's history. Thomas likely wanted to use them for one of his ongoing projects. During the 1770s and 1780s he worked on a constitution for Virginia, a corpus of state laws and a history.

Thomas mourned the record losses that had already happened by the 1770s and wrote that 'our experience has proved to us that a single copy, or a few, deposited in manuscript in the public offices, cannot be relied on for any great length of time. The ravages of fire and ferocious enemies have had too much part in producing the very loss we are now deploring.'[1] So he kept this precious volume on his bookshelves at Monticello, his own home. Thomas Jefferson was state governor from 1779 to 1780, a diplomat in France from 1784 to 1789, secretary of state on his return and, at last, became the third president of the United States in 1801. If he'd ever intended to give the manuscript back to the Williamsburg Courthouse, he forgot. And, surprisingly, this was a good thing. During Thomas's state governorship, all the other early records of the General Court went into storage in Richmond, Virginia's new state capital. During the American Civil War, on the night of 3 April 1865, retreating Confederate forces set fire to them. All were burned, centuries of irreplaceable history powdered into ash and smuts. Except, of course, for the volume in protective custody on Thomas's shelves, which contained details of America's first documented witch trial, contemporary with the trials of Kari and Kirsti.

When you think about the history of American witchcraft, perhaps you think first about Salem, the Massachusetts town where a witch-hunt broke out in 1692, your mind filling with images of sour-faced Puritans amid New England snows (a later chapter of this book tells that story). Few people know America's first witch-hunt happened six hundred miles south and seventy years earlier than Salem, among worldly merchants and property developers in Jamestown, Virginia, who were not Puritans at all. Here, Joan Wright was charged with using witchcraft in 1626. She did not know her accusation would become a significant historical moment, the first-known American witch trial. Nor would she have been impressed to know that it was recorded in a book prized by the president of the new nation she helped to found. For Joan, the witch trial was simply an ordeal, one of many in a very eventful life.

She was born in the English city of Kingston-upon-Hull in around 1580 to 1590. Hull – as it's usually known – is in the East Riding of Yorkshire, on the east coast of northern England. Colonists set out from Hull and other English ports to make a better life in America, setting a shining example to the 'old' world in what were meant to be the ideal cities of the 'new'. But instead, Joan Wright's story shows us a terrible reality: settlers hoisting sail with lofty words, only to sink into persecution, racism, misogyny and a witch trial that was exactly like those of old Europe. How did this calamity happen?

Let's begin with a housemaid labouring in a provincial English dairy in the early 1600s. In her youth, the Virginian 'witch' Joan was a servant in the Hull household of a superstitious employer. She worked in the dairy, processing milk into butter and cheese. Many seventeenth-century people milked their own cows and made dairy products for home use and neighbourhood markets. It demanded skill, specialist equipment and chilled space. In the cold hush of her employer's dairy, Joan skimmed and strained milk, pressed and drained curds to make cheeses, and churned cream into butter. A butter churn is a conical wooden barrel with a vertical plunger or 'staff' inside – remember that, it will be important later. Inside the churn, cream separated from liquid milk to concentrate its fat is agitated by the pounding of the plunger. As fat globules rupture and coalesce, butter forms. It's scraped out, compressed, salted and stored. Churning isn't easy. In seventeenth-century England it was confined to late spring and summer, when lush grasses make fatty milk. However, in the days before refrigeration, milk curdled easily. If that happened, the fat would not coalesce, and hours of churning would still produce no butter. Puzzled dairy-maids often concluded witches had cursed their churn, souring the near-magical transformation of cream into butter. They were left with nothing to show for a whole morning's work but a churn full of smelly liquid.[2]

One day when Joan was churning in her employer's house, a woman called at the door who, as Joan told her American neigh-bours many years later, was suspected of witchcraft. The woman might have come to the big house to ask for a charitable handout, which was one way witchcraft accusations started. While sometimes accusations could result from a direct argument – like that between Helena Scheuberin and Jörg Spiess or Kirsti Sørensdatter and Anders Blom – even ambiguous encounters could prompt suspicion. Poor people who went from door to door asking for a few apples, some yeast or a pint of milk were sometimes accused of witchcraft. If they got what they came for and went away smiling, all was well. But if their request was turned down or they looked disappointed with their gift, things could turn nasty. In particular, if they grum-bled and then disaster struck the property they'd visited, householders might decide their home had been cursed. While demonologists insisted Satan must always have been involved in any such witch attack, often these neighbour-against-neighbour accusations didn't mention him. They believed in witchcraft, but they didn't buy into all the detailed theories of demonology. The supposed victims didn't always take the matter to a church or state court, either. Instead, they would often find their own remedy, known as 'counter-magic'. This meant performing a magical rite or deploying a charm to nullify the supposed witch attack – the sort of magic practised by Anny Sampson. This was what Joan's employer planned to do.[3]

On that hot day at the turn of the seventeenth century, Joan's employer – the 'dame', as her servants called her – was lying in wait to confront her visitor with an accusation of witchcraft and take action against it. Stomping into the dairy, she ordered Joan to interrupt her churning. 'By directions from her dame', Joan explained years later, she 'clapped the churn staff to the bottom of the churn and clapped her hands across upon the top of it'. Holding down the plunger with both hands, she stood still and expected more orders. Silence fell, replacing the thump and swoosh of the churning. Joan's employer smiled triumphantly, told Joan to keep the plunger rammed down to the bottom of the churn and swept out of the door. The suspected witch loitered awkwardly. Sometime later, Joan's employer returned. Both her maid and her unwelcome guest were still there. Relieved but confused, Joan begged her dame 'to ask the woman why she did not get her gone'. Then the point of Joan's long wait gripping the churn plunger was revealed: it was counter-magic, designed to get the 'witch' to confess and remove her evil spell from the milk in the churn.

An astonishing thing happened, Joan explained years later. The witchcraft suspect 'fell down on her knees and asked forgiveness' of Joan's dame. She 'said her hand was in the churn and could not stir before [the] maid lifted up the staff of the churn'. Flabbergasted, Joan let go of the staff and immediately 'the witch went away'. Joan's employer had, apparently, trapped the witch's hand – or at least, an imaginary, spiritual projection of her hand, known as a 'spectre' – under the staff so she could not move. This magical hand had been holding back the butter from forming. Now the witch was snared by her own attack and had removed her curse, allowing butter to be made.

Joan's story is an indication of just how strong belief in witchcraft could be. Not only Joan and her dame but also the suspected witch all agreed that projecting a spectral hand was possible, and the hand could be caught. Did the 'witch' really think her hand was in the churn? Did Joan invent the woman's confession to make a good story? Whatever the truth, the confrontation demonstrates that magic was part of ordinary experience; it was all just as real as a wooden barrel or the salty tang of butter on the tongue. And it didn't need demonology to make sense of it. When there was no churchman or royal official to ask questions informed by demonology, people dealt with the suspected magic in their own way, and sometimes a witch trial was avoided.[4]

Later in her life, four thousand miles away, Joan told this story to her American neighbours, along with a second tale of witchcraft and informal counter-magic. One time, Joan said, her dame thought herself bewitched. Perhaps she believed she'd been cursed by the woman whose hand was trapped in the churn. Joan's dame might have imagined her creeping spectrally through the house, rubbing her bruised hand and sighing out sickness onto her victim. The dame asked Joan, her maid, for help. As with the previous incident, Joan was to wait for a woman to come to the door. When the woman arrived, Joan must seize a horseshoe she had ready in the kitchen and 'fling it into the oven'. The oven was a domed brick box built into the fireplace and Joan was to bake her horseshoe inside. Once it was 'red hot' Joan would use it in a charm against witchcraft. The horseshoe was made of iron, thought to be powerful against witches. In counter-magical spells, iron-tipped arrows were fired into beer vats to 'unwitch' them and iron knives were stuck into tables where food was prepared. The horseshoe, with its wide smile and reassuringly heavy heft, was especially lucky. So, taking it out of the oven, Joan was to 'fling' it into a pot of 'her dame's urine'. 'As long as the horseshoe was hot, the witch was sick at the heart,' Joan explained. As the urine hissed, the witch would clutch her own body in agony and lift her curse. Apparently, Joan's horseshoe charm worked. As it cooled, her employer recovered. This anti-witchcraft charm and her earlier experience with the butter churn were Joan's introduction to witches. She talked about this when, about twenty years later, she was put on trial as a witch herself in Virginia.[5]

Sometime before 1610, Joan left Hull and undertook a terrifying sea journey to America, just like Kirsti Sørensdatter migrating north to Finnmark at the same time thousands of miles away. Kirsti travelled with her husband, Joan perhaps with an employer, following her job, or perhaps alone. Since she was not a wealthy woman, her passage was likely paid for by a colonial investor. Paying for an American immigrant's passage entitled the bill-payer to fifty acres of colonial land, an entitlement called a 'head right'. Servants and other labourers who were shipped to America were thus treated as a property investment. Joan's head, bouncing queasily across the Atlantic waves, was worth a lot to a sponsor. By 1610 she had arrived in Virginia and married a tobacco-planter and sawyer, Robert Wright. For the first time in Joan's life we have a surname for her: Wright was her married name. Robert had been in Virginia since 1608, arriving on a ship called the *Swan*. In Virginian terms, he was an 'ancient planter': a man or woman who landed in the colony's earliest days, stayed at least three years and had paid for their own passage. Robert Wright was a solid prospect as a husband for Joan.

Robert had raised enough money to ship himself halfway round the world, and later – as the new colony flourished – he was entitled to be granted at least one hundred acres by the Virginia Company for financing his own migration. The land didn't come as a usable package at once, however, so he had to do other work in the meantime. Why did he choose Joan as a wife? It might have been a love-match or a matter of mutual convenience. Convention dictated that planters needed wives to run their homes – ideally sensible, hard-working women who would have children to help out on their farms and inherit their businesses. Our Joan fitted that specification. She married Robert in 1610, probably soon after her ship docked in Virginia's James River, and probably in the new wooden church at the village known as Kecoughtan or Elizabeth City. Things had worked out for her so far. Soon she also became the mother of two children. She had done what was required of her by the practical, hard-headed founders of the colony.[6]

*

Once in Virginia, the Wrights lived at Kecoughtan, which early records call 'Kickotan'. Until 1610 Kecoughtan had been a Native American settlement, with eighteen houses surrounded by maize fields. The villagers had opened their homes to passing white explorers like Captain John Smith, who had visited them in 1608, and shared their food – oysters, fish, meat and bread. But in 1609 trouble began. There was conflict between the neighbouring Nansemond people and the colonists, who had extorted food from the Nansemonds, burned their homes and destroyed the burial place of their elders. In July 1610 this colonial warfare brought disaster to Kecoughtan. A party of soldiers got into trouble on the creek twenty miles from the village. One of them tried to retrieve a longboat from the Nansemond shore and he was killed by the people there. Lieutenant General Sir Thomas Gates, the leader of his troop, decided to attack Kecoughtan in retaliation, although its people were a separate grouping. His men drove the villagers out, killing over a dozen of their former hosts and burning their homes. They also seized their crops. The staging of the attack during harvest was not a coincidence: over one hundred and fifty bushels of corn were cut from Kecoughtan's fields and shipped to Jamestown Island to feed the hungry colonists there and then the settlers took over the cornfields and the village.

Having gained their objective, Sir Thomas's militia built two wooden stockades at Kecoughtan and named them in tribute to the sons of our old acquaintances King James VI and Queen Anna, who now ruled both Scotland and England. The stockades, Fort Henry and Fort Charles, formed the base for a plan to settle the area. Kecoughtan was renamed Elizabeth City, for James and Anna's daughter. A church was built, the one where Robert and Joan Wright were probably married soon after its construction.[7] Robert and Joan prospered, working for other families on their plantations and building side businesses as independent sources of income. In the mid-1620s we find them living at Elizabeth City with the Bonall family, French wine-growers who had come to America to plant vines. The Bonalls had a vineyard at Buck Row, or Buckroe, near

Elizabeth City, east of the main settlement on a creek. In 1625, when a military muster or census was compiled, Robert and Joan Wright and their two children were living with Anthony Bonall and Elias Legardo, two vine-planters, two young English servants, William Binsley and Robert Godwin, and two other Frenchmen. Outside the Bonall home, Robert's physical skills as a sawyer were in demand clearing new land, building forts and homes, and providing planks for shipping barrels and crates.[8] Meanwhile, Joan was working medically and spiritually as a midwife and fortune-teller. Unfortunately, as in Austria, Scotland, Norway and England, this type of work tended to attract suspicions of witchcraft.

Around her Elizabeth City was growing rapidly, with migrant boats arriving regularly packed with colonists. Most new arrivals were English, but there were also Scots, Irish and mainland European people – Dutch, Poles, Italians, bringing a rich mix of magical traditions. By the mid-1620s there were at least twenty Africans in Virginia, the first of many arrivals for whom the 'new world' was a prison. Black enslaved people were brought to the colony to farm tobacco, so some of Joan's neighbours were enslaved people or traffickers. Soon plantation-owners were leaving African people to their descendants in their wills alongside livestock, crops and weaponry, beginning a history of violent exploitation. Wealthy Virginians also held white indentured servants in conditions that led some to say they were 'sold here up and down like horses'. In 1624 there were accusations that employers John and Alice Proctor had beaten to death two of their servants. Some were forced to work for their employers for many years after their indentures – or contracts – had expired, half-starved and unpaid. Unlike their enslaved co-workers, however, they had entered into contracts and could fight in the courts for freedom and a pass allowing them to return home. But the freewheeling power of the Virginian elite meant the notional rights of others were often ignored.

The colony was a hard place to live. Joan and Robert Wright had survived until 1626 because they were tough and mostly lucky. So far the court had favoured them, and in April 1626 Robert was awarded damages against George Fryer who failed to pay him for three weeks' work.[9] The Wrights were employable and adaptable, which was why they were in Virginia in the first place. From the flat, marshy shore at Buckroe they could look towards the old world and think how far they had come. Despite hardship, they kept sane, focused and entertained through dark nights and long winters. Perhaps they walked the golden-sanded beach, picked the strawberries that jewelled the grass, fished in brown marsh pools, paddled in the surf. The Wrights had practical attitudes and skills and Joan also had a stolid religious faith that things would turn out well. She needed this faith as the Virginia Colony grew. By the mid-1620s, Elizabeth City and the colonial capital Jamestown were densely populated, with over 1,300 inhabitants across the two settlements, but these were the survivors of famine, Native American attacks and an epidemic, which together had killed over 3,000 colonists.

In the background of Joan's life looms an enormous, awful fact: she and her neighbours lived under the daily shadow of starvation or murder because they were inexpert invaders of somebody else's land. They did not know how to cultivate unfamiliar crops, so they stole them. They did not understand Native American cultures, so their leaders failed to create meaningful alliances, just as the Norwegians failed with the Sámi. This was not sustainable, and on 22 March 1622 a Native American force attacked the Virginian colonists' villages with the intention of killing every settler. Plantations south of the James River were overwhelmed. Across the colony over three hundred people were killed – shot by arrows, hacked by axes, chased down and stabbed, driven into swamps and drowned. A few survived by hiding or fighting back until their attackers moved on. Afterwards, lost and traumatised, they crept out of the undergrowth and ruins and ran towards Jamestown. Where were Joan and Robert that day? Probably at Elizabeth City, safer on its peninsula than the lands south of the river. Did they run for their lives or stay put and hope for the best? Whatever happened to Joan later in her life, it would never be as bad as those spring days in 1622 when highly skilled hunters roamed the fields trying to kill her.

The settlers who survived 'the Massacre', as they called it, had not seen the last of trouble, however. The colony's records are spattered with casualties 'slain by the Indians'. Accordingly, after 1622 the colonists lived under harsh military rule, with sentinels patrolling their communities watching for external attackers but also increasingly for faults in their fellow colonists' lives. In some ways this was merely a tightening of existing restrictions on their freedom. Sometime between 1611 and 1616 a woman named Jane Wright – who may be our Joan but likely isn't, as both a Jane Wright and a Joan Wright are listed in colonial records – was actually whipped for sewing poor-quality shirts for the colonial forces. Protests had always been harshly punished.[10] But in 1623 in addition to, and partly because of, external threats, Jamestown ran short of food. People gave up farms inland 'in regard of the great danger of planting [farming] the same'. As is often the way, illness followed famine and a fever epidemic spread, killing many of the malnourished families who had escaped the massacre. Because of these disasters, the Virginia Company that had founded the colony went bust in 1624. So, in 1626 a new governor attempted a tighter grip on colonial life. Colonists stockpiled weapons and practised military drilling, movement was further restricted and there were religious changes. Daily prayer was now mandated along with stricter conformity to Protestantism – specifically the Anglican doctrine of the Church of England – and there was a crackdown on 'sin'. The colonists' private lives were no longer private, and the spotlight fell on women: several were prosecuted for drunkenness, 'whoredom' or adultery. And Joan, with her medical and magical work, was drifting into danger.[11]

In founding their colony, Virginians had imported into their laws the 1604 Witchcraft Act introduced by King James VI and I a year after he became King James I of England as well as King James VI of Scotland. As you would expect from James and his courtiers, the Act was informed by careful reading in demonology. It banned 'any invocation or conjuration of any evil and wicked spirit' and any further interaction with such spirits. No one should 'consult, covenant with, entertain, employ, feed or reward any evil and wicked spirit, to or for any intent or purpose'. Grave-robbing for magical purposes was specifically forbidden, suggesting anxiety about the use of body parts such as the bones and flesh mentioned in the Innsbruck and North Berwick accusations: no one should 'take up any dead man, woman, or child, out of his, her, or their grave, or any other place where the dead body resteth; or the skin, bone, or any other part of any dead person, to be employed, or used in any manner of witchcraft, sorcery, charm, or enchantment'. Anyone using any type of witchcraft to kill or harm a person would be executed along with any accomplices: 'aiders, abettors and counsellors'. Lesser offences like the use of magic to find stolen goods were punished by imprisonment.[12] Three decades after the Witchcraft Act, and thousands of miles away, Joan Wright would be tried under an anti-witchcraft law framed partly in response to the trials of Anny Sampson and Gillie Duncan, and formulated by one of their judges. It was intended to have the same outcome: the execution of witches who were a threat to the state. However, where some of the most sensational claims of demonologists were played out in the North Berwick trials, the Virginians were practical folk not much interested in demonological theory, and that lack of interest would shape Joan's trial.

State concern about witchcraft was directly embodied in the military men who came forward to accuse Joan Wright in September 1626. As with Anny, Gillie, Effie and the others in Scotland, and Kari, Kirsti and their co-accused in Finnmark, Joan's witch trial was staged in the context of interlinked crises. In Scotland in the 1590s there were anxieties about the succession, civil war and religious change that crystallised around fears the king and queen would be lost at sea. In Norway a mass shipwreck similarly came to be linked with worries about governance and religion, with the addition of fears about the indigenous Sámi. In Virginia the problems were similar: famine, disease and Native American attack, military rule and financial collapse. In all these places, religious beliefs driven by the Reformation framed fears about Satanic enemies within the community, which were then further defined by local concerns. Especially vulnerable were women who stood out in some way: in their speech, beliefs, skills, actions or attitude. Perhaps if these witches could be found and rooted out, the Virginian soldiery now reasoned, then God would smile on the colony. Their luck would turn and the military governors, traders, farmers and their wives could live the dream of freedom and plenty they'd imagined when they left the 'old' world and sailed over the edge of the map to start new lives in Virginia.

The first of Joan's accusers was Lieutenant Giles Allington. In his statements about himself and her, made to an unnamed magistrate in late summer 1626, Giles shows us both the context of his suspicions – the wider stresses of colonial life – and the reason for his fears to focus specifically on Joan. Like Robert Wright, he was an ancient planter, holding one hundred acres at Blunt Point, seventeen miles west of Buckroe. He came from a wealthy English family and was building a successful life in Virginia. He ought to have felt secure, but he didn't. Firstly, he explained to the magistrate, he and his fellow officers had experienced poor hunting recently. 'Having very fair game to shoot at', some of them had been unable to actually hit anything for over a year, he fretted. Another accuser, Thomas Jones, a weaver from Pasbehays near Jamestown, confirmed Giles's claim. Their prime example was Sergeant Reynold Booth, who both men said had gone out with his 'piece' or gun, 'came to good game and very fair to shoot at, but for a long time after he could never kill any thing'. Reynold had been in Virginia since 1609, so his local knowledge and skills should have been adequate to boost the colony's desperately vulnerable food supplies. But they weren't. So, although it was unusual to blame witches for disrupting hunting, Joan's hungry neighbours including Giles had begun to think only witchcraft could explain the twitchiness of the deer and wildfowl and the starvation of those who needed meat.

Giles's other fear about Joan was a more personal one. About six months previously, he'd made some bad decisions about the care of his pregnant wife. Childbirth was dangerous for mother and baby, and worrying for the wider community, which depended on rearing children. In 1625, a shipment of women was brought to Virginia to provide mothers for future colonists, and a few months later the General Court heard a negligence case against the physician Dr John Pott for failing to feed an expectant mother meat, supposedly causing a miscarriage.[13] With this level of sensitivity around childbirth, Giles had a delicate task in picking a midwife. He asked Joan, who must have had a good reputation for medical skill to have attracted the attention of a lieutenant's family. But when Giles told his wife, she objected to his choice because Joan was left-handed. Left-handedness was sometimes thought unlucky: the left hand was the 'sinister' one in Latin terminology, while the right hand was 'dexter', dextrous and blessed. Caught out by his wife's unexpected fears, Giles had to withdraw his invitation to Joan, depriving her of the lucrative work. He was reluctant to confront Joan about the lost job – so he didn't. Awkwardly, he avoided her.

Instead of having Joan deliver the baby, Giles's wife then asked him to get another woman, either Katherine or Eleanor Graves, to be her midwife. But being passed over rankled with Joan, and when she finally heard about the slight she exploded. She went to the Allingtons' farm the day after their baby's birth and Giles recounted how she 'went away from his house very much discontented, in regard the other midwife had brought his wife to bed'. Suddenly Joan was in the position of the 'witch' who had come to her dairy door in Hull all those years ago: a troublesome figure scowling on the step. No one wanted to upset a midwife and healer; like Anny Sampson, such people were feared for their secret skill. Soon after Joan marched away angrily from the Allingtons, Giles's wife fell ill with an abscess on her breast. Although she recovered, Giles then fell ill himself, and finally their baby sickened and died at just four months old. Grieving and frightened, Giles came to believe Joan Wright was to blame.[14]

As well as her midwifery, Joan quietly practised another trade that would have made her suspicious to the Allingtons when they heard about it. She told fortunes. Either she did this for separate payment or as part of her medical mystique. She might have implied that she knew secret things; had special skills and insights. Unfortunately, many of her predictions concerned death. One of her accusers, Rebecca Gray, explained to the magistrate what kind of statements Joan made about the future. Rebecca said that Joan had told her she knew 'by one token [she] had in her forehead [that Rebecca] should bury her husband'. Joan was saying that by some invisible sign on Rebecca's face, she knew that she would outlive her man. Rebecca added that Joan had said something similar to the planter John Felgate. Joan told him he would lose his wife, and so he did. Finally, Rebecca said Joan had been able to tell Thomas Harris that his wife would die before he did, even at the stage when the couple were newly engaged. Thomas held seven hundred acres and was a good catch, but some people gossiped that he was a philanderer with several mistresses, and they thought his wife had died before her time. Apparently, Joan had known this would be the outcome years before the event: it must have been witchcraft![15]

With large landholdings like this at stake, anyone knowing which spouse would die first leaving all their worldly goods to the other was in demand. Rebecca Gray had a particular investment in such knowledge: she was herself the third wife of Thomas Gray of Gray's Creek, who held over five hundred acres. Rebecca understood the fragility of life and legacy; she had been a widow when she married Thomas, and her previous husband Daniel Hutton had died without a written will. He had bequeathed his land verbally to her and it was lucky his word had been accepted. No doubt Rebecca had reflected deeply on early death.[16] She wasn't alone. Alice Baylie said she had asked Joan 'whether her husband should bury her, or she bury him' but Joan had refused to answer. This must have been shortly before the witch trial because Joan said tantalisingly, 'I can tell you if I would, but I am exclaimed against for such things [accused of witchcraft because of such predictions] and I'll tell no more!' Although she would 'tell no more' fortunes, Joan's words show us she was proud of her authority and truly believed she could see the future if she wanted to.

Rebecca and Alice feared her foretellings, and so did several families who farmed south of the James River at Pace's Paines. In 1625, Joan and Robert Wright relocated to Pace's Paines from Elizabeth City. But they were not welcome. Giving evidence against her, their new neighbour Daniel Watkins said that soon after Joan's arrival, she had spoken unkindly to the farmer Robert Thresher about a gift of chickens to a newly orphaned girl. 'Why do you keep these hens here tied up?' she asked. 'The maid you mean to send them to will be dead before the hens come to her.' This prediction had caused the Pace's Paines plantation-owners, councilman William Perry and his wife Isabella, to voice their own fears.[17]

Isabella recalled Joan threatening a maidservant employed by Elizabeth Gates – wife of Thomas Gates, the invader of Kecoughtan – that 'she would make her dance stark naked' by magic. It was an alarming thought for respectable women, and so Isabella and Elizabeth 'charged the said goodwife Wright with witchcraft'. Some people, they said, had even asked Isabella 'why she did suffer goodwife [Wright] to be at her house, saying she was a very bad woman, and was accounted a witch amongst them all' when she had lived at Elizabeth City. Further accusations followed. Clearly people were talking about Joan's skills and her past. Joan too was looking back on her earlier life, as it was to Isabella Perry that she told the two stories about her first encounters with witchcraft back home in Hull.[18]

So, with suspicions that she had possessed magical skills for many years and that these had turned to witchcraft, Joan was denounced to a magistrate as a witch and tried by Virginia's General Court. The men assembled to hear her case on 11 September 1626 were three of the colony's leading officials: the governor, Sir George Yeardley; Captain Francis West, who would be governor from

1627; and Dr John Pott, who succeeded him as governor from 1629.[19] These judges heard the evidence against Joan. There was no jury, since military rule was in operation. No doubt it seemed a solid case, driven by genuine emotions: grief, fear, anger. Some of the accusers were leading citizens, such as the Allingtons and Perrys. But interestingly, no churchmen intervened and none of the more sensational demonological concerns are mentioned in the trial paperwork that survives. Instead, Joan's witch trial was framed as a practical exercise dealing with material matters: threats to the colony's food supplies and the lives and security of colonists current and future. Satan did not get a mention, nor did most of the crimes covered by the Witchcraft Act. While demonology informed colonists' thinking in general, therefore, their witch trial was a less a crusade against Satanic conspiracy than a do-it-yourself response to mundane concerns. This put Joan in a good position. The law did not allow torture, and she was not expected to confess to Satanic visions under duress. Although she had no lawyer, Robert Wright was permitted to speak up for her. He had 'been married to his wife sixteen years, but knoweth nothing by her touching the crime she is accused of', he said. It was a sturdy statement that would have helped her case.

Unfortunately, we don't know what Joan herself said at her trial. The court book does not even record a plea of guilty or not guilty. But it does report something Joan said before her trial that points to her probable response in court. When they were discussing Joan's supposed attack on Elizabeth Gates, Isabella Perry had asked Joan why she had not sued her accuser for slander: 'If thou knowest thyself clear of what she charged thee, why dost thou not complain and clear thyself of the same?' Joan answered with surprising Christian calm. 'God forgive them,' she said simply and, Isabella thought, she 'made light of it' – meaning that she shrugged off the accusations. So, although there is no recorded plea, Joan had already said she was not a witch, claiming the moral high ground as a good Christian woman.

Perhaps she believed the anti-witchcraft skills she learned in

England and her prophetic knowledge made her a special sort of Christian – a mystic who knew God's secrets. We'll meet other women of this ilk later in this book: in eighteenth-century France and again in wartime Britain, both of whom were subjected to witch trials. Like Helena Scheuberin, even pious women were accused of witchcraft if they asserted themselves too loudly or criticised powerful men. But perhaps that 'God forgive them' did save Joan, because she was not immediately judged a clear and present Satanic danger and her case was adjourned until the next court sitting. On 18 September two witnesses confirmed at another hearing the stories that Daniel Watkins and Isabella Perry had told about their dealings with Joan, but no verdict is recorded.

And there the record ends. It's shocking that such an important matter as this woman's life or death should go unrecorded. The gap in the record makes one horrifying point and one comforting one. Firstly, by the seventeenth century the lives of witchcraft suspects were often not much valued. By 1600 accusations were common across Europe and had spread to America, where they would proliferate. Across much of the Christian world, Reformation changes stripping the church of legal powers meant that suspected witches were no longer investigated by church courts, where attention was at least paid to questioning the accused in detail. In the new state and colonial justice systems, courts often spent only as much time on a witchcraft accusation as on a minor theft. Joan would have been given only a brief trial: the Virginian General Court based its practices on the English Assize Court, where most trials took fifteen to twenty minutes. Witch trials were no longer new and, shockingly, no longer special. Secondly, however, the first high excitement of demonologically driven investigations led by church and state was ebbing across many jurisdictions by the mid-1620s. While anti-witchcraft laws remained in place and state agents still pursued witches, some regimes failed to enforce their own laws. Some had banned torture because they associated it with the abuses of the Inquisition. Even King James had begun to display doubts about witch-hunting after witnessing some false accusations, and in the years immediately after his 1604 Witchcraft Act, he was involved in several English trials where suspects were acquitted and accusers charged with lying instead.[20] So state courts might acquit witchcraft suspects, especially if accusers looked uncertain or prejudiced, suspects were pitiable or offered a smart self-defence. Any of these things could have determined Joan's fate.

On the one hand, there is no evidence that Joan was convicted or executed, but on the other hand, she might have been. Other colonists were sentenced to death, such as Daniel Frank, executed in 1622 for theft from the governor, so we know that capital punishment was in use, but there are no records of witch-executions. In some cases, however, a death sentence is not recorded in the court book but only mentioned by chance in a later record. Richard Cornish was executed for raping a crewmate in the early 1620s, but we only know this because of a later record detailing that his friends were prosecuted in 1625 for protesting his conviction. More cheeringly, lesser penalties than were formally required by law were also handed down. A sentence of whipping or a fine were mandated for contracting an engagement with two possible husbands, but when Eleanor Sprague was convicted of this in 1624, she was sentenced only to confess her fault in church. In 1626 John Ewins received eighty lashes for repeated fornication with Jane Hill, but she, like Eleanor, had only to confess her fault in church.[21] The Virginian authorities treated some women harshly, whipping them for minor offences, but sometimes they chose mercy. Potential wives and mothers were in short supply and executing a young woman – someone both vulnerable and useful – might have seemed to the court both ethically harsh and practically wasteful. A demonologist might have insisted on killing Joan as a Satanic heretic, her soul forever tainted by sin; the Virginian administration cared more about her body and her practical contribution to their project.

Joan Wright probably survived, then, perhaps being acquitted or sentenced to a lesser punishment than hanging. Certainly, no one mentions a witch-hanging in Virginia's remaining records. Joan did what she could to save herself: she spoke mildly in conventional Christian terms about her enemies, a good strategy. But her trial's consequences are still profoundly disturbing. We do know the Wright family had to leave their home and their business suffered. On 13 January 1627, Robert Wright petitioned the General Court to be allowed to move back across the James River from Pace's Paines to Jamestown. The court agreed and on 27 August he was given twelve acres to the east of Jamestown, to build a house beside a marsh. However, the land had the unpromising name of 'Labour in Vain' and was of poor quality. In October Robert found a new business opportunity. With Andrew Rawleigh, he took a ten-year lease on a joiner's yard at Jamestown, which the previous lease-holder, Thomas Grubb, had left them in his will. But life was not easy. On 14 January 1628 Robert was arrested for a debt of one thousand two hundred pounds of tobacco, and on 2 March he was imprisoned for two separate debts. The Wrights had sustained huge reputational damage. They had been driven from the lives they'd built at Elizabeth City, then at Pace's Paines. Perhaps Robert was mistrusted as the 'witch's husband' and his business collapsed as a result.[22] In any event, we can be confident in thinking that Joan's, her husband's and her children's futures in America had been permanently damaged by her witch trial.

The Trial of Bess Clarke: Disability and Demonic Families in the English Civil War

Although the first wave of demonology had ebbed somewhat in western Europe by the third decade of the seventeenth century, the malign influence of the theory persisted. Despite differences of opinion over the role of Satan and some concerns over false accusations, the era of witch trials was certainly not at an end. The colonial edges of Europe and the Americas, places like Vardø or Jamestown, weren't alone in holding witch trials either, although the clash of cultures there helped create the fears that led to accusation. Witches were also being accused in their hundreds across the old European heartland: in the 1630s trials took place in Würzburg in Germany, Loudun in France, Trentino in Italy. Across Europe, renewed wars raged between and within Catholic and Protestant factions over the continuing religious changes of the Reformation, and whichever sect was currently dominant persecuted the others.

Twenty years after Joan Wright's Virginian ordeal, Protestants on the east coast of England from which she had emigrated were in the middle of a civil war, partly driven by religious disagreements and partly by a crisis in royal authority that would end with the execution of King Charles I, son of James VI, in 1649. During this national trauma the people of south-eastern England held an extended witch-hunt from 1645 to 1647. Dozens were executed without even a record of their name surviving today. Friction between religious sects was dramatised in many accusations, with breakaway Protestants who had rejected Anglican control both driving accusations and becoming victims of them. But although high-level demonological theory and fears of heresy lay behind the trial – as had happened in Austria, Scotland and Norway – the English investigators of the 1640s were amateur witchfinders, like the people of Virginia. They were lower-level church and state officials joined by enthusiastic citizens with general fears about witchcraft rather than professional demonologists.

This devolution of witch-hunting came about because the English church and state had effectively collapsed: even if he had wanted to, the king could no longer authorise witch trials because by 1645 he was on the run. The Anglican Church of which he was head had also lost its authority. Although it was not alike in all ways, governance in parts of England resembled that of a devolved colonial authority and people in these partially autonomous areas – military governors, clergymen and private citizens – were left to discover their own priorities and invent their own practical procedures. In this way, the eastern English witch trials were like Joan Wright's trial in Virginia. The people of eastern England designed processes to investigate witchcraft that were based on the advice of amateur witch-hunters: men who had read demonologies and internalised many of the basics of demonological theory but had no official role or fixed doctrine. They were open to hearing from suspects about their own magical beliefs as a process of experimental 'discovery', literally the dis-covering of Satan's hidden ways. The result was a chaotic, controversial series of witch trials that engulfed communities across seven counties and served to establish the authority of local witch-hunters for a time before overturning it forever. The witch-hunters were broadly aligned with the insurgent and ultimately victorious side in the civil war, and with the religious grouping that we know as 'Puritan'.

Puritans were pious, fundamentalist Protestants who felt the

Reformation had not gone far enough in sweeping away Catholic rituals from English church services and believers' lives. The Anglican state church was not pure enough for them and they felt it should reform further or be abolished. They split into multiple factions trying to purify their own worship too. In wider society, Puritans wanted an end to sins such as swearing, drunkenness and fornication and also an end to frivolity of all kinds: wearing fine clothes, dancing and many forms of art, music and literature. In their hands, witch trials were a revolutionary act, seeking out those who polluted their communities with devilish sin. As Puritans began to win the civil war, holding witch trials aided them in establishment of purer government in parts of England previously under the control of the king (whom the Puritans saw as the swearer-, drunk- and fornicator-in-chief). Witch trials were also an opportunity for these pious people to learn more about their enemy the devil by personal contact with him – a must for wannabe demonologists. They required only plausible witches – mostly women, inevitably – and godly activists. In 1645, these witchfinders included a troubled and suggestible twenty-something called Matthew Hopkins, the son of a clergyman. His chief suspect was a young disabled mother, Elizabeth Clarke.

Elizabeth – known as Bess – grew up in the village of Bradfield in Essex with her father Bartholomew and her mother. Bradfield's long fields sloped down from its stubby stone church to the River Stour, and villagers raised cattle on the marshes and fished the muddy river. Across the water, Matthew grew up with his parents James and Marie ten miles north-west in Great Wenham, Suffolk. They had a comfortable rectory with a leafy garden. No doubt Matthew played decorous games there and in the adjacent church-yard, with his brothers James, Thomas and John. When his father James Hopkins died in 1634, when Matthew was in his teens, his mother Marie remarried and Matthew found himself the stepson of another churchman, Thomas Witham, rector of Mistley-with-Manningtree in Essex.[1]

The children grew up during the first disputes between King

Charles I and Puritans in the English parliament. In Bradfield and Great Wenham, as elsewhere, religious radicals challenged Anglican authority, quibbling over details of religious rites, and in the early 1640s these national tensions exploded into civil war. During 1642 to 1645 the battleground moved closer to Matthew's and Bess's homes. Traditional forms of governmental control such as criminal courts were disrupted. Judges and magistrates appointed by the toppled royal regime lost their jobs, and in some places court sessions ceased. People did not stop suspecting their neighbours were witches, however, and as well as the old counter-magical remedies they found ways to organise impromptu trials. This was even more dangerous than usual for suspects. Trials were no longer overseen by legal experts answerable to a central authority, and courts were often staffed by one political faction or the other, leading to groupthink. We've seen what happened when elite churchmen and royal governors tried witches during a demonological crackdown, which was bad enough. But the English witch trials of the 1640s show that ordinary groups of citizens acting independently in revolutionary circumstances could do just as much harm, if not more.

Matthew Hopkins was well placed to flourish in the changed circumstances of civil war Britain: not too close to the old regime but benefiting from many of the advantages of its elites. He was the son of the rector of a wealthy parish; he was well educated and destined for a prosperous career. He was also fortunate in that he had no financial or geographical need to become a soldier when fighting began. But despite this privileged position, he also had no formal power, and he lived in violently changing times. His future was less clear than before the national collapse of 1642, and he appears to have been an anxious young man, one who easily imagined himself as a victim despite his many social advantages. There's some evidence that he might have been seriously ill and was worried about how long he had left to live. Matthew was only in his early twenties when fighting began, and shortly after that time he decided his stepfather's community – Manningtree, to which

Matthew had moved with his mother – was full of witches: people like Bess Clarke. She now lived in Manningtree, three miles from her birthplace. But being young and believing himself to be smart, Matthew had an opportunity to make a difference in her and his new home.

In the 1640s, Manningtree was a riverside village of traders, sailors and hauliers, bigger than Great Wenham and Bradfield combined. It was prosperous, although its shipping businesses had been disrupted by the war and its citizens were keen to keep in favour with the winning Puritan side. Some members of Matthew's step-kin, the Witham-Edwards family, had always been pious, wanting their village to be known not just for goods but for godliness. In the 1630s, Richard Edwards senior – whose son was married to Matthew's stepsister Susan Witham – funded the rebuilding of a long-derelict church in Manningtree as a chapel. It was a separate meeting place from the official parish church at Mistley and, as an affiliated extra space, it allowed some reformist Puritan experimentation: subtle changes in ceremonies to suit more fundamentalist taste. When Thomas Witham preached there, he refused to wear the Anglican priest's uniform of cassock and surplice (a long black gown and a white tunic) because Puritans considered these Catholic-looking. Mostly, however, he conformed to Anglican norms when told to do so, and he kept Manningtree-with-Mistley calm.

The new chapel drew many worshippers, among them Bess Clarke. But in 1643 Thomas took a new posting in London, and no new rector arrived to replace him, the appointment process having broken down during the war. The absence of the old Anglican authority, and of Thomas's religious balance and personal care – he'd been rector for thirty years – unexpectedly made room for young Matthew to be heard as the voice of deepening religious conflict.[2]

To be fair, Matthew Hopkins was not the only villager to suspect witchcraft in Manningtree-with-Mistley and to agitate for its prosecution; he was just the leading member of an activist group, notable because of his social status as the rector's stepson. Like

Heinrich Kramer, James VI and John Cunningham, Matthew's group of Essex witch-accusers drew on pre-existing tensions to lay the groundwork for a witch-hunt. Formal accusations were first made on 21 March 1645, when a Manningtree tailor, John Rivet, went to see the local magistrates Sir Harbottle Grimston and Sir Thomas Bowes – probably at Harbottle's family home, Bradfield Hall, three miles from Manningtree. John Rivet's wife had begun to have fits so violent that John thought them 'more than merely natural', and so John had been to visit a 'cunning woman', a diviner with magical knowledge like Anny Sampson or Joan Wright. John did not think of his advisor as a 'witch', however; to him, she was an enemy of witches, someone who could tell him if his wife had been cursed. The diviner confirmed John's fears: two women had bewitched his wife, she said. One lived on the hill above John's house in Manningtree, and one in the town below. John immediately knew who she meant by one of these identifications: Bess Clarke lived up the hill from his house. He was sure she was to blame. And so John Rivet gave a statement to the magistrates naming Bess as a witch.

There's some unclarity about the sequence of events after that, but it's likely Bess was summoned to be questioned. A warrant was issued for her arrest, using one or both of her official names, Elizabeth Clarke and Elizabeth Bedingfield, and she was detained at her hillside cottage and marched off to be questioned by the magistrates. It's often assumed Bess was a widow – that her birth name was Bedingfield and her married name Clarke, explaining her double identity. But in fact she was probably born Elizabeth Clarke, daughter of Bartholomew Clarke of Bradfield, in April 1606. She had a younger sister, Jane Clarke, born in 1609, who then married Richard Benifield (or Bedingfield) in Manningtree in 1621. It's likely that Bess moved to Manningtree with her father – he was buried there in 1614 – and after 1621 she lived with Jane and Richard Benifield, taking on Jane's married name by association. But Jane Benifield died in 1640 and Richard Benifield remarried by 1643.[3] Was Bess forced out of his home by her remaining in-law family? The Benifields might have wanted to dissociate themselves from her because, as John Rivet tells us in his accusation against her, 'the said Elizabeth's mother and some other of her kinsfolk did suffer death for witchcraft and murder'. Horrifyingly, Bess and Jane Clarke were the daughters of a convicted 'witch'. Records of their mother's trial appear to be lost with her forename – we only know her as Bartholomew Clarke's wife – but Bess must have seen her dragged from her home, shoved onto a cart and driven away to prison, after which she was tried and killed. It left a legacy of trauma.[4]

As well as the mental wound of her mother's killing, Bess's body was also scarred, marking her out. She had only one leg. Perhaps this was why she depended upon her sister Jane and had come to live with her. It could have been a congenital disability but more likely it was due to an injury: limb absence in newborns is rare, and seventeenth-century infant mortality was high even for conspicuously healthy babies. The commonest cause of amputation was gangrene in a wound – perhaps caused by a bone fracture or untreated cut. Amputations were performed by village surgeons: beefy, butcher-like men who also pulled teeth and barbered hair. They were adept with knives, razors, pliers, choppers and saws. There were no anaesthetics, and little pain relief. Patients lay on their back while the surgeon stood or knelt between their legs. An assistant lifted the diseased limb. Together the men tightly bandaged the soft parts of the thigh. The assistant held the foot and everyone else held their breath. If the patient was lucky, the surgeon had cleaned and sharpened his knife out of earshot. Now he would plunge its razor-edged blade into the outer side of the leg and draw it around towards himself, under and up the inside. As it crossed the top of the leg, cutting to the bone, the assistant had a saw ready. The now-exposed bone was sawn away. Afterwards came tight binding of the blood vessels, swabbing, bandages and anointing the exposed flesh with egg yolk and oil.[5]

Whether Bess was born without a limb or went through a traumatic amputation, by 1645 she had survived against tremendous odds. She would have needed walking sticks, a crutch or maybe a crude wooden leg, made by a relative or friend or paid for by parish taxes. Professionally made prosthetics were expensive and most were for naval or military officers. The figure of the one-legged veteran stumping manfully home from the battlefield was respectable in seventeenth-century culture. In the 1620s Manningtree was home to 'John Evered with the wrang leg' – 'wrang' is an old word for 'wrong' – whose disability gave him a nickname distinctive enough to be recorded at his burial. But one-legged women were rare, and there was no room for them in ideals of feminine beauty. Even if Bess was fortunate enough to have a wooden limb, walking would have been painful, and she would have limped badly. It is more likely that she would have had only a crutch, and hopped and swung herself along, making her disability more obvious. John Rivet had certainly noticed her, and her unusual appearance would have made her memorable to the magistrates Harbottle Grimston and Thomas Bowes too.

It was an exposed position in a society where disability was known as 'deformity' and often presented as God's punishment for sin. In February 1643, Bess's neighbours were given a reason to think she deserved such a punishment. Historians have often represented her as an 'old woman' or 'aged' at the time of her trial in 1645, because that's the stereotype of the witch. But records from two parishes show she was a young woman of childbearing age, and when she was in her mid-thirties, she gave birth to an illegitimate daughter. Bess named her baby Jane, after her own sister who had died three years before. She chose to have little Jane baptised at Thomas Witham's chapel in Manningtree on 12 February 1643. That meant naming the baby's father, Joseph Applegate, partly so he could be forced to pay child support. Bess was a poor woman, speaking openly during her later interrogation about 'her lameness and her poverty', and she needed Joseph's money to feed her baby.[6] It didn't matter that he had apparently abandoned Bess – whether after a single encounter or assault, or after a more sustained affair – he was still Jane's father, and she would carry his name. Bess would be associated with him forever in the eyes of her neighbours and would have to rely on his financial goodwill.

By 1645 everything in Bess's life – illegitimate child, appearance, poverty, family history – made her vulnerable. She was considered immoral: an unmarried mother, her body marked by God and her purse empty by his will too. Worse, people speculated she'd inherited witchcraft, just as Bessie Thompson was thought to have inherited it from her mother Anny Sampson, leading to John Rivet's accusation. Others followed. Just four days after John had made his accusation, on 25 March 1645 Matthew Hopkins also spoke to the magistrates about Bess. Matthew may have got some of his suspicions from John, but he was already prejudiced against Bess, and he later said that he'd identified her as one of a group of witches who'd awoken him by holding meetings near his house every six weeks for several months before making his accusation. He'd overheard strange conversations with and about animals, he explained: surely these were witches' Sabbaths, and the animals must be familiar spirits. Matthew knew about Sabbaths and the Satanic 'covenant' imagined in demonological theory – he had read King James's *Daemonologie* and perhaps other textbooks too. He wanted to investigate further, particularly focusing on the witches' animal familiars. Compared with Scottish or European confessions, English witch stories were full of demonic dogs and curse-bearing cats, so Matthew was excited by the idea that his noisy neighbours had evil pets. The young witchfinder said he had overheard one woman telling her animals to go to Bess Clarke's house.[7]

After Bess was arrested on 21 March, Matthew spent part of the next three days and nights keeping her under observation with a group of his neighbours. This 'watching' was one of several investigation techniques suggested. Matthew called them 'trying ways' by which he 'gained . . . experience' in witch-hunting. His wealthy friend John Stearne proposed another 'way', throwing Bess into water like the Vardø witches, but that was vetoed as an unusual practice in Britain. Instead, the watching strategy was pursued. It was hypothesised that the witch's familiar spirits might arrive to catch up with her and be spotted by watchers, providing clear evidence of guilt. Bess was therefore watched for three days and nights by a team of Manningtree tradespeople together with Matthew and John. Four women also checked her body for demonic marks – just as Anny Sampson was examined sixty years before. Women as well as men believed witches were God's enemies and helped to interrogate them. Because they thought she had multiple animal familiars, the female watchers of Manningtree looked particularly carefully for marks made by teeth on Bess's body: small bites, blood spots. In England familiar spirits were thought to suck blood from witches with whom they'd made a Satanic pact, both as a sign of that agreement and as payment for doing harm. They would report their evil deeds to the witch and get a sip of blood as a reward. The demonic mark they left behind as a sign of their deal might look like a fleabite, wart or teat. While Bess's watchers hoped to see her familiars they also, conversely, thought they might be invisible, so it was necessary to inspect any bodily mark that might reveal their presence. Like a keen team of scientists, the watchers were combining the demonological theory that Matthew Hopkins had read with practical experimentation.[8]

Fatally, Bess was not only kept under intrusive surveillance on the nights of 21–24 March but was also kept in constant motion, a process that came to be known as 'watching and walking'. It was a cruel ordeal for her as a one-legged person and would have been debilitating even for a fully fit and mobile suspect. The purpose of watching and walking was to maximise the time when a witch's familiars might come to consult with her and be identified. Today such coercive sleep deprivation is recognised as a form of torture. It disorientates the victim, inducing despair and scattering thoughts. It also prompts confession, and that was its effect on Bess.

Matthew was especially keen to hear what she had to say. Later, he described his visits in casual terms. He just popped into Bess's holding cell on the long, dark night of 24 March, he said, 'for the better discovery of her wicked practices'. He 'intended not to have stayed long there', he told the magistrates next day. But when he and John Stearne strode into her cell, Bess surprised them. Suddenly she exclaimed, 'If you will stay, I will show you my imps!' – she meant she would summon her familiar spirits. Why did she make this offer? Because the men had so insistently wanted to meet her familiars? To end her ordeal and get some sleep? She was exhausted and frightened, woozy-headed and unsteady on her one foot. The fact that she explicitly told Matthew, John and the others to 'sit down' suggests she wanted to sit down herself. Anything to end the demands that she drag herself painfully up and down the room.[9]

Matthew and John pulled up chairs and listened. They and the other watchers asked questions: general, unscientific ones like the anxious enquiry: 'Will they [the spirits] do us no harm?' and specific ones such as: 'Hath not the devil had use of your body?' With this demonology-inspired prompt to talk about sex with the devil, Bess started to tell her listeners the story they wanted to hear. But it was also her own story. In Matthew's words, given later to the magistrates, she said that she had 'had carnal copulation with the devil'. The devil had been her lover for six or seven years, she continued. He came to her bed three or four times a week, saying firmly, 'Bess, I must lie with you!' and stayed half the night. He was 'a proper gentleman with a laced band', she said, meaning a lace collar. John Stearne said she added he was 'a tall, proper, black-haired gentleman'. 'Proper' meant that he was a respectable, middle- or upper-class devil, like Matthew and John, and perhaps like Bess's lover Joseph Applegate. Proper could also mean 'good-looking'. But, like Joseph, Satan betrayed Bess. He seduced her and drew her into sin. Now she was ready to confess her wickedness to these other gentlemen and deliver on her promise by summoning her familiars, as her watchers demanded.

What did this mean? Unless we accept that Bess did indeed call animal-shaped devils into her cell, we have to try and explain. What we do know is that she made 'smacking' noises with her mouth and beckoned with her hand. And 'within a quarter of an hour after there appeared an imp like unto a dog', Matthew and John said later – a dog 'which was white with some sandy spots, and seemed to be very fat and plump, with very short legs'. The watchers must hardly have dared to breathe: the devil! Sure, he looked like a harmless puppy dog, but he was Satan, winged and clawed, lusting to snag their souls so he could drag them to hell. But what did they really see? The words 'seemed to be very fat and plump' suggest something glimpsed in the shadows, or even that the watchers could see nothing. If you see a fat dog, you say 'there's a fat dog' not 'there was a dog that seemed to be very fat'. So instead of seeing the familiar, the watchers were perhaps relying on Bess's description of what she said *she* could see. This imagined creature was a spaniel-like lapdog, and Bess told her questioners that 'she kept him fat' and he was called something like Jarmara or Jeremarye.

Matthew, John and the watchers gave slightly different accounts of the appearances of Bess's familiars – something a good defence counsel, had Bess had one, like Helena Scheuberin, could have used to get their evidence thrown out of court. She was not allowed such representation in an English trial, so her accusers were free to report whatever fantastical evidence they wanted, more or less unchallenged. Matthew said Jarmara the dog was the first familiar spirit to appear. John Stearne and the other watchers said that it was a white cat called Hoult that appeared first, followed by Jarmara. But both John and Matthew agreed that when Jarmara vanished, he was replaced by the even better-named Vinegar Tom, 'a greyhound with long legs', although Matthew later added that he had a head like an ox and transformed himself into the shape of a child, another inconsistency suggesting how far Bess and her watchers had departed from observable reality. Then came a black rabbit called Sacke and Sugar – the name of a popular tavern drink – and a polecat. John added that Bess referred to all of the spirits as 'my children'. It's another sign that in telling the story of her seduction by Satan, Bess was reliving her own experience of sex and pregnancy. Like her daughter Jane, Bess's animal children were, in her tormented imagination, born from a fall into sin.[10]

When the watchers asked Bess how many 'children' she had, she said she had five familiars and shared two others with another witch. The spirits tormented her and would 'never let her rest or be quiet', like her torturers. Remember how Kari Edisdatter also conflated her real-life racking with the imagined 'stretching [of] her limbs' by demonic spirits? Now, in Manningtree, Bess told the watchers that her familiars had harassed her until she agreed to let them kill some pigs belonging to Richard Edwards, Matthew Hopkins' stepbrother-in-law. Later she would also be charged with killing his little son, and a horse belonging to shopkeeper Robert Taylor. Bess then accused Anne West and Anne Leech, both widows, and Elizabeth, wife of Edward Goodwin, of being witches like her. Matthew and John duly went to the magistrates carrying a list of new suspects, so they could be arrested. Some churchmen also questioned the accused. One suspect, Anne West, lived about a mile from Manningtree at Lawford with her daughter Rebecca. Rebecca was a confused, pious young woman who was already caught up in the witch-hunt when Bess accused her mother Anne. On 21 March she had been questioned by the magistrates regarding her own involvement in witchcraft. She was interrogated again on 28 April by John Edes, Puritan rector of Lawford, during which she elaborated further on religious fantasies that – like Bess Clarke's stories – were saturated by puritanical concerns about sin. John Edes, whose questions will have shaped Rebecca's story, had likely been reading demonologies, like Matthew Hopkins.[11]

Like Bess – and perhaps under similar duress – Rebecca confessed that she had had sexual 'familiarity with the devil' in the shape of 'a proper young man'. Rebecca's demon lover promised her revenge on her enemies, so she told him to kill the son of her neighbours Thomas and Prudence Hart and then cause Prudence to have a miscarriage. This all happened just as she wished. Horrified by Rebecca's claims, the minister must have asked her, 'What? Do you think that the devil can kill people? That would mean he could do the same things as God! That you could do the same things as God!' Puritan churchmen had worried for decades that their congregations didn't understand the power differential between God and

Satan. In the 1590s, George Gifford, the vicar of Maldon – just twenty-five miles from Lawford – had written that while God was 'the ruler of the whole earth', some heretical people thought Satan might be his spiritual equal. 'To spread this opinion among the people,' he said, witches' familiars would 'have them openly confess that they have done such great things, which all the devils at any man's request could never do'. God did give devils 'power some-times to afflict both men and beasts', George confirmed, but to believe that the devils handed over any of this power to witches themselves was 'most absurd'.[12]

So, John Edes asked Rebecca if she had evidence of witches' power to go around killing people with the devil's help. And Rebecca solemnly said yes, 'she conceived he could do as God'. That was any demonologist's worst fear come true: a witch who described Satan as the alternative deity of an anti-Christian religion. John probed further and Rebecca detailed how she knew Satan's abilities. She, her mother Anne West, Anne Leech, Elizabeth Goodwin and another woman, Helen Clarke (Anne Leech's daughter but maybe also a relative of Bess Clarke), had all met at Bess's house in Manningtree and there 'they together spent some time in praying unto their familiars', Rebecca said. Afterwards, 'some of them read in a book, the book being Elizabeth Clarke's'. 'Every one of them', she said, 'made their several propositions to those familiars', asking for things that they wanted. Bess wanted Richard Edwards's horse to unseat him on the middle bridge at Manningtree – a potentially fatal accident, since the bridge was part of a long causeway over the River Stour. The other women wanted, less ambitiously, to attack pigs and cattle. Rebecca wanted to hurt her enemy Prudence Hart. Anne West asked simply that 'she might be freed from all her enemies and have no trouble'; Anne had been accused of witch-craft by the Harts before, in 1641, but acquitted. She didn't want all that 'trouble' again.[13]

The formal meeting Rebecca described, with its prayers, books and argumentative 'propositions' – a form of theological debate enjoyed by some Christian congregations – sounds in many ways like an ordinary church gathering. Like the North Berwick Sabbath, it's a parody of a church service, although this time in a home-church. Maybe it was completely imaginary, a response to demonological fears of a Satanic sect. But perhaps it had more reality than that. Rebecca lived among Puritans who really did hold meetings of this kind. Perhaps she was recalling a prayer meeting attended by her family and friends. Some of the people rounded up during the 1645–47 witch-hunt, including Anne West, were described as apparently godly, clean-living Christians even by their enemies. Like Helena Scheuberin with her Hussite leanings, or Effie McCalzean and Barbara Napier, 'reputed for as civil, honest women as any that dwelled within the city', perhaps some of the accused women of Lawford, Manningtree and Mistley were truly pious Christians. Maybe they did meet at Bess Clarke's house in the early 1640s to pray in Christian community, and perhaps Bess did own a prayer book. The civil war had set Puritan sects against each other, as well as against Catholics and the Anglicans of the state church, and perhaps Rebecca knew John would disapprove of her home-church, so she included it in her confession.[14] But she also added Bess's fantasies of magical animals, which would have pleased Matthew. It's hard to tell which aspects of her story were inspired by demonology, which described folklore beliefs, and which were verifiably true.

Other accused women told folk-magic stories under duress. Anne Leech, from Mistley, was questioned on 14 April and confessed she had worked with Bess Clarke and Elizabeth Goodwin, sending her familiars to kill Richard Edwards's cows. She'd also killed Elizabeth, daughter of Robert and Jane Kirk, in July 1642, and Thomas and Rachel Rawlins's daughter in autumn 1638. Anne explained that Elizabeth Kirk had angered her by refusing to give her a cap, and Rachel Rawlins had been allocated Anne's land when Anne was evicted by her landlord.[15] Anne had also been accused by Mary and Edward Parsley – two of Bess's watchers – who suspected Anne and her daughter Helen had murdered their child. The Parsleys' little girl had died on or around 1 March, just six weeks before Anne Leech was questioned. With their grief so raw, no wonder Edward and Mary Parsley were committed to finding witches in their community, so much so they agreed to sit up all night with suspects waiting for their imaginary animals to appear.

On 11 April, Helen Clarke was questioned. Like the other women, she admitted keeping a familiar spirit, in this case a white dog called Elemanzer. The dog had told her to 'deny Christ, and she should never want'. The idea of 'not wanting' or not lacking anything suggests that Helen was another poverty-stricken woman, thought to have been tempted by the sort of food, comfort and worldly possessions that people like Richard Edwards and his stepbrother Matthew Hopkins enjoyed every day. But Helen said she had not killed the Parsleys' daughter, and so Edward and Mary could find no closure in an admission of murder.[16] Yet whether they confessed or not, all of the accused women were sent to prison in Colchester Castle to await their trial.

The accused were kept in the castle's dungeons, stone-paved and iron-barred cells, cold, dark, damp and deep underground. Here Matthew Hopkins visited them. He had no official role in their trial, but he couldn't let go of the fascinating information he'd discovered about the ways of witches. In particular, he wanted to follow up Rebecca West's evidence about devil-worshipping meetings at Bess Clarke's cottage. Falling in obediently with his obsession, young Rebecca told Matthew about her conversion to witchcraft. It had happened on an evening about a year ago at Bess's house, she said. Five women met there with their familiars, and one of them asked Rebecca's mother Anne West 'if she had acquainted her daughter with the business'. Anne said she had, and immediately her fellow witch Anne Leech 'pulled out a book, and swore the said Rebecca never to reveal anything she saw or heard'. If she did, she would be tormented, she said. Then the devil appeared to Rebecca and kissed her. From that moment onwards, she was a witch. Later she was 'married' to the devil and 'took him for her God', she said, following up her discussion with John Edes.[17] It

seemed crystal clear to Matthew Hopkins: the Manningtree witches
were devil-worshippers, they'd hurt and killed their neighbours as
Satan had instructed them, and they had been joined by women
from neighbouring villages in their diabolical crimes. He had his
answers. All that remained was a courtroom trial, which he believed
would rubber-stamp their convictions.

Bess Clarke and the other accused were sent for trial under the
1604 Witchcraft Act at the next assize, the state court that judged
almost all serious crimes in seventeenth-century England – crimes
such as theft, murder and arson. From Colchester jail they were
driven in guarded carts to Chelmsford, the town where the assize
was to be held. The court met in the market hall in the high street.
It was a two-storey, galleried building where normally Chelmsford's
farmers sold vegetables and meat and merchants haggled over cloth
and grain. The hall was open-sided; townspeople could cram inside
or spectate from surrounding streets and windows. Much of the
town's population would have risen early to secure a good spot to
view the witch trial and the important men who would judge it.
The Earl of Warwick, Robert Rich, presided as chief judge with
two juries, a grand jury and petty jury, totalling thirty-six men.
But Robert was not a qualified judge. He was a nobleman and
military commander in the civil war, fighting on the Parliamentarian
and Puritan side.

Before the civil war, assize judges were experienced specialists.
They were still capable of convicting 'witches' quickly and unjustly,
but they expected some acquittals. Like many European and
American state courts of their time, no defence lawyers were allowed
at the assizes, so the judicial system relied on trained judges to
analyse accusers' stories. They would weigh them in the light of
their long experience and take into account circumstances that they
thought mitigated the alleged crime or worsened it. They then
advised juries, steering the decision-making that led to a verdict.
The aim was orderly government, with wrongdoers quietly disposed
of to jail or gallows. Almost by default, few judges were religious

fundamentalists but instead were sceptical, worldly men who spent their time with legal textbooks rather than Bibles.

The Earl of Warwick was, contrastingly, only acting as a judge because the assize system had broken down during the civil war and he was a Puritan in his religious beliefs. He was also a naval commander and colonial adventurer with almost unlimited power across a large part of Britain and the Atlantic world. Robert was an earl by birth, rather than a lawyer by character and education, and in his social position he had more in common with James VI and I than with a typical assize judge. He was extremely wealthy, with a powerbase at the gigantic Warwick Castle in the English Midlands. In some other respects he resembled Vardø's John Cunningham. Earl Robert was an admiral with interests in founding European settlements in North and South America. He held lands in Virginia, New England and Bermuda and was a slave-trafficker. In 1619 his agents sold Angolan people to the governor of Virginia, Joan Wright's judge Sir George Yeardley. Earl Robert was used to making bold, unscrupulous decisions fast and pursuing enemies with murderous vigour. He thrived on change and conflict and spent much of his time on battle strategy. He was not an expert in the checks and balances of legal procedure. Even if he had been, he was surrounded at the assize trial by other militant Puritans. Beyond them, pushing and shoving, were anxious, angry spectators – people hungry for something they could control. Bess, Anne and the others smelled the sweat of hot, hostile bodies packed around them that stiflingly hot summer day. The noise of the high street market stilled, and a hush fell over the crowd as the prisoners laboured into court wearing their clinking iron fetters.

Looking down from his dais at the filthy, exhausted women huddled below him, Earl Robert did attempt to replicate usual assize procedures. First, he had his clerks summon a grand jury to inspect the written charges against the accused. It was the grand jury's job to see that these charges, or indictments, contained all the essential information about the case and focused on crimes correctly matched to the 1604 anti-witchcraft law. The jurors – local

gentlemen and merchants – approved two indictments of Bess
Clarke. Firstly, she was charged with feeding familiar spirits, a crime
explicitly forbidden by the law and to which she had confessed in
great detail. But she was also charged with killing John Edwards,
son of Richard and Susan, in summer 1644. We don't know how
the accusation originated – previously the story had been that she
had attacked Richard's livestock – but it was a crime likely to win
sympathy from any jury and was punishable by death. The grand
jury forwarded these two indictments to the petty jury, ordinary
townsmen also summoned by the earl, and these filed into place
at the front of the courtroom to hear the evidence.

Matthew Hopkins, John Stearne, Richard and Susan Edwards,
Edward Parsley and Robert Taylor stood up before the judge and
jurors and made statements against Bess. Richard and Susan no
doubt spoke movingly about the loss of their son. Matthew and
John presumably spoke about the spirits – florid evidence that must
have made eyes pop. The court heard their own anxieties about
Satan's power brought to life in their testimony. So, Earl Robert
and the jury all accepted what the witnesses said. The jury conferred
briefly, and, within just a few minutes, Bess was found guilty.[18]

Stood with her in the dock was Anne Leech, tried by the same
jury along with three other witchcraft suspects from other villages,
Rebecca Jones, Helen Bretton and Margery Grew. By now witchcraft
accusations had spread across the religiously divided communities
of Essex, driven by wartime fears and belief that the devil was
rampaging through England. As the Chelmsford Assize trial wore
on, other juries appointed for specific groups of prisoners heard
the cases of other 'witches' from all across Essex: Helen Clarke,
Anne West, Mary Sterling, Anne Cade, Alice Dixon, Mary Johnson,
Joan Rowle, Mary Coppin, Sarah Bright, Elizabeth Goodwin, Susan
Cocke, Joyce Boones, Margaret Landish, Sarah Hating, Susan Went,
Elizabeth Harvy, Marian Hockett, Bridget Mayers.[19] Some of them
we know almost nothing about, beyond a name and a few accusations. They were all local women, although later in the developing
witch-hunt, some men were accused too. All were variously charged

with keeping spirits, killing animals and children, and belonging to Satan's church. Some accusations linked back to the witch-hunt's origin in Manningtree. Helen Clarke was charged with killing Anne Parsley, the daughter of the watchers Edward and Mary. Some accusations grouped women from different villages together in supposed conspiracies. Margaret Moone from Thorpe-le-Soken – a village nine miles from Manningtree – was accused of participating in the murder of Richard and Susan Edwards's son John, along with Bess Clarke.

The outcome of the trial was a disaster for the accused women and for the communities of Essex from which they came. Joan Rowle, a widow from Leigh, is the only suspect who we know was immediately acquitted of all the charges against her. There may perhaps have been others, but if so no records of them remain. Some of the accused were later pardoned but died in prison of fever or plague. Rebecca West may have survived, perhaps because of her cooperation with the authorities, although this did not always ensure survival. She was charged with keeping spirits and an indictment was drawn up against her naming this crime. But although the grand jury approved it and two accusers, including her original accuser Thomas Hart, were waiting to give evidence against her, she was not actually tried – no trial process or verdict is recorded for her in surviving documents. Instead, she was called as a witness against her mother, a depressing, enforced act of betrayal that may have saved her life physically but must surely have destroyed her mentally. Four women died in jail before they came to trial: Rose Hollibread, Joan Cooper, Elizabeth Gibson and Mary Cooke. In all, at least thirty-six women had been imprisoned, a very high number compared with previous witch trials. Matthew Hopkins reported from the court that twenty-nine of them were sentenced to death; John Stearne thought twenty-eight.[20]

On 18 July 1645, most of the women were walked down the lane out of Chelmsford town to the west, past the church and rows of shops, to where the gallows stood next to a field of prehistoric burial mounds. One of the people herded in breathless terror down what is now Duke Street was Bess Clarke. The women had to queue to be killed, and during the wait Margaret Moone died of fear, perhaps suffering a heart attack or stroke. Her co-accused clustered round weeping, unable to help her as she died, but the executioner smoothly continued his professional duties. He must have paused when he came to Bess, to consider how to hang a one-legged person. She could not use the ladder that led to the noose. Condemned people were expected to climb the rungs and stand still until they were pushed – 'turned off' as it was called – by the hangman. But Bess could not reach the rope and gain the necessary height for the drop that would kill her, eventually, by breaking her neck or strangling her. Her killer must have helped her, perhaps with other men who held her until she was correctly positioned to fall into space. After Bess had died, she was likely buried among the prehistoric barrows under the bleached summer grass.

On the orders of the court, several of the convicted witches were taken from Chelmsford to Manningtree to be hanged there, as an example to other villagers. Further accusations spilled out across Essex, Suffolk, Norfolk, Huntingdonshire, Cambridgeshire and beyond. Women and some men confessed harming their neighbours and keeping familiars in the form of cats, moles, mice, frogs, sparrows and other creatures. Appointing themselves eastern England's unofficial witchfinders, Matthew Hopkins and John Stearne began a tour of seven counties, travelling from one community to another with their witchfinding roadshow. But they did not go unchallenged. At a witch trial in Norwich in 1647, the judges presented to Matthew a list of questions delivered to them by an anonymous objector who wanted to stop the witch-hunt. The questions, Matthew reported angrily in a published account of his witchfinding, went so far as to accuse him of witchcraft himself! The objector argued that Hopkins would have to be a witch in order to know so much about other witches.[21] Sadly this, admittedly weak, charge did not stick, and the executions continued. By the time Matthew and John had finished their rampage in late 1647, John estimated that two hundred people had been executed. The fact he could not give a more precise figure reveals his contempt for the lives that he and Matthew had ended.

Matthew Hopkins died young, in summer 1647. He may already have been sick when he accused Bess Clarke – perhaps with an illness prompting his fears of witchcraft. His death helped halt the witch-hunt. By 1647 he had many enemies, some of whom claimed he profited from his murderous work. Matthew did admit charging up to twenty shillings, gathered from the citizens of each town he visited, to cover expenses. If he found three or four witches or just one, he wrote, that was 'cheap enough'. It was an ugly statement in a peevish ten-page demonology that he published after the trials in self-defence: *The Discovery of Witches*. In it, Hopkins mythologised himself as 'the Discoverer' and 'Witchfinder General', which looked needy and arrogant. It did his reputation no good. When he died his stepbrother John Witham, the new rector of Mistley-with-Manningtree, recorded his burial at Mistley on 12 August and described Matthew as the 'son of Mr James Hopkins minister of Wenham'.[22] That was correct, but avoided mentioning his connection to the Witham-Edwards family. By 1647 the sheer number of accusations had forced a rethink, and it was realised a terrible injustice had been done to hundreds of people. A flood of criticism poured in. John Stearne feared being sued and also wrote a demonology in self-defence. Neither added new theories; both looked amateurish and belligerent. Witch-hunting had been dealt a severe blow. But although it slackened it did not end. Matthew's and John's books were sold across Britain and the British colonies. Once again, printed books spread demonology. Readers learned new 'facts' about witches and how ordinary folk could find Satan's agents by experimental investigation in their own towns. The most famous experimenters lived at Salem, Massachusetts.

CHAPTER SIX

The Trial of Tatabe: Slavery and Survival on the Salem Frontier

In mid-January 1692, two young girls living with Salem's Puritan minister Samuel Parris began to suffer fits. They went on to accuse women in their town of bewitching them. Their tale is a famous one, and we'll get to it later on in the chapter. But let's go somewhere else first, back to a time many years before that bitter Salem spring. Far to the south, a young woman was growing up in Barbados. She was called something like Tatabe or Titibe or Tetaby or Tituba – such a distinctive name it appears unique in the historical record. It is certainly unique in the records of the Salem witch trial, in which the young woman became tangled in 1692. She was accused of witchcraft because she was unfortunate enough to be enslaved in Samuel Parris's household when accusations were being made. First things first, however: this is her story, not Samuel's. As an enslaved person, Tituba, Titibe or Tatabe had no official surname but also, unusually, no European name of the kind often bestowed on people when they were enslaved. Both African and Native American people were enslaved by white settlers in the Americas and renamed as part of the horrifying erasure of their identity. New names were chosen for them either during Christian baptism or by the brutally simple allocation of a couple of syllables to each captive. Other Black and Native American people whom

Heretics from the 'Vaudois' group based in the French Alps, imagined in a fifteenth-century manuscript as witches riding on broomsticks. Ideas like this fed Heinrich Kramer's interest in the links between heresy and witchcraft.

The Witch, an early sixteenth-century engraving by Albrecht Dürer. The woman is shown riding a goat backwards through the air, showcasing the unnatural abilities and inverted morality of witches.

An early image of an English witch's familiar – presumably a hedgehog? – from a news pamphlet.

The golden-roofed house –
'Goldenes Dachl' – in Innsbruck.

A 1489 woodcut showing a witch
dancing with and being seduced
by the devil, from a book by the
lawyer Ulrich Molitor. Although
Molitor actually criticised Heinrich
Kramer's credulity, the images are
often mistaken for endorsements of
demonological fantasy.

An early edition of *Malleus
Maleficarum*, the 'Hammer of
Witches'. Its lengthy Latin title
displays Heinrich Kramer's learning
and amplifies the threats posed by
witches.

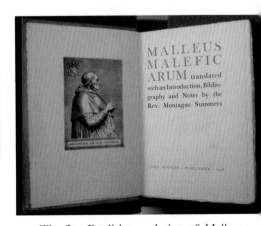

The first English translation of *Malleus
Maleficarum* by Montague Summers – note
his title 'the Rev.'. The illustration shows
Innocent VIII, pope from 1484 to 1492,
whose decrees underpinned Heinrich
Kramer's witch-hunt.

A bespoke 1591 woodcut in *Newes from Scotland* showing the witches meeting to brew potions and raise a storm at sea, hearing the devil's sermon in North Berwick church and causing other magical mayhem.

A nineteenth-century image by Edward Armitage of Gillie Duncan playing her 'Jew's trump' to James VI, a real event contributing to his 'delight' in attending the interrogations. Stereotypically, she's portrayed as an elderly woman.

Adrian Vanson's 1595 portrait of James VI.

Witches raising a storm, from Olaus Magnus' 1555 history of Scandinavia, *Historia de Gentibus Septentrionalibus.*

The 2011 memorial to the Finnmark witches, Steilneset, designed by Louise Bourgeois and Peter Zumthor with texts by Liv Helene Willumsen. In Bourgeois' section, glass and mirrors surround an eternal flame burning on a chair, suggesting torture as much as remembrance.

Steilneset, with Peter Zumthor's wood and fabric structure in the foreground. It houses a hallway where the witch-hunt's victims are named in Willumsen's texts. Each is commemorated by a lightbulb shining through a window.

A witch-burning in sixteenth-century Derenburg, Germany, from a printed broadsheet, or leaflet, produced in Nuremburg. At least two women were executed, although the broadsheet claims one was rescued from the flames by the devil.

A page from the record of Joan Wright's trial, in the court book belonging to Thomas Jefferson. This page shows the testimonies of Daniel Watkins and Isabella Perry, given during Joan's reappearance in court on 18 September 1626.

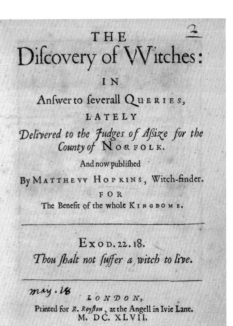

THE
Difcovery of VVitches:

IN

Anfwer to feverall QUERIES,

LATELY

Delivered to the Judges of Affize for the
County of NORFOLK.

And now publifhed

By MATTHEVV HOPKINS, Witch-finder.

FOR

The Benefit of the whole KINGDOME.

EXOD. 22. 18.
Thou fhalt not fuffer a witch to live.

may. 18   LONDON,
Printed for R. Royfton, at the Angell in Ivie Lane.
M. DC. XLVII.

Matthew Hopkins' book *The Discovery of Witches*, with its woodcut depicting Matthew himself as the 'Witchfinder General', Bess Clarke and some of her familiar spirits as well as those named by other women. Bess is shown, inaccurately, with two feet.

The gateway of Colchester Castle, where Bess and her co-accused were imprisoned.

The underground prison at Colchester Castle. Today it houses a display about the victims of the Essex witch-hunts, including a dramatisation of their interrogation staged by projecting shadows onto the cell walls.

Tituba and the Children.

This 1870s illustration by Alfred Fredericks shows Tatabe as Native American. But it misrepresents her as an elderly woman performing rites that frightened Abigail, Betty and their fellow-accusers. There's no evidence she practised any magic.

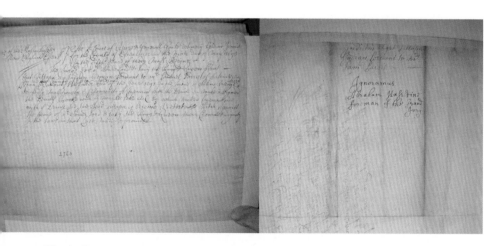

The indictment that charged Tatabe with witchcraft and with signing the devil's book, showing the signature of the jury foreman Abraham Haseltine on its reverse under the grand jury's verdict of 'ignoramus', which meant the charge did not proceed to trial.

A nineteenth-century depiction of the Salem witchcraft trial by Joseph Lauber. It shows a classic courtroom setting with witness box and judge's dais, more formal than the inn and meeting house used in 1692, with a suspect pleading for her life.

Regni *ANNÆ* Reginæ Decimo.

A R
SEMPER EADEM

Province of the Maſſachuſetts-Bay.

AN ACT,

Made and Paſſed by the Great and General Court or Aſſembly of Her Majeſty's Province of the Maſſachuſetts-Bay in New-England, Held at Boſton the 17th Day of October, 1711.

An Act to Reverſe the Attainders of *George Burroughs* and others for Witchcraft.

FOR AS MUCH as in the Year of our Lord One Thouſand Six Hundred Ninety Two, Several Towns within this Province were Infeſted with a horrible Witchcraft or Poſſeſſion of Devils ; And at a Special Court of Oyer and Terminer holden at Salem, in the County of Eſſex in the ſame Year One Thouſand Six Hundred Ninety Two, George Burroughs of Wells, John Procter, George Jacob, John Willard, Giles Core, and his Wife, Rebecca Nurſe, and Sarah Good, all of Salem aforeſaid : Elizabeth How, of Ipſwich, Mary Eaſtey, Sarah Wild and Abigail Hobbs all of Topsfield : Samuel Wardell, Mary Parker, Martha Carrier, Abigail Falkner, Anne Foſter, Rebecca Eames, Mary Poſt, and Mary Lacey, all of Andover : Mary Bradbury of Salisbury : and Dorcas Hoar of Beverly ; Were ſeverally Indicted, Convicted and Attained of Witchcraft, and ſome of them put to Death, Others lying ſtill under the like Sentence of the ſaid Court, and liable to have the ſame Executed upon them.

A   The

The Act clearing the names of the Salem 'witches' by reversing their convictions and restoring their confiscated property.

The memorial in Salem town remembering those executed as witches in 1692. It was completed in 1992 to mark the tercentenary of the witch-hunt.

the young woman knew during her life were called names like Mary, Hannah, Candy, John and Peter. Sometimes they had a surname referring to their racial identity, such as 'Mary Black, a Negro'. This young woman, however, had a singular name, with many variant spellings in the English records of her trial. The name's uniqueness suggests she was given it because of some distinctive origin, perhaps even before she was enslaved.[1]

The names Tattuba and Tatabe are the ones used in the first and the last record we have of the young woman. Tituba is a more familiar label for her in history books and Tattuba echoes that name. But scholars have pointed out that the ending 'uba' seems to relate to west African names in records of enslaved people. It may have been a spelling chosen by slave-holders who were used to that ending. The ending 'abe' better reflects the most common spellings from the Salem records: 'Titibe' and also 'Tetaby'. Because of the phonetic nature of much of the spelling in these records, it seems likely to mimic actual pronunciation. Meanwhile the 'tat' variant of the name pre-dates the young woman's contact with Samuel Parris and post-dates her time in Salem. It was the name under which she apparently exited her witch trial. Therefore, this book uses the variant 'Tatabe' to name her, because it is the nearest approximation we have to a name possibly used by her to describe herself. It also frees her to some extent from the myths attached to 'Tituba', which – as we'll see – are multiple. It's not an ideal restitution of her identity, but I hope it's a way to retell her story – one that respects her existence before and after she was labelled 'witch'.

In any of its forms, Tatabe's name suggests she was a Native South American. Although she's usually portrayed as of African origin and Black, that identity was created for her in the nineteenth century. At that time it was assumed all America's enslaved people, from the seventeenth century onwards, were Black. In fact, although the vast majority of enslaved people, over twelve million, were Black, there were at least two and a half million enslaved Native Americans. Before the mid-nineteenth century, Tatabe was uniformly described as one of these – an 'Indian'. In the paperwork from her witch trial, she is always Native American. From the 1970s onwards, scholars attempted to trace a more exact origin. Most promisingly, an Arawak people called the Tibetibe or Tetebetana lived in the Orinoco-Amacuro delta in the seventeenth century and observers documented Tetebetana women calling themselves 'tetebetado' as a group name. In the 1990s historian Elaine Breslaw suggested this self-labelling originated the name Tituba or Tatabe. If she was a tetebetado, then Tatabe lived in what is now Venezuela. It seems likely her 'Indian' birth identity was Arawak, although she may have had both Native American and African ancestry – enslaved Black people worked plantations on the South American mainland. Possibly Tatabe was born into slavery there, although her unusual name means it's more likely she was enslaved as a child, already with a distinctive Native American identity.

What would Tatabe's world have been like? Native South American culture was polygamous, so a little girl would have grown up with multiple siblings and cousins, tens of people living together in a straw-roofed hut. Venezuelan and Caribbean summer temperatures steamed up to a humid thirty-five degrees centigrade, so the huts had open sides for ventilation. The community slept close together in *hamakas* (hammocks) cooled by night air and lulled by whistling frogs and chirping crickets. Life was deeply communal, with families bound by shared gods, and cooperation was essential. Seventeenth-century outsiders commented frequently on the gentleness of Arawak behaviours.[2] Narcotics were used, in the form of smoked and chewed tobacco and a strong cassava-based wine – what a contrast with seventeenth-century Massachusetts! Enslaved Native Americans carried their culture onto sugar plantations, too, sharing local knowledge and custom with the desperate African people they met there. Wherever she grew up, and whoever her parents were, Tatabe's cultural world was soft-textured and intricately decorated, materially as well as psychologically. Homes, hammocks and baskets were woven of grass fibre, cotton and reed. Hair was plaited with rainbow-bright feathers and men's bodies were oiled and painted by women with vegetable dyes and coloured earth.

Although it was not a feminist or any other kind of paradise, in South American societies women were not secondary in quite the way they were in seventeenth-century European cultures. Although Arawak men had multiple wives, there was a balance of power in the extended household since husbands joined the extended families of their wives rather than the reverse. They became subjects of their wife's father, so daughters were prized as bringing new workers to the family. A woman was also free to evict her husband from the family home if he displeased her. Girls grew up in the belief that their lives were important. Daily, they helped their mothers pound cassava roots into flour and make stews of fish, meat and peppers. Women as well as men fished and processed forest resources – fruit, vines, nuts, roots, bark – and all Arawak people were good swimmers and foragers.[3] It was on hunting and fishing trips that they encountered Europeans also gathering useful local plants such as maize and tobacco. Some Europeans were also, however, hunting and – disgustingly – what they were hunting for was people to kidnap and enslave.

White West Indian slave-traffickers mounted expeditions specifically for this inhuman enterprise. They captured Arawak people from fishing boats and river shores, often to become house slaves.[4] Native American girls and women were stereotyped as skilful cooks, adaptable, cooperative and unlikely to threaten colonists. So, at some point before 1676, when we first find her name in a document, Tatabe was likely enslaved for this purpose – a terrifying kidnapping that dragged her from a beach or canoe near her home onto a seagoing ship which set sail for Barbados. There she became one of the uncounted 'great numbers of negroes and other slaves' held on the coral island.[5] Day after day ships arrived in the island's primary port, Bridgetown, carrying newly enslaved, utterly wretched African (Yoruba, Dahomean, Hausa and others) and South American (mostly Arawak) people listed as cargo. They were rowed ashore, chained and traded between ships' captains and middle-men who sold them to landowners. An enslaved person cost twenty-five or thirty pounds. A child like Tatabe, perhaps included in a 'lot' with her mother or other people unlucky enough to be captured with her, would have been valued less. But this enslaved child was still a marketable commodity.

Around the central horror of the slave markets, Bridgetown harbour teemed with life. Ships manoeuvred and porters sweated under sacks, planks, rolls of cloth and barrels. The dockers were mostly enslaved people, black- and brown-skinned men straining under the whips of white overseers. Already traumatised – grief-stricken, sickened, panicked – the child Tatabe would have staggered onto the quayside and noted immediately that people who looked like her were abused in her new 'home'. As enslaved Africans and Native Americans had replaced white workers in Barbados's industries during the later seventeenth century, definitions of race had hardened to Tatabe's disadvantage. Characteristics such as skin colour, facial features, hair and body types were crudely labelled and began to be seen as categorical differences, establishing a supposed hierarchy of white superiority. It was an excuse for inhumanity, even more acute than what we saw in the Arctic Circle or Virginia but based on the same lies about human difference. In this racial hierarchy, Native Americans like Tatabe were categorised with African peoples as less human than their white captors. Herded off ships into Carlisle Bay, Bridgetown's harbour, they were marched to the market, sold summarily and set to work in the fields of sugar cane and plantation houses.

Native South American and Caribbean people had once lived safely on Barbados. Although most of them fled to other islands when Spanish colonists arrived in the 1620s, Tatabe would have seen evidence of their presence: potsherds in the sand, hut ruins by the river. Because of this evidence of former inhabitants, the first Barbados settlement was named 'Indian River Bridge'. The white settlers there were initially Spanish, Portuguese, English, Dutch,

French, Scots and Irish. Like the settlers of the Virginia colony, some were wealthy speculative planters, some merchants, craftspeople, medical practitioners or sailors. Some were white indentured labourers who had signed long-term contracts to serve a particular employer. There were similar models of labour, governance and repression in Barbados as there were in Virginia because the same people were in charge: a mixture of fortune-hunters, military adventurers and religious hardliners. Trade grew between the east-coast colonies like Virginia and the Caribbean islands, and there were other trading links with New York and New England, especially Massachusetts.

In the early days of Barbados's settlement, there was some religious as well as cultural diversity. Some settlers were Catholics, Puritans, Quakers or Jews. But increasingly the dominant religious culture was a severe Anglicanism. There were attacks on the Quakers and Jews, with greater accompanying oppression of enslaved people. Island society gradually became more English and militarised. The shifting political situation of the civil war and its aftermath in Britain, and the fact that most Barbados people were held in slavery or indentured service, meant that by the 1670s it had a fortress mentality, with the threat of violence and torture everywhere. There was a populous prison holding thieves, debtors and 'maroons' – escaped slaves and servants – and also a large 'Cage' alongside a pillory and stocks in the town centre. The Cage held escaped or resistant captives, whose punishments were public events. They included lashing with a whip and sometimes extraordinary executions such as burning alive. That was the sentence for the alleged leaders of organised rebellions, one of which occurred in the 1670s.

Coming from a Native American forest-dwelling people, Tatabe would have dreaded the reeking brick and stone maze of Bridgetown. Chained and helpless, she and other prisoners were shuffled through this strange environment, passing horrendous scenes of racism, oppression and cruelty. The port town had three thousand inhabitants in the 1670s and was growing almost daily. The bellowing

of traders and the clink of fetters accompanied Tatabe and her
fellow slaves as they walked, and their panic prompted only sneers
and indifference from crowds of white shoppers.[6] As Bridgetown's
seething street markets, its Cage and prison, its warehouses and
stalls fell behind her, perhaps there was a brief sense of relief.
Tatabe's Bridgetown was an urban enclave in a tranquil wetland.
It straggled along the Indian River amid dunes, islets and salt-
marshes. Where its quays and causeways ended, mangrove swamps
began. Yelping gulls filled the sky above the careenage, where ships'
hulls were cleaned and repaired, and silent herons stalked roadside
ditches. Tatabe walked into open countryside, a gentle, green landscape whose rising folds were spiky with the chimneys and
windmills of sugar refineries. Fronds of sugar cane waved in the
warm breeze. She followed a dirt road, meandering into the island's
interior, towards wooded hills.

Tatabe's destination was a three-hundred-acre sugar farm and
refinery owned by Samuel Thompson, likely the land now called
Clifton in St Thomas parish. Samuel was a young man, born in
1655, who had inherited the plantation from his father at the age
of four. He took formal control in 1676 aged twenty-one and lived
there with his widowed mother Elizabeth. But Samuel was not a
happy youth. Like Matthew Hopkins, he may have had a terminal
disease, since he died in 1680 at the age of just twenty-five. As if
anticipating his death, he had sold most of his land by then. A
relative, Anthony Lane, bought one third and in 1676 Samuel
part-leased, part-sold the rest to Nicholas Prideaux, a Cornish
slave-trafficker who was based in Bridgetown but also owned other
land. With these sales came an inventory of Samuel Thompson's
goods, including the people he owned. Among these was Tatabe,
listed as 'Tattuba' in two inventories of 1676. She was one of
sixty-seven enslaved people and is identified as still a child. No
'Indians' are separately labelled in this list, which is headed
'Negroes'. As we saw, Tatabe may have had ancestors from both
sides of the Atlantic or may have been conflated with the Africans
among whom she lived. A predominantly Black community had

certainly sheltered her since her arrival. Now all her protectors and friends were sold.[7]

Tatabe might have changed hands several times when the Thompson estates broke up. Perhaps she was sold first to Nicholas Prideaux, who took most of Samuel Thompson's land and maybe most of the people he had enslaved. But if so, Tatabe was then sold again. In Bridgetown lived a sugar dealer and banker sunk deep into the slave trade: Samuel Parris, a London-born nonconformist who had emigrated in the 1660s. Samuel had attended Harvard University in Massachusetts until 1673. In that year his father died, and Samuel had inherited his Barbados lands, worth around seven thousand pounds, a huge sum. The Parris family had been in Barbados since the 1640s: Samuel's uncle John had been a slave-trafficker as well as a planter. The Parrises owned two plantations near Prideaux land, one directly adjacent to Nicholas Prideaux's second plantation, land known as Newbold in St George parish. It's easy to imagine how Tatabe might have been traded by Samuel Thompson to Samuel Parris via his neighbour Nicholas Prideaux.

However, Samuel Parris did not intend to stay in Barbados after he had taken possession of his father's assets. Rebellions of enslaved people, declining soil fertility, a damaging hurricane and falling sugar prices had begun to undermine his business. He had also evidently been happier at Harvard, where his brand of Puritanism was the norm instead of Barbados's Anglicanism. Now he wanted to return to Massachusetts. Samuel sold all his land and, by 1680, he had wound up his business in Bridgetown. Documents of the time show him holding only one slave and one servant, neither of whom are named. Tatabe is probably the former, and so she was forced to leave the island with him. Later she would recall 'my own country' in her witch trial testimony as a place where she supposedly learned magic. Whether she meant the South American mainland or Barbados, by 1692 that magic place must have seemed very far away. She was hustled onto a ship and endured a stormy, miserable voyage over grey seas, travelling three-and-a-half thousand miles north.[8] This history of unsettled, trafficked movement and repeated loss of home and friends was what Tatabe brought to her witch trial in Salem.

The ship carrying Tatabe and Samuel docked in Boston, Massachusetts, where they lived for a decade. Samuel married and had children with his wife Elizabeth: Thomas, Betty and Susannah, born between 1681 and 1687. Tatabe was reclassified as a 'servant' because enslaving Native Americans was technically illegal in Massachusetts. Like Virginia, Massachusetts was a colony run under a charter from the British government, but it had its own laws and customs. The prohibition of slavery and Tatabe's apparent new status meant nothing in practice, however: Tatabe was not free, and, even if she had been, she had nowhere else to go in this strange new world. In Boston, leaves turned scarlet, pink and lemon in autumn, whirling from the trees. Winter meant sousing rains. Snow frosted the washing line and vegetable patch with sharp crystals that numbed Tatabe's fingers. None of her clothes warmed her and she envied wealthy Bostonians in their woollen serge coats and padded silk hoods. But Boston was a luxurious, bustling hive compared with Salem village, where Samuel was appointed minister in 1689. Since arriving in Boston in 1680, he had reinvented himself from businessman to Puritan clergyman, one of a new Massachusetts elite aiming to remould the colony on extreme Protestant lines. When its charter was revoked by King Charles II in 1684, the Puritans feared direct rule from London and especially the imposition of religious tolerance – an idea they hated. Samuel and his Puritan friends wanted freedom to persecute Quakers, Baptists and other sects who disagreed with them; they hadn't come to America to make nice with heretics. And where people feared heresy, they often feared witchcraft too.

The villagers who invited Samuel to lead their church were Puritan fundamentalists like him. They'd built their own church in Salem, a wooden meeting house with a fine pulpit. But that was not enough for them: now, with Samuel, they wanted to create a more exclusive sect within that church. This inner circle offered membership only to the most radical believers. These literally signed up to all the church's teachings, entering into a written covenant binding them to their God and each other. Non-members could use the church building to hear Samuel's sermons but would then be shooed out and excluded from the sacrament of communion – whose name marks its normal function within Christianity, the act of coming together as a community. Samuel did not want to bring together a community; instead, he explained in an early Salem sermon that his mission was to 'cleanse and purge' his church and later insisted that 'our Lord Jesus Christ knows how many devils there are in his churches and who they are'.

He sounds like Heinrich Kramer, itching to turn upon members of his congregation whom he disliked and regarded as Satan's agents. We know some church members had criticised him and refused to raise his salary, so that he regarded himself as the victim of their injustice. Even worse than opponents within his church were those who would not commit fully to it; Samuel refused even to baptise the children of non-members, who made up three-quarters of the village population. Salem was the antithesis of the inclusive societies Tatabe's people prized, being divided, angry, judgemental.[9] As well as looking and sounding different from the white Massachusetts villagers, she was now an outsider for yet another reason: she did not join the inner sect – no enslaved people could do so – and so was unfairly thought defective in the Christian faith forced on her by her enslavers.

It was the same for another Native American living in Samuel Parris's parsonage – a man known as John Indian. Tatabe is described in some sources as John's wife, and it is possible that she was married to him by Samuel Parris as a convenient arrangement for their employer. Marriage would allow Tatabe and John to share a room and bed. But we don't know Tatabe's feelings about John and whether he helped or hindered her in her daily struggle. We can imagine other aspects of her life, however. The Salem parsonage was a small, cold, damp two-storey house with a lean-to kitchen and storehouse and a stone-built cellar and chimneys. Tatabe was responsible for its cleanliness and what warmth could be conjured within its wooden walls. These were different housekeeping challenges from those in Bridgetown. In her testimony, Tatabe describes 'washing' rooms: mopping mud off floorboards; swabbing the elegant furniture to remove the ash breathed out by open fires. Firewood had to be burned sparingly. It was provided to Samuel by the church community, and at times he had to beg for more: he 'had scarce wood enough to burn till the morrow', he complained in November 1691.[10] Tatabe had to manage her fires efficiently to dry clothes, heat water and stew food in the iron cauldrons and skillets that steamed daily over the flames.

The house was a workplace and a prison. But Tatabe might also have seen it as a defence against local people. Although they were like her in many ways, they were also unlike her, with different languages, knowledge and spirituality, and no liking for the settler society which she'd reluctantly joined. As in Virginia seventy years before, Salem villagers greatly feared conflict with local Native Americans, although the Naumkeag band of the Massachusetts people who lived around Salem were peaceable neighbours. However, several of the girls who were friends with the Parris children were refugees from the frontier of the 'Indian War' in Maine. Like Joan and Robert Wright in Virginia, they had seen neighbours shot or clubbed to death – this time by angry Wabanaki people whom the colonists had sold illegally into slavery and whose leaders they had murdered. Several of the girls caught up in this horror had lost family members and had themselves to flee from attackers. Although Tatabe was unrelated to these northern Native Americans, or the Naumkeag whom the traumatised girls saw hunting in the woods and riding into town to trade, white villagers identified her with them. Recognising the similarities but not the differences, they called her an 'indgen' or 'Indian' or 'Mr Parris's Indian woman' and viewed her with prejudice that became hate.[11]

Significantly, in the aftermath of the 'Indian War', a new family member joined the Parris household at Salem: Samuel's eleven-year-old niece Abigail Williams. Abigail seems to have been orphaned, perhaps in the war. Whatever her story, she was relocated to her uncle's house in a time of crisis. There was warfare, political turmoil over the charter, and religious conflict, and it was a long, snowy, hungry winter. In mid-January 1692 Abigail fell ill and then her nine-year-old cousin Betty, Samuel's daughter, did too. Perhaps their malady was a cramp or fever but soon their symptoms were alarming. The girls twitched and shrieked as if in pain. Their bodies contorted into strange positions, arms and necks at unnatural angles. Soon they began saying they were being 'bitten and pinched' – something outside their bodies seemed to be hurting them. At times they would be struck dumb so that they could not even describe it. In a community that believed in devils, it was obvious what the girls were claiming: they were bewitched. Samuel called a doctor, who agreed with the diagnosis of bewitchment, and so the minister and his church members launched into sermons, fasts and prayers to try to break the curse with their pious energy. Other ministers were invited to view the girls' contortions, and the parsonage house became a central focus of attention. A battle with Satan was being fought there, and the godly congregation revelled in the drama.

One church member, however, responded overenthusiastically to the need to heal the girls. To discover who the witch was that afflicted Abigail and Betty, Mary Sibley decided to use folk-magic to supplement her prayers. Like Joan Wright with her butter churn and hot iron, maybe Mary thought herself an expert on anti-witchcraft charms. She asked John Indian to bake a witch cake, a mix of cereal flour with the urine of the 'bewitched', which was then baked and fed to a dog to carry away the curse. But Samuel Parris found out about the witch cake. He was horrified that such irreligious activity, magical in itself although designed to combat witches, was happening in his house. On 27 March, he reproved Mary in church for giving 'direction to my Indian man in an unwarrantable way to find out witches' by 'making of a cake'. By this act, 'going to the Devil, for helps against the Devil', as he put it, Samuel believed Satan had been let loose in the village.

Now everything was worse. More girls and young women began to have fits, writhing, screaming and crying. It seemed evident they could not be cured without discovering the witches who were attacking them.

In late February 1692, Tatabe was accused of witchcraft by Abigail and Betty. Abigail seems to have led the accusations. Betty's name was later erased from documents and only Abigail signed them – with her mark, because she could not write her own name.[12] To start with, the accusations were verbal, made to Samuel Parris and repeated by him to neighbours and magistrates. Details went unrecorded; even later they would be written down only in summary form as events accelerated. However, the main charges are clear. Both Abigail and Betty accused Tatabe of bewitching them in conspiracy with two white colonists, Sarah Good and Sarah Osborne. They said they 'had been much afflicted with pains in their head and other parts and often pinched by the apparition of Sarah Good, Sarah Osborne and Tituba Indian'. By 'apparition' they meant the spectral body of the witch, like the hand that Joan Wright trapped in her butter churn nearly a century before. The girls alleged Tatabe and the other accused had drifted into their rooms and assaulted them. Later they also accused other Salem villagers: Martha and Giles Corey, Rebecca Nurse, Bridget Bishop, George Jacobs, Elizabeth and John Proctor and many more.

Once the first accusations were made, Samuel Parris himself interrogated Tatabe. He had no formal role in proceedings against her, was not a magistrate and should not have questioned her – but as a minister and guardian of the two supposed victims he evidently felt justified. He was also Tatabe's owner-employer, and sometimes employers would intervene to question suspects, like Gillie Duncan's brutal employer David Seton.[13] Like Matthew Hopkins and John Stearne, Samuel Parris wanted to know more, to test the demonological ideas that had structured his prejudices during theological training. At Salem, therefore, pre-trial questioning was partly run by amateur interrogators, very much like the Manningtree witch-hunt and possibly using the same cruel methods.

The result was the same: a fast-spreading witch-hunt with farmers and traders eager to speak up. The notion of recording personal testimony was important in Puritan culture: it was 'witness' both in a legal and in a religious sense. Salem church members imagined their relationship with God in these legalistic terms. They had literally signed a covenant offering him worship. Abigail and her fellow accusers imagined witches making a similar written agreement with Satan. It was the usual demonological idea of inversion – Christians covenanted with God, witches with Satan – but it was no longer articulated only by top churchmen such as inquisitors. The Reformation's overall outcome was to democratise religious knowledge, and one consequence of this was that the power of demonological analysis was devolved to ordinary people: witch-finders like Matthew Hopkins, wider church congregations and even children. Going one better than Rebecca West's account of the Satanic prayer meeting at Lawford fifty years before, Abigail said she'd actually witnessed the covenanting process. She'd been haunted by the spectral form of Martha Corey 'by which apparition she was sometimes . . . tempted to put her hand to [sign] the Devil's book'. She had often seen Martha at 'the Devil's sacrament' and now Martha was signing up demonic converts right in front of her. George Jacobs, too, had appeared spectrally 'bringing the book for her to set her hand unto'. Satan had 'two books' in which 'there was many lines written'. Sometimes he brought a book to her himself in the form of a 'black man'. The devil was often portrayed as a coal-black creature with hooves, flowing hair and a tail, but of course his darkness also recalls white colonists' perceptions of people of colour like Tatabe.[14]

As these revelations began to emerge in pre-trial questioning, Tatabe, Sarah Good and Sarah Osborne were arrested for formal interrogation on 29 February 1692. The warrant for her arrest describes Tatabe as 'Titibe an Indian Woman servant' and then as 'Titibe Indian', the composite name that Samuel Parris used for her when he was not referring to her dismissively as 'the Indian woman'. The three suspects were summoned to Nathaniel Ingersoll's inn at

ten o'clock next day by magistrates John Hathorne and Jonathan
Corwin, but their interrogation was later moved to the meeting
house so more villagers could participate. A crowd gathered, among
whom were three men who each wrote an account of events. Their
versions differ at times, but what is clear is that Tatabe's interrogation was in a crowded and threatening room. Abigail, Betty and
new teenage accusers Elizabeth Hubbard and Ann Putnam screeched
and pointed; the crowd gasped and groaned. The magistrates
assumed Tatabe's guilt. Rather than asking if she had caused the
girls' fits, they asked, 'Why do you hurt these children?' Tatabe
tried to resist: 'I no hurt them at all,' she replied.[15] When she was
asked who was hurting them, she drew on her knowledge of
Christian doctrine: 'The devil,' she hazarded tentatively, 'for ought
[anything] I know.' We can almost hear the question mark in her
voice. Was this the right answer? In one version of the account,
she adds defensively, 'I can't tell when the devil works.' But the
questioners wanted more.

If anything, the arrival of the devil into Tatabe's statements –
perhaps prompted by questioners or her own knowledge of
Christianity – encouraged her interrogators. Had she 'never seen
the devil?' they probed. It seemed safe to Tatabe to say that she
had; after all, the devil tempted good Christians. 'The devil came
to me and bid me serve him,' she ventured, hastily adding that
it was four other women who were hurting the accusers. Sarah
Good and Sarah Osborne were two of them, she admitted. They
had wanted her to help them, but 'I would not', she concluded
hopefully. 'She further saith', the transcript continues, 'there was
a tall man of Boston that she did see.' Her narrative was shifting.
So, there were four women and this man? And they were the
witches, not she, and 'they said hurt the children'. 'And did you
hurt them?' wheedled the magistrates. 'No,' she said. But it was
hard to remain brave. 'They lay all on me,' she faltered in one
account, meaning that the five people laid all the blame on her.
The witches had told her that if she would not obey them, 'they
will hurt me', she said – a threat of punishment she must have

encountered in reality many times. They had said her 'head shall be cut off'. 'But did you not hurt them?' the magistrates insisted. And eventually Tatabe said 'yes'.

Her confession was probably inevitable. We don't know if she was subjected before her interrogation to the watching and walking that had been so effective on Bess Clarke, but this certainly happened afterwards. On the night of 1 March, some of the accused were watched by village constable Joseph Herrick and others, using the technique adopted during the Manningtree witch-hunt. In the morning, Sarah Good's arm was covered in blood from the elbow to the wrist. This was explained as an injury inflicted in spirit upon her apparition as it wandered out to attack her victims, rather than evidence of mistreatment of her actual body – but of course this was nonsense.[16] We can imagine how vulnerable the two Sarahs and Tatabe were. Although Sarah Good and Sarah Osborne had refused to confess, their assertions of innocence were not believed. Sarah Good had been suspected of witchcraft for years. Regarded as a 'turbulent' person, she and her husband had often been home-less in recent years, being evicted from lodgings and chased out of barns because it was feared Sarah's tobacco pipe would set the hay on fire. Even her husband William now turned against her.[17] Sarah tried telling her questioners, 'I am falsely accused', but they attrib-uted her firmness to her 'wicked and spiteful manner' rather than to outraged innocence. Sarah Osborne was less assertive but the outcome was the same.

What hope did the enslaved and reviled Tatabe have? She broke down completely, promising she would not hurt the children anymore and apologising. Her confession shows particularly clearly how demonologists and other amateur questioners could plant ideas in witchcraft suspects' heads and force them into confessing what-ever they wanted to hear, by violence and intimidation. Tatabe's confession is all about this type of coercion. The witches and their spectral forms had threatened her, she repeated. Coming to her in the spirit-shapes of hogs, dogs, rats and a man with a yellow bird,

they had told her to 'hurt the children' and 'kill the children' or
they and the devil 'would do worse to me'. Over and over again,
Tatabe described threats: 'he would do worse to me', 'he said he
would hurt me', 'he looks like a man and threatens to hurt me'.
When she was physically examined by the innkeeper Hannah
Ingersoll to see if witch marks could be found, her story that the
apparition of Sarah Good had 'pinched her on the legs' was apparently confirmed. We 'found it so', wrote magistrate John Hathorne,
credulously unable to perceive the bruises that were discovered
might have been inflicted by – who? Tatabe's enslaver Samuel Parris?
Joseph Herrick, the constable who arrested her? Other people who
had beaten her? There were many hard-hearted and hard-handed
people in Salem, but instead John decided that the marks on Tatabe's
legs had been made by a ghostly spectre.[18]

Tatabe gave him – and us – all the clues needed to come to a
different conclusion. Her confession showed she expected abuse
from everyone and concocted her story of witchcraft because of it.
But she wove in, as all 'witches' did, something of her own story
too: real feelings, fears and experiences that can help us recover
something of her voice. Some of the witches that she described
were wealthy-sounding people, like those she would have known
in Boston: a Bostonian man with a black cloak and serge coat; a
woman with a serge coat and silk hood. They would 'pull and haul
her' to the houses of Elizabeth Hubbard and Ann Putnam. Tatabe
knew about being dragged from her home by finely dressed
gentlemen and ladies. In contrast to being manhandled through the
streets she described magical transportation, perhaps a wish-
fulfilment fantasy. Witches 'ride upon sticks', she said, drawing on
images of Europeans like Kirsti Sørensdatter whirling through the
skies to Sabbaths. Perhaps Tatabe hoped she could fly home in this
way. Her descriptions of familiar spirits suggest her imagination
returned to the Caribbean as well as dwelling miserably on experiences in Massachusetts. Sarah Good had animal familiars, Tatabe
said – a normal cat but also a hairy 'thing' two or three feet high,
a harpy-like creature and some kind of spectral wolf. Some of these

sound like monsters from Arawak and African nightmares: the hairy thing has no parallel in English stories of familiars. But Tatabe framed these stories from her own imagination in the way her questioners wanted, eventually leading to the confession they sought: yes, Sarah had signed the devil's book, Tatabe confirmed, and soon she was charged with making a mark in it herself.

As if to emphasise her disempowerment, throughout Tatabe's examination her supposed victims screamed abuse and pointed at her. They may have done more. Another convicted Salem witch, Rebecca Eames, later said she had been 'hurried out of my senses' into confession, because the girls were 'mocking of me and spitting in my face, saying they know me to be an old witch and if I would not confess it I should very speedily be hanged'. She had been 'amazed and affrighted' into confession, she said. So was Tatabe, and, as Samuel Parris put it, when she 'began to confess' her tormentors 'were immediately all quiet the rest of the said Indian woman's examination'. Having got what they wanted, they shut up. 'As soon as she began to confess,' Elizabeth Hubbard claimed, 'she left off hurting me.'

Once she had broken under the pressure, Tatabe succumbed to despair and began to have fits herself. Observers Samuel Parris, Thomas Putnam and Ezekiel Cheever all testified that 'she was herself very much afflicted' and 'in the face of authority' she turned on Sarah Good and Sarah Osborne, accusing them as 'the persons that afflicted her'. This granted her the status of an accuser, which might save her life.[19]

First there was a final interrogation, however. Tatabe was questioned for a second time on 2 March. She was asked what Satan had told her. 'He tell me he god,' she replied, 'and I must believe him and serve him six years.' She had refused, saying, 'I ask my master' (Samuel Parris), but eventually accepted him as her deity, worn down by his persistence. So far, Tatabe had served Satan only six weeks, since a mid-January Friday night, just 'afore Abigail was ill'. The Wednesday after that the witches had held a Sabbath in Samuel Parris's house, she said. The devil gave her the power to be invisible there, a welcome relief. Then the demands that she hurt the children began. 'I would not hurt Betty, I loved Betty,' Tatabe said sadly, but she did agree to pinch her. She ended this fantasy by confirming she had made her mark in the devil's book.[20] She was imprisoned on 7 March to await trial.

A special court, known as a court of Oyer and Terminer because of its judge's power to hear and determine cases, was then set up by the colony's governor, Sir William Phips. All that had to be proven to the judge under Massachusetts law – distinct from English law – was that an accused witch 'hath or consulteth with a familiar spirit', an offence that boiled down demonological complexities into one simple prohibition readily understood by ordinary witchfinders. Tatabe's indictment stated that in late 1691 she 'wickedly, maliciously and feloniously a covenant with the devil did make and signed the devil's book with a mark like a : C by which wicked covenanting with the devil she the said Tittapa is become a detestable witch'.[21]

However, that indictment was not drawn up until 9 May 1693, over a year after her arrest. Before then there had been a series of initial successes followed by alarming setbacks for Tatabe's accusers. Along with Sarah Good she was sent to Boston prison in early June 1692, Sarah Osborne having died miserably in jail in mid-May. The warrant for Tatabe's removal to Boston describes her as 'Titiba an Indian Woman, belonging unto Mr Samuell [sic] Parris'. Once again, Tatabe was in chains. She was carted through the marshy coastal countryside, scrubby woods brooding under summer skies. Boston jail lay on Prison Lane, now Court Street. It was cold even in June, its unglazed windows barred with iron, its walls three feet thick. Over the next two months Tatabe was joined there by over fifty other witchcraft suspects. The jail had to be remodelled to house them and new fetters and chains ordered. French and Native American prisoners of war added to the overcrowding. One was an 'Indian Girle', captured as Tatabe herself had probably been twenty years before.[22] As Tatabe languished in prison, other accused people were put through formal trials by the court of Oyer and

Terminer, convicted and hanged. Nineteen were executed, while Giles Corey refused to enter a plea of guilty or not guilty and suffered the cruel death appointed as a punishment for that. He was pressed to death by having rocks loaded onto his body. But Tatabe was not one of those tried. We don't know why. Perhaps she was considered too useful as a witness against others? It's one of many crucial gaps in her story.

Time worked to her advantage. By mid-1693 an astonishing two hundred people were awaiting trial. The majority of Massachusetts' citizens had begun to realise something was terribly wrong and to protest: whatever demonology said, there could not be so many witches. As well as becoming theologically implausible, the number of trials was organisationally unsustainable, and the court system collapsed under a backlog. Trials were paused and a new court, the Superior Court of Judicature, was invented to try the remaining cases under a revised anti-witchcraft law. This law, based more closely on the English Witchcraft Act of 1604, confirmed it was illegal to 'use, practise or exercise any invocation or conjuration of any evil and wicked spirit' or to 'consult, covenant with, entertain, employ, feed or reward any evil and wicked spirit to or for any intent or purpose'. Tatabe's supposed crime was covered by the new law as well as the old one. But when her indictment was presented to a grand jury at Ipswich, working for the new court, the jury rejected it. Just as in England, it was their job to scrutinise charges and check all relevant information was present to try an offence. Having looked over Tatabe's paperwork, their foreman Abraham Haseltine wrote 'ignoramus' (meaning 'we don't know', we don't approve) on the back of her indictment. This meant she would not go on to further trial.[23]

The jury's reasoning is not given. They might have thought the accusation vague. Normally the date when an offence was said to have been committed was required but this indictment only mentioned a broad time range. Jurors might also have reflected that evidence based purely on visions or confessions was, by mid-1693, regarded as potentially unsound. Perhaps the jury had begun to doubt the wisdom of holding witch trials at all. If so, it was a defining moment in witch trial history. Abraham Haseltine's Ipswich jury was asked to commit for trial a suspected witch whose accusation had famously begun a mass hunt involving at least two hundred suspects across multiple settlements in Massachusetts, from Ipswich to Andover, and whose supposed crime was a hanging offence in law – and they said no. Amazingly, this was to be Tatabe's only trial. A few convictions continued around her, because some personnel from the old court were unchanged in the new one, but there were no more executions. Anyone condemned was reprieved by the governor, who had lost confidence in the decisions of his colony's courts. As bereaved families spoke out and ministers admitted they had made mistakes, it was gradually accepted that a terrible miscarriage of justice had occurred. Protestors besieged the colonial government. The Salem village congregation split. People who had seen family members hanged because of Samuel Parris's accusations petitioned for his removal and he left Salem in disgrace. The surviving accused and the families of those who had been executed were compensated by the state, public recantations were made by some of the accusers in 1697 and 1706 and eventually, in 1711, the government apologised too.[24]

A misspelled and heavily edited note from the Salem prison-keeper written sometime after 9 May 1693 is the last evidence we have of what happened to Tatabe when her trial was over. In the note, the prison-keeper pleads with the court to pay the food bill of the witchcraft suspects during their time in detention. Tatabe's name is first on a list of detainees, and she is referred to as 'Tatabe Indian'. The note explains Tatabe has been in prison for 'a whole year' and several months, costing the prison over four pounds. And these lines are crossed out, which shows the debt was paid – perhaps by Samuel Parris, perhaps someone else.[25] Stories have circulated ever since that Tatabe was sold to pay her jail fees. That might be true. There was no slave market in Massachusetts, however, and the costs of transporting Tatabe to a market somewhere else would have been large. Only someone who had never heard of Tatabe or believed her innocent would have been likely to buy her. It's therefore possible that she was freed by the state or by well-wishers, of whom there were many by 1693. Where does that leave Tatabe? We don't know. She survived her witch trial and was freed from prison, but we can only hope that she eventually gained real freedom.[26]

Intermission: From Demonology to Doubt

As demonology's hold on the human imagination weakened across Europe and North America, early eighteenth-century legislators began to reconsider how best to handle the witchcraft accusations that were still made from time to time. Even before the Salem debacle of 1692–3, some had doubted whether existing anti-witchcraft laws and trial processes were appropriate. In 1647 Matthew Hopkins and John Stearne were accused of profiting cynically from witch-hunting and found themselves in disgrace. After Salem, it was clear to almost everyone that baseless witchcraft accusations had killed innocent people. Perhaps tighter definitions of the crime would have saved lives, ministers argued – refusing to trust victims' visions of the witch's spectral body, for instance? But bigger questions followed: did magic really work? If so, how? Even if it did, were witches' spectacular confessions of Sabbaths and murders mere fantasies? Or were they devil-worshippers, as traditionally claimed, abusing religion heretically to do real harm? This led to a practical question: how was it possible to decide in a court of law? How were inquisitors, judges, juries expected to test accusers' and accused people's stories? They could not command suspects to summon the devil, as Matthew Hopkins had contentiously done in pre-trial questioning in 1645; that was itself regarded in many jurisdictions as an illegal act. Accusers could not produce physical evidence of witchcraft in action either. Meanwhile, witnesses could lie or speak under the influence of demonic illusion or their own mistake. The questions arose whether a law court was even the place to be asking these questions, because if the wrong decision was made an innocent person died.[1]

Gradually the demonological definition of witchcraft that had originated with churchmen in the late Middle Ages and spread across the world through the secular courts came to seem unlikely to many intelligent, educated and moderate people, who reinforced each other's scepticism. While many ordinary people continued to believe in witchcraft, increasingly their social superiors did not. Seventeenth- and eighteenth-century scientific discoveries demystified life, and even where some mystery remained it was expected that new, clearer explanations would be demanded. Solutions were less often sought in Christian theology as power seeped from churches and individual rulers towards parliaments, stock exchanges and technocrats. In law, many factors came together to reduce the desire to prosecute witches.[2] And although the men who staffed public institutions often continued to believe in God, demons, magic and – as a logical part of that worldview – the power of witchcraft, they questioned its provability and punishment. Yes, Satan existed but could it really be right to execute this illiterate peasant, or churchgoing grandmother? Yes, this accuser had experienced terrible visions of named women bewitching them, but could observers be sure these were not demonic deceits? For intersecting reasons of secularisation, education and scepticism, witchcraft prosecution began to *feel* wrong ethically, as well as being judged wrong scientifically. But the formal decriminalisation of witchcraft was a long process across Europe, America and the Christianised world.

In France a progressive but flawed Royal Edict is a good example of the indecisive squirming of legislators. In 1682, the government of King Louis XIV decided that while in theory witchcraft – *maléfice* – did exist, it should be redefined in law. The Edict stated that witches who used *maléfice* should be executed, but only if they were also blasphemous, had committed sacrilege or used poison to kill their victims. A recent scandal at the royal court had uncovered courtiers who used inversions of the Catholic Mass to call on Satan. They believed, it was claimed, that he would supercharge their spells and poisons, granting them sex and success, killing off rivals and buying political influence with the king. At their Sabbaths, or 'Black Masses' as they became known, babies were supposedly sacrificed.³ The Edict came out of attempts to close down this sensational royal scandal. However, although the Edict accepted that some people did abuse the Mass, were sacrilegious poisoners and witches, it did not describe such people as heretics or devil-worshippers, despite the fact that their gatherings had many features of Satanic Sabbaths. The idea that witches replaced God with Satan was no longer considered officially credible. Further, the Edict did not actually support the idea that witches' spells worked; it stated that they used poison, not curses, to kill their victims. Therefore, witches should be punished, the Edict stated vaguely, according to the severity of their actions – whatever that meant. Sounding even more sceptical, the Edict then listed various kinds of fakery and superstition, as it called them: astrology, divination, fortune-telling; activities once believed to be potent realities and part of the crime of witchcraft. Now they were condemned as con-tricks, and those who practised such arts were ordered to desist or leave France. Overall, the Edict left a lot of questions unanswered, which would later lead to difficulties in court.⁴

In Britain and those of her colonies that used British law, a Witchcraft Act of 1735 repealed both the Scottish and English anti-witchcraft laws of 1563 and 1604. The Act stated simply that 'no prosecution, suit, or proceeding, shall be commenced or carried on against any person or persons for witchcraft, sorcery, inchantment, or conjuration . . . in any court whatsoever'. Instead, anyone who pretended to have magical powers, such as cursing their neighbours or conjuring up spirits by chanting spells and performing rituals, would be punished. Specifically, no one should 'pretend to exercise or use any kind of witchcraft, sorcery, enchantment, or conjuration, or undertake to tell fortunes, or pretend, from his or her skill or knowledge in any occult or crafty science, to discover where or in what manner any goods or chattels, supposed to have been stolen or lost, may be found'. 'Ignorant persons are frequently deluded and defrauded' by such claims, the Act added. The penalty for this crime was a year's imprisonment. The Witchcraft Act's definition of con-trickery was much the same as Louis XIV's list: fortune-telling, summoning spirits, divining, dowsing for treasure and so on. So, the 1735 law specifically prohibited traditional witch trials but, like the Edict, it substituted trials of pretended or imagined witches instead.[5] Crucially, the witch trial did not end: instead, it changed its processes and meaning.

PART TWO

Echoes

CHAPTER SEVEN

The Trial of Marie-Catherine Cadière: Witches Reimagined and a French Revolution

In the first decade of the eighteenth century, Joseph and Élisabeth Cadière's olive oil business was thriving on Rue de l'Hôpital in the city of Toulon, Provence. It was a cramped and dirty alleyway, its grey stone tenements echoing to the shouts of delivery drivers and the thump of wooden barrels, but it was well placed for brisk trade, near the naval port. The Cadières' oil went into stews and sauces, ointments and soap. Outside, bewigged and gold-braided officers strutted while sailors and hauliers pushed by, streaming into and out of the dockyard each day. Today the alleys around their shop hold quiet apartment houses, with multi-coloured graffiti spattering metal shutters and washing garlanding upper floors. Signs advise 'no parking' – anything wider than a scooter would block the narrow space – and forbid ball games, noise and fuss: 'Jeux de ballon, balles et projectiles interdits!' The alleys are still on a summer morning, smelling of diesel, coffee and urine. But with a bustling market a few minutes east, packed with patisseries, boulangeries and stalls selling anchovies, olives, kebabs and couscous, they retain their association with fine Provençal and north African food.

Joseph had done well to gain a foothold in the Provençal olive business, marrying his boss's daughter Élisabeth Pomet and taking over his father-in-law's trade: the next alley to Rue de l'Hôpital is named Rue Pomet, after her family. The couple had three sons, Laurent, François and Étienne-Thomas, a daughter who died in infancy, and then their youngest child Marie-Catherine was born in November 1709. She and her family lived much of the time in the block over the shop. Every day she woke to the mew of gulls wheeling in the square of sky above the alley and squabbling among the chimney pots. Sometimes a poor family would scuttle up the street supporting a sick grandmother or child to be treated by the nuns at the free hospital, the religious foundation that gave the alley its name.[1] When Marie-Catherine walked with her mother to the baroque Cathedral of Notre Dame de la Seds, with its soaring white marble columns, its curly ironwork and intricately carved altarpieces, she may have thought about the church's charity: its obligation to help the poor and afflicted; the love of Christ promised to faithful worshippers. Although her family were comparatively secure artisans, she was often anxiously in need of comfort.

Her father Joseph died young, leaving her mother Élisabeth to manage the oil business until the Cadières' son Laurent grew old enough to help. Times were hard when harsh winters damaged the olive groves. Although Provençal summers are hot, in cold years frost and snow could spill down from the mountains, killing the trees, and this happened in the early eighteenth century. But the Cadières' business endured. Outside Toulon, they owned a small olive farm with a house and oil mill, a place where they could grow food and retreat from the city.[2] Marie-Catherine spent many childhood summers there, when the city was thought – rightly – to be unhealthy, full of rotting rubbish and disease. The Provençal olive groves smelled healthily of thyme and rosemary as well as of the fat green olives. But, as events were to show, for all its hazards Marie-Catherine preferred the excitements of Toulon to the peace of country living – the opportunities to do charitable work among her neighbours and to attend religious services and festivals with her friends were especially rewarding to her.

She was an extremely devout Christian, proudly part of France's state-backed Catholic Church. Élisabeth raised her children to revere the church, seeing sainthood as an ideal. François became a priest, having studied with the Jesuit order, and Étienne-Thomas became a Dominican monk, like Heinrich Kramer three hundred years before. Laurent, too, would have been ordained if he had not been needed in the family business. That left Marie-Catherine, torn between competing futures: become a nun or marry a pious merchant, if one asked her. She'd received a basic education – a new and wonderful freedom for middle-class girls in the eighteenth century – but still limited in its scope compared with her brothers' opportunities. Her studies taught her to read holy texts but not write at length herself. She was raised to pray quietly under the guidance of male priests and then, if she did not become a nun, she could do charitable deeds and raise good Christian sons and daughters. Marie-Catherine had little power except through piety. In this way she was like Salem's Abigail Williams or Betty Parris, more literate but still a provincial, dependent young woman taught that dutiful passivity would earn her a reward in heaven. She likely did not expect much from her earthly life, because no one imagined much for her.

Compounding this anxiety over her own prospects, like Abigail and Betty Marie-Catherine was born into a community under strain. Toulon was a border city, facing France's enemies around the Mediterranean. Its people lived with fear of invasion. The city was heavily defended, with four forts and hefty gun batteries trained on its harbour. While the walls hadn't fallen recently, historically there had been bombardments and even occupation. In the 1540s Ottoman forces led by corsair admiral Khizr Khayr ad-Din Barbarossa had overwintered in Toulon. They were the French king's allies against the Holy Roman emperor, and in 1543 the king ordered all Christians except household heads to leave Toulon to accommodate them. If the Toulonnais stayed, they faced execution by their own govern-ment. The city's cathedral became a mosque for thirty thousand Muslim guests. But the overwintering became an occupation, until the Ottoman sailors were eventually paid to leave. Smarting, Toulon's church authorities reconsecrated the cathedral – despite many shared views of God they still, inaccurately, regarded Muslims as devil-worshippers. Religious enemies kept coming. In 1707, two years before Marie-Catherine's birth, Toulon was attacked by an Anglo-Dutch-Italian force, led by Protestants. The city was besieged, causing near-starvation even for merchant families like the Cadières.[3]

On top of these threats, bubonic plague dominated Marie-Catherine's teenage years. In a scene now grimly familiar, during the plague years 1720–1 there were no social gatherings, no Christmas festivities, people lived in fear and the death toll mounted daily. Appallingly, half of Toulon's population died between autumn 1720 and summer 1721: it was later described as a 'dead city . . . the end of the world'. For a time, there were no Masses, no religious processions, very few large gatherings even for prayer. The Cadières fled to their farm when they could. Marie-Catherine's small pleasures lay in ruins. Would she ever again enjoy a saint's-day feast? Would she ever meet a husband? For the next four or five years, the city endured waves of infection and many people were in permanent mourning. So, when a new Jesuit priest, Jean-Baptiste Girard, arrived in Toulon in 1728 looking to make a splash in religious life, he knew that he would have to offer something more than frustration, tears and panic to his new congregation.

Jean-Baptiste's speciality was the guidance of women and girls; previously he had acted as confessor to nuns and now he aimed to inspire women beyond the convent. He told his pupils stories of female saints and mystics: St Teresa of Avila, St Catherine of Siena, Anne-Madeleine Remuzat and Marguerite-Marie Alacoque. The last two were famous French nuns who had promoted meditation on an image of Christ's sacred heart as a way to strengthen faith.[4] They were compelling role models. Particularly striking was the local woman Anne-Madeleine Remuzat, who lived until 1730. Her visions had shaped a Festival of the Sacred Heart, a vast public church service now being used to combat the plague by prayer. Of course, the event was a super-spreader, but few Toulon people knew that. Marie-Catherine must have blessed Anne-Madeleine for giving her the excuse to attend a religious festival at last. Now this saintly woman's meditations provided the opportunity to pray and dream in a small, newly hopeful group of students, led by kindly Father Girard. He knew Anne-Madeleine personally and shared tales of her visions, torments and prophecies with his pupils. If only Marie-Catherine could be more like Anne-Madeleine! Jean-Baptiste would be so pleased with her.

Jean-Baptiste's devotees found him welcoming, respectful and charismatic. He listened to them individually, which was rare in their experience. He prescribed charitable works and reading material and led them on outings. But you can see where this story is going. Innocently or knowingly, Jean-Baptiste was building a cult. His students began to fall a little in love with him. He was in his late forties, craggy and intense, with an austere authority that drew worshippers. The teenagers and twenty-somethings Marie-Catherine, Claire, Anne and Marie-Anne, the older Anne-Marie (a joiner's wife), Anne-Rose (a single thirty-something) and Thérèse (a fifty-year-old widow) all loved his stories. They enjoyed imagining the emotions of the saintly Anne-Madeleine, who found joy and fame through suffering.[5] Marie-Catherine was just eighteen and star-struck. She already had a confessor, but he was busy. He nodded wearily as Marie-Catherine revealed her sins and hopes, formally forgiving her on the church's behalf. But she wanted more engagement. Her spiritual dilemmas were not just petty frettings! When she met Jean-Baptiste by chance, she said a voice spoke to her, saying 'ecce homo': behold the man! These words label the crucified Christ in many paintings, so although Marie-Catherine was not taught Latin she knew their meaning. She had been chosen to recognise Jean-Baptiste as Christ-like.[6]

Once she'd joined his group, Marie-Catherine was delighted with Jean-Baptiste's teachings. He became her personal mentor. 'No matter how busy he was,' she said later, 'he never was too busy for me, and when I asked for him, whether it was at the street door or the confessional, I never met with any delay.' Indeed, Jean-Baptiste was so concerned for Marie-Catherine's religious development that he began to visit her at home and loan her books. He lent her his own letters to and from the saintly Anne-Madeleine Remuzat, prayed with her and helped her brothers.[7] To all the Cadières, Jean-Baptiste offered hope of heaven, but also the opportunity to imagine a significant religious role on earth. Through his teachings, he told his listeners, direct access to God was possible: an answer to life's questions; an individual revelation. It was emotive stuff. As a result, in the summer of 1729, Marie-Catherine began to experience what she believed to be an intense personal relationship with God. But, unusually, it went beyond prayers and meditations. It caused her to fall into extremes of joy and agony, to weep and scream, and to experience what appeared to be fits or convulsions. These were the sort of behaviours that throughout history had characterised religious revolutionaries: saints – or heretics.

Marie-Catherine began to describe visions that, she said, filled her head with images of the sins of the world. In deeply religious societies like eighteenth-century France, it was common for pious people to focus on everything ugly in life as they explored their faith. Just as young activists now rage at the callousness of corporations and the prejudices of voters, so at nineteen Marie-Catherine wept for humanity. Why were people hurting God with their evil deeds? She began to see Christ's sacred heart in her visions, throbbing with love and compassion. This had been a favourite component in the visions of Anne-Madeleine Remuzat and Marguerite-Marie Alacoque. Marguerite-Marie had devoted herself to the heart's image to the extent of self-harming with knives and fire as she attempted to mark a heart shape on her breast. This story was well known to Marie-Catherine Cadière, and she too began to exhibit physical marks that bled. These were identified by Jean-Baptiste and others as 'stigmata', representations of the wounds of Christ. Marie-Catherine presented Jean-Baptiste with bloodstained cloths showing the face of Christ and a wooden cross she said had been given her by Jesus in a vision. Priests and pious citizens began to visit Marie-Catherine's house to see her trances and wounds, and gossip spread that she was an oracle, a saint, a prophet. Her visions were welcome when they confirmed the church authorities' own religious traditions. But what if they did not? Was everything really as it seemed?

As Marie-Catherine writhed and wept, there at her side was Jean-Baptiste, the discoverer of this prodigy. He examined her wounds, prayed with her in private, and she turned to him constantly for guidance and attention. In one vision, she described seeing John the Baptist, Christ's disciple after whom Jean-Baptiste was named. The disciple showed her that her name was registered in a book that he held, and the name was expressed as 'Marie-Catherine Jean-Baptiste'. It was as if the two had become one! What a miracle! Less pious citizens started to snigger and make jokes. Even churchmen and their congregations who were convinced of the reality and holiness of Marie-Catherine's visions began to worry. Surely there was potential for misunderstanding when a priest spent so much time alone by the bedside of a half-conscious, semi-naked young woman? Why were her visions so filled with imagery of love and passion? Was it modest that the body of the visionary should so often be exposed and touched by men seeking to verify her stigmata? And finally, a bigger question: what if Marie-Catherine's visions were not sent by God, but by the devil? We've seen how at Salem the tormented girls described visions of a demonic figure bearing a book full of worshippers' names. What if Marie-Catherine was not seeing John the Baptist, but a Satanic illusion?[8]

Demonic visions were, unfortunately, regarded as more common than godly ones. All Christian sects stressed that Satan slipped sinful images into human minds. Who knew which thoughts were holy meditations and which demonic temptations? Usually, this question was resolved by further church investigation, and in Marie-Catherine's case it appeared proven by Jean-Baptiste – a Jesuit priest, a supremely holy man – that she was a vessel for God's passion. But increasingly her health suffered: she fasted, wept, hurt herself and at times became catatonic. In June 1730, Marie-Catherine was asked to visit a local convent at Ollioules, whose nuns would manage her condition. There she remained for several months, visited regularly by Jean-Baptiste. They also communicated by letter – in Marie-Catherine's case, letters dictated to her brothers. 'I have a very great desire to see you,' wrote Jean-Baptiste, 'and to see everything . . . write to me twice a day.' But then there was a dramatic development. In autumn 1730 Marie-Catherine suddenly left the convent. After her flight, she told her family and friendly churchmen that Jean-Baptiste had abused his position to seduce and rape her. She had become pregnant with his child, she said, and he dosed her with a drug that caused her to miscarry. It was an utterly shocking turn of events.

Marie-Catherine's accusations hit Toulon like the shells of the recent bombardments and spread like the plague through the crowded streets. In barbers' shops and inns, prayer groups and kitchens, everyone wanted to discuss the details. Satan must surely have been at work to cause such a ruckus among God's people! Had he created Marie-Catherine's visions, fooling everyone? Or was he deluding her now, planting false memories of abuse to discredit Jean-Baptiste? There were other demonic possibilities too. What if one of the two had been working quite consciously with Satan: the innocent maiden or the holy father? Had one of the guilty pair got someone to cast a love spell on the other, like the ones reported at the French court fifty years before? How else to explain such a catastrophic fall from grace? At last, some people began to say openly that Marie-Catherine was a witch, an abortionist baby-killer and seductress, enchanting the trustful priest with charms. Others began to respond with a counter-accusation: their precious Marie-Catherine was guiltless, and the witch was that 'holy lecher', rapist and abortionist Jean-Baptiste Girard![9] In this confusion of claim and counter-claim, both of the accused were said to possess characteristics once thought to identify witches: suspicions of promiscuity, wicked knowledge of the female body and its fertility, the abuse of babies, heretical beliefs.

Imagine the horror of the Toulon authorities as gossip spread. The city's bishop, Louis-Pierre de la Tour du Pin-Montauban, thought Marie-Catherine a holy prodigy. When in autumn 1730 she had declared that she wanted to leave the convent and speak to a church official, he had sent a carriage for her. At her request he had assigned a new confessor, Nicolas Girieux, to help her with whatever was her problem. And it was to Nicolas that she revealed her claims against Jean-Baptiste. The accusations of sexual abuse were bad enough, but she added an even stranger story that troubled the bishop. Jean-Baptiste, she said, had one day blown into her mouth. As his breath entered her, Marie-Catherine felt changed. She could not pray as she had before; the words just wouldn't come. Her visions became sexual, and it was then Jean-Baptiste began his seduction. Soon Marie-Catherine was awaking from trances to discover she had been raped. Her new confessor Nicolas told the bishop he suspected love magic. Among many methods of bewitchment, blowing into a person's mouth could be a magical act. It was a flexible spell, depending on the intention of the blower: it might bewitch someone, or grant them occult powers. It could force unwilling people into an infatuation with their bewitcher or render them vulnerable to attack. Both these things seemed to have happened to Marie-Catherine.

Hearing her confession, Nicolas decided that she had been bewitched, but he went further: he believed she was probably now possessed by Satan. It would explain her indecent visions, and why she had first loved and now hated Jean-Baptiste. It would context-ualise her self-harming and illness. Jean-Baptiste had blown the devil into his victim, Nicolas feared. He shared his suspicions with the bishop and confirmed to Marie-Catherine's outraged family that he thought she had been sexually abused and was demonically possessed. The Cadière family would have known that Satan might enter the human body and control it; it was a pious fear that stretched back to biblical times when Christ threw a devil or devils named 'Legion' out of a man into the bodies of pigs. Since two of the Cadière boys were churchmen, they believed they had inherited Christ's exorcising power. They began rituals to cleanse Marie-Catherine's body, driving Satan out. Now not only the bishop and Father Nicolas, but Étienne-Thomas and François (a Carmelite monk and a Dominican, respectively) were involved in the scandal.

The bishop stepped back and launched an investigation. It was damaging his diocese, with religious sects now competing over control of Marie-Catherine and her story.[10]

On one side, the Jesuits were lobbying the bishop regarding their man Jean-Baptiste's innocence. Of course he was not a witch – it was a slander made up by a foolish, corrupt girl pretending to be a saint! If anything, she was a blasphemous witch who had deceived him with fake visions. On the other side, many of Toulon's monastic orders and also Protestants were proclaiming Jean-Baptiste's guilt. They disliked the Jesuits, whom they believed to be a secretive, arrogant organisation. Priests had been convicted of witchcraft in French history, the Jesuits' critics pointed out – like Louis Gaufridy in Aix-en-Provence in 1611 – so Jean-Baptiste might indeed be a witch. As in past times, witchcraft accusation was being used as a weapon in sectarian conflict. Already unstable, Toulon society was in uproar, and under this pressure of claim and counter-claim both Marie-Catherine's supporters and the Jesuit order bypassed the bishop's authority and appealed directly to the king for help. Louis XV referred them to Provence's highest court, the Grand'Chambre du Parlement: twenty-five nobleman-judges who met at Aix-en-Provence, thirty-five miles from Toulon, under the distant authority of the king. It was agreed the case would be judged by the Grand'Chambre court's members, and lawyers were appointed to represent the two parties before these judges. What had begun as a local enquiry into sexual abuse mushroomed into a witch trial in southern France's highest royal court that would be publicised across Europe.[11] By the time it came to trial in 1731, both Marie-Catherine and Jean-Baptiste had been accused of witchcraft as vaguely defined by the Edict of Louis XIV.

The Parlement's pre-trial investigation leaned towards exonerating Jean-Baptiste, in part because many officials who carried out the questioning had links to the Jesuit order. Some felt that even if a priest had sinned sexually it was not right to expose him, and they did not believe he was a witch. Accordingly, before the trial began,

Marie-Catherine was imprisoned by court order in a Toulon convent whose nuns had Jesuit connections. Two of her friends from Jean-Baptiste's class of devotees were pressured to accuse her of fraud. They claimed she had intended all along to deceive Jean-Baptiste with fake visions. The Ollioules nuns were asked to sign pre-drafted statements rejecting the validity of her trances. One was threatened for saying she had seen Jean-Baptiste kiss and hold hands with Marie-Catherine. A priest from Ollioules was asked to denounce Marie-Catherine and in return a charge against him – that he had raped a thirteen-year-old girl – was dropped. Pornographic images of Marie-Catherine and Jean-Baptiste began to circulate, making her look like a prostitute. This all seemed preposterously unjust to observers, and the upcoming trial began to stoke a campaign against both religious authority in Toulon and the nobility who ran the Parlement court in Aix-en-Provence.[12]

Further evidence of court bias came in late February 1731, when formal summonses to trial were issued. These documents obliged Marie-Catherine, her new confessor Nicolas and her brothers to appear in person for interrogation but intended to allow Jean-Baptiste to skip attendance and be represented by a lawyer. It looked like the Parlement was inventing trial procedure based on political expediency and enabled by the vagueness of the law. This impression was strengthened when Marie-Catherine was questioned three times for up to eleven hours per session. She was allowed a lawyer to sit with her but had to answer in her own voice and from the resources of her own mind. She was not tortured, but she was bullied and shamed. Marie-Catherine was a young woman from a lower-middle-class home in a back street. Now she was being interrogated by velvet- and ermine-robed noblemen with long experience of courtroom rhetoric. Their questions are not recorded, but more general accounts show they were aggressive. During the final round of questioning, Marie-Catherine broke down. Dripping tears, she confessed her story of sexual abuse was a lie. Father Nicolas, she said, had invented the accusations against Jean-Baptiste, who was innocent both of seduction and witchcraft.

Later, Marie-Catherine alleged she was forced to drink wine
before her interrogation. She felt 'outside of herself', adding, 'I knew
not what I said.' She had also received an anonymous threatening
letter ordering her to withdraw her accusations. Now, on 6 March,
she was made to confess to Jean-Baptiste that she had lied. But by
10 March she had gone back to her lawyer, retracted her retraction
and launched a legal protest concerning the abuse she had endured
from the Parlement and Toulon authorities.[13] She would not give
up. She was allowed representation in court, and her lawyer, Jean-
Baptiste Chaudon, went on the offensive as her formal trial began
before a panel of Parlement members. He charged Jean-Baptiste
Girard with witchcraft, 'spiritual incest' (which meant rape in a
confessional relationship), abortion and the heresy of Quietism.
Quietism was a theological position urging Christians to accept
sinful impulses quietly. They should trust their own consciences
and – at least in the lawyer's caricature of Quietism – give in to
sin. Jean-Baptiste Chaudon argued that Jean-Baptiste Girard had
seduced Marie-Catherine with both magic and theological argument, had cast a love spell by blowing into her mouth and then
told the girl that her attraction to him shouldn't be resisted. But
in answering, Jean-Baptiste Girard's lawyer Claude-François Pazery
de Thorame made a bold claim. Witchcraft, he said, was a 'nursery
tale'. His client had made no pact with the devil: what a foolish
fantasy! There was no blasphemy, sacrilege or pretended magic, at
least on Jean-Baptiste's part. Arguments about witchcraft belonged
in 'a school of philosophy', not a law court.[14] Claude-François
came very close to saying witchcraft did not exist.

This was in some ways the most important outcome of the trial
of Marie-Catherine Cadière and Jean-Baptiste Girard. During this
witch trial, both sides made accusations of witchcraft whose mutual
incompatibility made it clear that the truth was evasive and the law
was confused by differing definitions of the crime. There was no fully
transparent and accepted legal procedure to test these definitions in
court. So people began to say aloud witchcraft was not real. After
all, both Marie-Catherine and Jean-Baptiste were exceptionally

religious people. Could they really be Satan's agents on earth? Surely neither of them were sacrilegious blasphemers. Meanwhile, the king's own Edict suggested witches were no longer regarded as heretics. Finally, if Jean-Baptiste's lawyer said he could not be a witch because there were no such things as witches, then Marie-Catherine could not be a witch either. Confusion reigned, stoked by the 1682 Edict's unclarity about both crime and punishment.

This delay served Marie-Catherine well. As the case continued in summer 1731, her Parlement representative Jacques-Joseph de Gaufridy made progress on her behalf. He obtained a ruling freeing her from prison and instead imprisoning Jean-Baptiste Girard. As Jean-Baptiste entered jail on 30 July, a crowd of two thousand people gathered to shout abuse. 'Villain!' they roared, 'Devil! Sorcerer! Witch!'[15] Perhaps some truly believed in witchcraft, but others were beginning to use the term 'witch' as a handy insult, particularly of people thought to be superstitious or secretive – like the Jesuits. The mob was on Marie-Catherine's side. Instead of dragging the young woman to the stake, they were screaming for the execution of a churchman. The world had changed.

Many of the noblemen in the Parlement, however, had not changed their view. The full Parlement of twenty-five men had heard the evidence, including testimony from over one hundred and twenty witnesses. They were all present when a panel of five of them, appointees chosen from among the Parlement's members because of their legal expertise, delivered their summary of the evidence as a steer for the other members. Each of the five panellists spoke separately, explaining their own conclusions. Three blamed Marie-Catherine entirely, judging her a fake mystic. They wanted to sentence her to be hanged because she had 'abused religion and profaned the sacred mysteries'. The other two panel members delivered a minority report. They believed Jean-Baptiste Girard was a sex offender and heretic who should be both hanged and burned. They also wanted Marie-Catherine sent to a convent for three years for lying about her visions. None of the panellists accepted her claims to be a prophet and, while two of them believed she had been raped, if their summary was reflected in the final verdict she would be hanged. When the panel's summary was announced in public, riots began. Crowds gathered outside Marie-Catherine's cell, to which she'd been returned after the summary, to show their support. They did not believe Marie-Catherine had committed sacrilege or blasphemy or had lied, so why should she be executed? Even if the panel thought her a pretend mystic, the law allowed them room to reprieve her. The crowd thought the trial a sham: the upper classes – a coalition of noblemen and churchmen – defending one of their own at the expense of an ordinary city girl.

With a mob running through the streets, the Parlement was under great strain. Its twenty-five members would go over the trial's evidence again before the final verdict: this time all twenty-five would rule on the outcome. They had to appear just, or revolution might follow. The accused and witnesses were all requestioned. In a late September interrogation, Jean-Baptiste wept as he described Marie-Catherine's deception. In early October Marie-Catherine maintained her innocence. There was stalemate. So, Marie-Catherine made a bold request: she would confront Jean-Baptiste Girard again face-to-face. On 4 October the court met to watch. The confrontation tipped the power dynamic of the trial because, for the first time, Marie-Catherine was the questioner. The young woman from the back street had come a long way and 'with a serene air and much modesty', as an observer reported, she faced Jean-Baptiste. Calmly, her lawyer recited his alleged crimes with interjections from her – incomplete notes survive.

It was true, Marie-Catherine probed, he had seduced her – wasn't it? He'd called her his 'idol', impregnated her, given her abortion drugs? Why hadn't he given the court all eighty letters they'd exchanged? Wasn't another of his devotees 'with child by him'? Jean-Baptiste accused her of being a hussy, interrupted her, denied her claims. It was generally agreed that Marie-Catherine won the exchange: 'such modesty, spirit and firmness, in a girl whose age, birth and education does not allow for such performances, seemed a wonder'. But it was noticeable that among the catalogue of other offences Marie-Catherine did not accuse Jean-Baptiste of witchcraft and he did not accuse her.[16]

The final judgment was delivered on 10 October 1731 by the full Parlement. First Jean-Baptiste was judged. Of the twenty-five Parlement judges, twelve acquitted him of any wrongdoing. One broadly sided with them, finding that he had behaved foolishly but was not guilty of the major offences alleged against him. This judge argued that Jean-Baptiste should be suspended from the priesthood, but not otherwise punished. Twelve judges, a minority, ruled he should be burned as a witch, rapist, abortionist and heretic. Then the verdicts against Marie-Catherine were handed down. Thirteen of the twenty-five judges acquitted her of any crime. Twelve voted to imprison her in a convent or prison, for periods of between two and ten years, as a liar and fake mystic. The Parlement was split, but both Marie-Catherine and Jean-Baptiste had been acquitted, more or less. Laws had been bent and procedure twisted to ensure both walked away from their trial. Both were released from prison and allowed home, with both cases dismissed. Amazingly, nobody was convicted of witchcraft in the traditional sense, and no one was convicted of anything else either. It was France's last witch trial. Jean-Baptiste retreated to northern France where he died two years later, 'few people, even of the priests themselves, believing him innocent'. Marie-Catherine 'having thank'd the judges' went home 'where she was met on the road by great numbers of people who congratulated her arrival, with all possible demonstrations of joy'. Then she disappeared from history – perhaps into hiding.[17]

The trial of Marie-Catherine and Jean-Baptiste was a turning point in witch trial history. Opinions that witchcraft was both real and fake shaped it and the outcome was a fudge. But the court eventually judged Marie-Catherine to be innocent of any form of witchcraft. She was not guilty of sacrilege or blasphemy, and even the accusations had steered clear of the old fantasy acts of killing a neighbour's children or worshipping the devil, so she was no witch. Neither was Jean-Baptiste Girard. Yet both were accused of new versions of the demonologists' imagined crimes and the charges wavered between old and new definitions of witchcraft. The heretical Quietist beliefs attributed to Jean-Baptiste were obscurely linked to the old kinds of demonic temptation to worship Satan. Jean-Baptiste also appeared to be guilty of 'baby-killing' – by abortion, not curses. Both he and Marie-Catherine were imagined as sexual sinners, seducing people by magic – not at Sabbaths, inducting them into a demonic cult, but merely luring them into bed. Both were accused of attacking pious people's reputations with poisonous words rather than murdering them with spells and potions.

By the 1730s, the crime of witchcraft was becoming a metaphor for other kinds of transgression and subversion. This was potentially an empowering idea. If witchcraft was unreal, no longer a matter for law courts but for private judgement, then all manner of imaginative possibilities were released. By the late eighteenth century, French radicals had seized on these in the wake of the French Revolutionary period of 1789–1799. If the historical witch was not a real criminal but a victim of tyranny – a young girl like Marie-Catherine menaced by evil old demonologists, judges and priests – then in revolutionary times could she be reimagined as a populist heroine? By the mid-nineteenth century the premier French historian Jules Michelet had turned this idea into historical orthodoxy.

In the 1850s Jules and his wife Athénaïs investigated historic French witch trials, including the trial of Marie-Catherine Cadière. They decided they were relics of superstition, part of France's pre-Revolutionary infatuation with religion, as they saw it. The Michelets had rejected traditional Catholicism and identified as pantheists, believing a universal spirit animated the world. As a result of their 'new age' investigations of witch trials, in 1862 Jules published an extraordinary book, *La Sorcière* (*The Witch*). It stated that medieval and Renaissance French 'witches' had been early pantheists too: revolutionary pagan priestesses, healers and mesmerists, sexually liberated, and in touch with an old deity wrongly demonised as Satanic. Jules's version of witch trial history was nonsense, but it was exciting nonsense. By liberating themselves sexually and imaginatively, Jules argued, witch-women had gained true magical power and resisted the predations of their feudal lords. They were executed, but they died glorious martyrs. For Jules and Athénaïs, women who were accused of witchcraft more recently, like Marie-Catherine, were as much victims of patriarchal conspiracy as their foremothers. Their religious ecstasies were the best they could muster as resistance against church and state tyranny. They should be celebrated as heroines!

Marie-Catherine would probably have been horrified to be equated with lusty pagan feminists. Jules's version of history did not offer an accurate depiction of her trial – revealingly, he repeatedly misremembered her name as 'Charlotte'. But his vision was probably quite accurate in its presentation of Marie-Catherine as a vulnerable young woman forced by corrupt churchmen into the mould of an outdated crime. She was not a witch, just a desiring dreamer wanting more from her life.

Despite its inaccuracies, Jules and Athénaïs's *sorcière* model caught on among scholars, novelists and suffragists. It inspired nineteenth-century women, corseted and disenfranchised, seeking new roles.[18] 'What does it matter if Michelet was the least trustworthy of historians,' asked one magically inclined reader, 'since he was the most personal and the most evocative?'[19] By the late nineteenth century, the Michelets' ideas were shared by other revolutionaries and spread across Europe, redefining the meaning of witchcraft and turning it into a resource for radicals. From being a tool of oppressive regimes, colonial powers and religious fundamentalists, the idea of witchcraft mutated to become a resource for passionate believers in liberty. Many future witch trials would not be about witches as real, Satanic enemies, but about the figure of the witch as a metaphor for freedom.

CHAPTER EIGHT

The Trial of Montague Summers: Satanism, Sex and Demonology Reborn

Notions of what was sexually acceptable shifted in the late nineteenth century: not just women's sexuality but same-sex attraction too. Magic came to be associated with both heterosexual freedoms and homosexuality, as well as 'new age' mystical experimentation like pantheism, and one of the freedoms that would be debated in future witch trials was sexuality, as Jules Michelet's book had suggested in the 1860s. Not all religious experimenters were on the same side in the debates about witchcraft and liberty, though – and some were not sure which side they were on. The gay man who called himself Montague or Montie Summers is described in his *Oxford Dictionary of National Biography* entry as a 'literary scholar, occultist, and eccentric', but more precisely he was both an occultist and an *anti*-occultist, a modern-day demonologist and witch-hunter. Like Marie-Catherine Cadière, Montie had a dual magical identity. He's best known today as a lover of demonology – the translator of Heinrich Kramer's *Malleus Maleficarum* who introduced its repellent ideas to a modern English-speaking readership. But his qualifications as a witch-hunter were as unclear as Heinrich's, or those of any of our other witch-hunters: James VI and I, John Cunningham, Matthew Hopkins and John Stearne, Samuel Parris. Montie's entry into witch-hunting was in some ways similar to theirs: a life-changing confrontation in which he appeared to be the victim, and a subsequent trial. For Montie Summers, this came when he was accused of both homosexuality and witchcraft.

In 1908, Montie was appointed to the curacy at St Mary's Church in Bitton, near the city of Bristol in south-west England. Montie was a Bristol boy, born into a mercantile financier family. His father Augustus was a magistrate, banker, brewer and owner of a mineral water bottling plant by 1880, the year after his son's birth. The British government census in 1881 shows the Summers household including a butler, cook, housemaid and Montie's nurse Annie, and in 1891 it also included an under-housemaid. By then Augustus and Ellen had seven children. They lived at Tellisford House, a few hundred yards from Bristol Zoo in the elegant Clifton district. From his nursery Montie heard the roar of lions; the sound of possibility, of exotic adventure.[1] He was the youngest Summers child, with an older brother Herbert and five sisters: Ellen, Frances, Edith, Florence and Marion. Herbert left home in 1887 to attend Lincoln College, Oxford, so from the age of seven Montie was the only son living at home – and the family baby.

Montie loved the lively women who surrounded him. Although he mocked his sisters' ignorance, their opinions pepper his autobiography. He was at odds with his father but adored his mother, Ellen. Tales of her Parisian schooldays in the 1850s – the Michelets' Paris – enchanted him. Ellen had lived a bohemian life there, in a tolerant society, at least compared to Bristol. Throughout his life, Montie admired women's desire for freedom and their artistic expression of it. Ellen had loved the scandalous French tragedienne Mademoiselle Rachel, and Montie continued her devotion to divas: the actors Ellen Terry and Sarah Bernhardt, and the Gothic fantasies of the novelist Anne Radcliffe. He loved women as companions, but it was clear by the 1890s that his sexual preference was for men. Although male homosexuality was acceptable in some circles, this did not include the families of provincial English magistrates. Acting upon gay desire was also illegal. When Montie's father Augustus discovered his son reading Oscar Wilde's *The Ballad of*

Reading Gaol, detailing the author's imprisonment for homosexual acts, he confronted him: 'Is this filthy thing yours?' Montie rebelled, affecting an effeminate lisp: 'Yeth, Father, I have all the workth of the Mathter!' Augustus forced his son to dump Wilde's books: either they left Tellisford House, he raged, or Montie did.[2]

Montie knew he was gay – an 'abnormality' or 'invert' in contemporary phrasing – but instead of feeling the shame his father expected, he celebrated his desires. Augustus beat and harangued him, but he thrived at school: an eccentric, assertive boy, ready with a savage retort or dirty joke in self-defence. Contemporaries described him as 'gentle and kindly' to friends and a wily deflector of enemies. He was a good actor, both in life and on stage, starring in amateur theatricals and writing plays. He especially loved melodrama, with its passionate feeling, beauty and violence, its immersive emotion. As a child, Montie staged puppet productions of shocking Renaissance dramas like John Webster's murderous, incest-driven Jacobean tragedy *The Duchess of Malfi*, acted by tiny dolls in satin farthingales and velvet doublets. His desire for drama – risk, confrontation, costumed role-playing and posing – increasingly spread from the stage into reality. Montie began to dress like an eighteenth-century dandy in his teenage years, wearing a cravat and frock coat, swishing a cane and flaunting purple silk socks.

After university at Trinity College, Oxford, where he did almost no work, and a grand tour of France, Turkey and Italy, Montie made what may seem to us a strange decision. He went to theological college in the small Midlands city of Lichfield and sought ordination into the priesthood of the Anglican state church. To Montie, there was no contradiction in his behaviour. He believed devoutly in God, as well as in other spirits and supernatural beings: demons, angels, vampires and werewolves. Why should he not pursue his research into demons and witches, and still officiate at church services on Sundays? Why should he not be both a priest and a gay man, dressing as a Regency fop, falling passionately in love with other young men? Not everyone would share his view. But Montie returned to the Bristol area and initially held a curacy in the city of Bath. Bitton village was his second posting. And it was here things went wrong. As his biography snappily concludes: 'Rumours of studies in Satanism, and a charge of pederasty, of which he was acquitted, terminated this phase of his career.'

We'll come back to 'studies in Satanism' later. But pederasty was a specific accusation: that Montie had engaged in anal intercourse with a boy. This made him a social outcast. It is worth noting that in 1908 a 'boy' meant an underage person, and in different contexts that could indicate someone aged under twenty-one, or under sixteen, or under thirteen. In Edwardian England it was a felony (a serious crime) to have sexual contact with a person under thirteen and a misdemeanour (a less serious crime) if the person was aged between thirteen and sixteen. But the law and its interpretation was confused by overlapping legislation referring to 'gross indecency' (homosexual acts) and prostitution. There were also conflicting medical and psychological opinions on consent and the age of sexual maturity in specific cases. Pederasty therefore covered a broad range of behaviours including both what is now paedophilia in UK law and what is consensual gay sex. The details of the accusations against Montie Summers have not survived, so frustratingly we can't tell which category they fell into.

Some decades later, Montie's biographers attempted to solve the mystery. In the 1950s Father Brocard Sewell, a Carmelite monk and literary scholar, began seeking information. A 1957 letter to Brocard from Sir Francis Meynell, editor at Nonesuch Press publishers, revealed one source of the pederasty rumours – a churchgoer who had lived in Bitton and subsequently spread gossip. 'I was told', said Francis, 'by someone who claimed to have been a parishioner of [Montie's] that he had been in Holy Orders of the Church of England but had been defrocked as a result of an accusation of pederasty. I repeat this with all the reservations proper to a complete ignorance of the facts.' Francis added that Montie 'gave me the impression that he had engaged himself in occult studies but I cannot recall on what that impression rests'. Brocard had heard both claims before. He responded with his belief that

Montie 'was never unfrocked in spite of his supposed misdemeanours in the C. of E.' Instead, 'he passed conscientiously to communion with Rome' – meaning he left the Church of England voluntarily and became a Catholic. Brocard's use of the word 'misdemeanour' is interesting. It doesn't fully rebut the accusation Francis had heard, but precisely echoes the legal definition of one category of sexual offence. Perhaps Brocard's information was that Montie had been accused of engaging in sex with a boy aged between thirteen and sixteen.[3]

Whatever the truth, the accusation also related to a book Montie had published in 1907, *Antinous and Other Poems*. Just a decade after Oscar Wilde's trial, Montie expressed overtly homoerotic thoughts in print. The boy Antinous was the Roman emperor Hadrian's lover and died mysteriously: perhaps by suicide or human sacrifice, scholars speculated. He was a well-known homosexual icon. In his poems Montie described Antinous's memory of 'the bitter thirst of Caesar's farewell kiss' and said of him that Hadrian 'deflowered thy boyhood'. Did the emperor 'bid thy blood incarnadine [redden] some sabbat altar?' he wondered, linking a witches' Sabbath to gay love – and all this on page one. Later in the book he hinted at homosexual desire between Christ and John the Baptist, celebrated sibling incest, imagined God seducing the Virgin Mary and praised the 'glorious eyes' and 'voluptuous joy' of 'a lad whose lips gleam sherbet-wet' behind 'the blue fume of a cigarette'. Montie's modern editors describe *Antinous* as 'hell-bent on shocking all and sundry'. But he had the serious aim of getting 'certain ways of love admitted or admired', they commented, and he hoped he could end the 'noisome ban' on homosexuality. Montie dedicated *Antinous* to his fellow gay activist Jacques d'Adelswärd-Fersen, a French baron whom he'd met abroad.[4]

Although admirably courageous, publishing a book of homoerotic poetry and dedicating it to Baron Jacques was a crazy thing for an English curate to do in 1907. Several years earlier, in 1903, Jacques had achieved notoriety through a scandal involving sex with underage boys, opiates and wider suspicions of Parisian 'Black

Masses'. Black Masses were the witches' Sabbaths of their day – Catholic church services supposedly held by rebel priests and dedicated to Satan. It was unclear whether these events, or some version of them, actually happened – perhaps as pagan experiments by radical bohemians, perhaps as role-playing orgies based on Jules Michelet's fantasies, who knew? Novelists and sensation-seeking journalists loved to imagine Black Masses, although few imagined the devil actually attended, and stories focused instead on sexual transgression. In this context, Jacques was charged with 'debauching' underage boys at theatrical evenings attended by fellow noblemen and priests. Convicted, he was pilloried by the press and imprisoned. Even Montie's parishioners in Bitton had heard of him. Many respectable English people regarded Paris as a playground of homosexuality and devil-worship. This part-real, part-imagined anarchy was publicised internationally in *Là-Bas* (*The Damned*), an 1891 novel by the French civil servant Joris-Karl Huysmans. The author dramatised every shocking allegation he heard about Parisian life or had read in history books.[5] His protagonists encountered sadomasochism, exorcism, murder, séances, orgies, a range of experimental magical rites, witchcraft and Satanism.

In the most shocking episode of *Là-Bas* the characters attend a Black Mass – essentially, a witches' Sabbath in a church like the 1591 North Berwick meeting. As part of his 'studies in Satanism', Montie was accused of wanting to stage or actually staging something similar, based on *Là-Bas*. In the novel, the Black Mass is celebrated by a witch-priest who's profaned his chapel with a crucifix on which a laughing, sexually aroused Christ hangs, before which the congregation fornicate. Naked, the priest defiles communion bread, screaming blasphemies. He worships Satan as the god of 'men who have been crushed by injustice', male and female prostitutes, sex addicts, revolutionaries – it's a Michelet-ish vision of witches as sexual, political subversives. Montie did later write that *Là-Bas* was a work of 'genius', a 'masterly study of Satanism', exemplifying 'a profound loathing for any kind of mediocrity'. He saw it as part of Huysmans's tortured road to a 'conversion' to Catholic truth. In 1946 he published his own edition of it. Although it seems unlikely that Montie ever staged a Black Mass at Bitton church, his editorial comments suggest he was fascinated by the idea and recognised aspects of his own religious journey in the novel. In the 1920s he was telling acquaintances – truly or not – that he had 'been frequently to Black Masses in Bruges, Brighton and London'.[6] Whatever happened at Bitton, it raised the eyebrows of churchgoers into their hairlines. The rumours they heard suggested that Montie was a sex offender and witch: he had to go.

As far as we know, Montie was not tried in a criminal court: his witch trial was less formal. If the sexual offences alleged at Bitton were classed as 'lesser', they should have been tried in the magistrates' courts in Chipping Sodbury or Gloucester, but the Chipping Sodbury records survive for 1907, late 1909 and 1910 and Montie is not mentioned among the railway fare-dodgers, burglars and traffic offenders. The Gloucester court also processed more serious crimes such as attempted buggery, attempted rape, 'indecent assault on a male person' and 'carnal knowledge of a girl under sixteen'. Penalties ranged from three to eighteen months. But again, the Gloucester court's complete records show Montie was not tried there.[7] In fact, accusations of pederasty were rarely tried in the criminal courts. In repressed Edwardian society the offence was prohibitively embarrassing and painful to discuss. The fact that Montie's father Augustus was a magistrate likely means the family managed to have the accusations suppressed. Unlike many of the other 'witches' in this book, although his desires made him a target, Montie's class, sex and career choice allowed him to escape formal trial. He was also lucky to live at a time when he could no longer be tried for Satanic magic in a criminal court. He had done nothing covered by the 1735 Witchcraft Act – con-trickery, fortune-telling, divination – and could not be prosecuted as a witch.

Regardless of his privileges, the accusation of 'studies in Satanism' still had terrible results for Montie. His fate was settled by informal trial within the church community. We don't know the details of this secret investigation, but Montie's likely judge was Henry Nicholson Ellacombe, the vicar of Bitton. Henry was an opinionated man, quick to judge and act, speaking sharply and to the point. He was still active into his eighties as a botanist, literary critic and traveller. Since succeeding his father as vicar in 1850 Henry had dedicated himself to improving church schooling, founding a boys' school in 1851. He hoped the boys would be 'trained up to take their station as good Christian Englishmen'. Montie's witchcraft studies and homosexuality were major threats to that vision, and he would have received no sympathy from his worthy, conservative boss. Henry would have called Montie to his study – as he did every day with his curate even in normal times – and shut the door tightly. He would have questioned him about the accusations and condemned him for sin or folly – his poems, his dress, his manner, his reading material, his essential being – whether he was guilty of pederasty or not. Then Montie was fired. Burning with rage and grief, he left Bitton and the Anglican Church.[8]

Quietly and quickly, Montie converted to Catholicism. While this was a legitimate religious choice, as his biographer later pointed out, it was also convenient. It allowed him to aspire to an ordained church role with a different sect and obscured other reasons for interim unemployment. Montie disappeared from Bristol into rented rooms in London: 61 Oxford Terrace, Paddington in 1911; 15 Eton Road, Hampstead from 1913 to 1921, and 4 Mount Ararat Road, Richmond by 1927. In between times he moved all over southern England to Beckenham, Bath, Hertford, Oxford and Alresford. His early relocations were for work, since his family no longer bankrolled him following his disgrace. Montie taught in schools and colleges, leading classes on Latin, French, English literature and history. For over a decade he taught at the Central School of Art (now University of the Arts), and for four years at Brockley School in Lewisham, both in London. Gradually he rebuilt his life and income, drawing on the literary and theatrical enthusiasms of his youth. He published editions of old plays and treatises, wrote reviews, articles and histories, all freelance. By 1926 he was sufficiently well known to make a living writing. He also founded a theatre company to revive plays neglected since the 1600s and worked with many of the top actors of his time: Edith Evans, Sybil Thorndike and Athene Seyler.[9]

But there's a continuing whiff of scandal about his relocations well into the 1930s – the sense of a man fleeing. Although he presented himself as an ordained Catholic priest, 'Father Summers', Montie troubled his neighbours. He burned incense, chanted religious services at all hours in a private chapel he had outfitted himself, and hosted lively parties attended by guests as unusual as himself. He had gentlemen callers who weren't fellow clergymen. Some are documented. The politician Chips Channon visited Montie several times in 1928. On the second occasion, the two men went to the chapel next to Montie's bedroom where, confessing to him 'my every temptation', Chips bent before the altar and had Montie spank his bare buttocks with a red-heeled, buckled slipper. 'The old priest wanted to seduce me,' Chips recorded. A fortnight later, he was perplexed: 'What am I to do about Montague Summers? The old libidinous priest is "gone on me" [in love, obsessed]. He rings me up nearly every day and sometimes more often.' Chips tried to drop Montie, but his desire won out and he visited again. 'That mad erudite old priest, with his tales of witchcraft, sorcery and esoteric beliefs fascinates me. After a bad dinner he whipped me with a dog-whip, which seemed to give him infinite delights.' It was the last visit: Chips concluded Montie was 'as dangerous as he is brilliant'.[10]

Yet for all his illegal and scandalous sexual activity, forbidden by both the Catholic and Anglican Churches, Montie was quite serious about his faith and his priestly identity. He described himself on the 1911 census form as 'Roman Catholic Cleric', pure and simple. He renamed himself from Augustus Montague to Montague Joseph Summers. The forename he dropped was his father's, and he took on Christ's father's name, Joseph, instead. The Bitton affair was unsurprisingly a watershed in his relationship with his father, after which Montie refused to be known as Augustus for several years. Later he readopted Augustus's name alongside Joseph, but then he added several other names to make a lengthy non-binary formulation: Alphonsus Joseph-Mary Augustus Montague Summers. Alphonsus referred to St Alphonsus, founder of the missionary order of Redemptorists. He checked a number of Montie's boxes: Alphonsus was an eighteenth-century Italian priest who argued for the importance of sensual beauty in worship. He was also a theologian of redemption, a blessing Montie badly wanted from his new church.

Whether he was ordained formally as a Catholic priest – which would have been a separate ordination ceremony from the Anglican one – has never been proven. Since he graduated from Oxford with a fourth-class degree and left the Anglican Church in disgrace, it seems unlikely, but biographers suggest he may have arranged a private, unofficial ceremony through sympathetic contacts. Whatever the truth, Catholic priesthood suited his love of drama and ritual. Montie moved beyond the cravats and purple socks of his undergraduate days and began to wear a flowing dress-like cassock in his leisure time and a frock coat for his teaching and theatrical work, a cloak, shoes with enormous silver buckles and a shovel hat. He wore his hair in a unique style, with rolled curls above each ear. This style imitated the look of an eighteenth-century clergyman's wig so that some of his pupils called him 'Wiggy'. In the 1920s Montie stalked the streets of north and west London in this historical costume, an eye-catching figure among the trams and motor lorries, the flappers and clerks. By 1924 he was a celebrity in London literary circles, so much so that a cartoon of him was published in the London *Evening Standard*.

By 1927, as Montie's writing became increasingly well known, he was employing a young secretary, John Lothar, for his editorial work. John also helped him to officiate in his private chapel: an unusual task for an employee, suggesting a close relationship, particularly when combined with Chips Channon's reminiscences.[11] And then, in the early 1930s, Montie met Hector Stuart Forbes,

known as Stuart and in his late teens. Stuart shared the next decade
and a half of Montie's life. He came from a Scottish family who
moved to England in the 1880s, where they kept a pub in Leicester.
The two began to live together in Oxford where initially Montie
presented Stuart as 'my adopted son'. In the 1930s they moved to
Hove, a suburb of Brighton on England's south coast. Here they
lived as more or less openly gay – with a light cover of Stuart's
employment by Montie as a literary secretary – at 47 Montefiore
Road. Stuart gardened, cooked and played the piano as Montie
settled into apparent domesticity. He had defied his enemies, moved
on from his reputation as a gay witch and set himself up as a
literary historian, moving from one side of the demonological divide
to the other. There were still disquieting hints of occultism, however.
Montie and Stuart walked on the Victorian esplanade with their
dog Cornelius Agrippa, a dachshund named after a sixteenth-
century German magician who, gossip said, had kept a dog as his
familiar spirit. The stories about Black Masses seemed to follow
Montie, as now there were rumours they were being held in
Brighton, too.

For all his outward respectability, Montie's interest in witchcraft
had not faded at all. His friend John Redwood-Anderson said
revealingly that in converting to Catholicism Montie was like 'an
actor who had found a new role more suited to his talents or . . .
the magician who had found a more authentic and powerful
magic'.[12] He was an actor and magician all his life. In 1926 he
wrote a *History of Witchcraft and Demonology* for a series on
'The History of Civilization' edited by the president of Cambridge
University's Heretics Society. He followed this with *The Geography
of Witchcraft* (1927) and went on to translate and publish editions
of various demonologies from medieval and Renaissance Europe.
There was the exorcist Ludovico Maria Sinistrari's *Demoniality*
(1927), the witch trial judge Henry Boguet's *An Examen of Witches*
(1929), the exorcist Francesco Maria Guazzo's *Compendium
Maleficarum* (1929), the witch-hunting magistrate Nicolas Remy's

Demonolatry (1930), the sceptic Reginald Scot's *The Discoverie of Witchcraft* (1930) and an account of the demonic possession of a nun who had obsessed Jules Michelet, *The Confessions of Madeleine Bavent* (1933). Both *Demoniality* and *The Confessions of Madeleine Bavent* were judged obscene by censors and ordered to be destroyed. The common note in this library of literature is that they are all works that combined Montie's interests in witchcraft and what his publishers called 'sex psychology'. But although they were controversial, all these books positioned Montie's reputation differently in literary and historical circles. He moved into the company of theologians, presenting his expertise as antiquarian, praising their piety and scholarship. Gradually and cleverly the suspected witch had joined the demonologists.

In 1928 Montie completed his journey from witch to witch-hunter by publishing the first English translation of Heinrich Kramer's *Malleus Maleficarum*. It wasn't just that he edited the witch-hammering demonology, as any scholar might do; what aligned him with the witch-hunters was his endorsement of it as a 'great work – admirable in spite of its trifling blemishes'. It was astonishing praise for Heinrich's paranoid, misogynist devil-worship fantasy. Across all his demonological scholarship from 1926 onward, Montie echoed Heinrich's condemnation of witches as a subversive cult. Once he had been a subversive himself, but, at least outwardly, age and history had changed him.

In the 1920s, subversives were more likely to be imagined as communists than witches, and Montie had come to regard the two as linked. The first chapter of his *History of Witchcraft*, 'The Witch: Heretic and Anarchist', defined a witch as 'an evil liver; a social pest and parasite; the devotee of a loathly and obscene creed . . . a blasphemer . . . an abortionist; the dark counsellor of lewd court ladies and adulterous gallants; a minister to vice and inconceivable corruption . . . an anarchist'.[13] He echoed all the accusations we've come across so far in this book as if they were true, and portrayed the lives of accused witches as a sewer of sin and rebellion: the adulteries of Helena Scheuberin, the Sabbaths of Anny Sampson and Kirsti Sørensdatter, the heresies and illegitimate children of the Manningtree witches, the devil-pact of Tatabe, the abortion procured by Jean-Baptiste Girard for Marie-Catherine Cadière, and so on. How this was consistent with his own activities remains an unanswerable question.

Because he believed in magic as part of his belief in God, angels and demons, Montie honestly thought that witches had power and worshipped Satan to get it. In his *History*, he revealed that 'personally I believe there is power for evil and even for destruction in such a bane, and that a deadly anathema [curse] launched with concentrated hate and all the energy of volition may bring unhappiness and fatality in its train'. He argued witches supplemented verbal curses or the making of wax images like Anny Sampson's with 'subtly administered poison' such as hemlock or belladonna (nightshade), echoing Louis XIV's Edict. 'Far from the confessions of the witches being mere hysteria and hallucination, they are proved . . . to be in the main hideous and horrible fact,' he fumed. He had once told Chips Channon that witches were part of a heretic conspiracy: 'demon-worship . . . thrives and breeds. It is of course tainted with communistic and Satanic, sadistic influences and is most subversive.' Witches are 'avowed enemies of law and order, red-hot anarchists who would stop at nothing to gain their ends. Terrorism and secret murder were their most frequent weapons' and their creed 'plain and simple Satanism'.

There was a sexual element to their revolt as well, Montie explained. When they had conjured up Satan, in animal form such as a goat, witches would hold an orgy. Montie imagined the authority figures of the conspiracy as male and women as their acolytes, explaining that 'each one of them as quickly as he can seizes upon the woman who chances to be nearest'. If a child was conceived, it would be subjected to 'the sacrifices of the old heathen' and 'burnt in the flames'. Witches also kissed the devil's backside, listened to Satanic sermons, exhumed dead bodies, ate dead children and so on – in other words, Montie believed everything demonologists had ever imagined, however extreme. It did not seem to occur to him that these were very poorly evidenced stories, based on monastic fantasies about religion, sex, femininity and motherhood and extracted by torture and intimidation from defenceless suspects. He liked imagining them.[14] He no longer identified with witches as innocent victims or legitimate radicals slandered by conservative enemies: instead, he joined in the slander.

Montie's story shows the persecuted becoming the persecutor, the accused witch becoming the witch-hunter – an idea that has haunted our story so far. Many witch-hunters saw themselves as victims: Heinrich Kramer, a shopkeeper's son rebutting accusations of embezzlement and heresy; James VI and I menaced by rebels and forced to marry; John Cunningham fearing that Sámi witches had murdered Finnmark governors; the colonial authorities in Virginia facing massacre and internal revolt; the English Puritans enduring civil war and emigrating to escape Anglicanism; Samuel Parris begging his congregation for better pay and fearing Native American murder. Each turned on witches, believing themselves to be the underdog, and used witch-hunts to deflect attention from their own sins and crimes.

Montie Summers had a better reason than most to consider himself oppressed. He was actually persecuted because of his sexual orientation and attraction to practising magic, and he was subjected to a witch trial for Satanism and pederasty, in as far as Edwardian England permitted one. He adopted the identity of a demonologist partly to deflect attacks – successfully, as it turned out. He did not hunt witches in person, but he publicised their existence as he saw it and encouraged others to hunt them.

Was Montie Summers deservedly persecuted as a child-molester? If he had sexual contact with boys under sixteen, he would today be a sex offender under British law. His friends included men reported to desire boys as young as ten and, as is well known, unwanted sexual attention causes lifelong harm to children. Montie and his circle of friends congregated in Capri, where Jacques d'Adelswärd-Fersen had settled, and there is no record of what happened at these gatherings. However, not all this group were alike. After Bitton, no allegations about underage sex were made against Montie despite a long career in boys' schools. Many former pupils wrote warm appreciations of him when his biographer wrote to them in the 1960s. Those who knew him often liked him, although he had some long-standing literary feuds. The actor Sybil Thorndike called him 'entertaining . . . never solemn' but 'very racy' in his anecdotes about 'black magic and diabolism, and all forms of decayed religions and ancient beliefs'. His biographer Brocard Sewell admits that 'some people found Montague Summers sinister' and that there was 'good ground' for rumours of participation in witchcraft rites. He knew as much as anyone ever will.[15]

Montie died in 1948 at his last home in Richmond, 4 Dynevor Road. He left everything to Stuart, who was buried with him in 1950. At the time of his death, Montie's sexuality was still illegal in Britain and would be for another nineteen years, and was then only deemed permissible between consenting adults over the age of twenty-one. It's no surprise that records of Montie's life are few and debated. Any single truth about him is inaccessible: all we can say is that he moved from being the victim of a witch-hunt – on trial, whether deserved or not – to being its perpetrator. One of his last literary acts was to contribute a Foreword to a 1947 book by Frederick Kaigh on the *Witchcraft and Magic of Africa*, a topic that was increasingly interesting anthropologists. The book explained that:

Satanists, that is to say out and out worshippers of the devil, have existed from earliest times, and still exist and practise today . . . material evidence of Satan worship, common witchcraft, celebrations of the Black Mass, convening of Sabbaths by the coven masters, horrid concomitants including human sacrifice, is overwhelming . . . it riddles the primitives, and particularly the African primitives and, in its immense power and malice, produces widespread horror and disease and blights and death and destruction.

In his Foreword to the book, Montie agreed. He wrote that it was:

> . . . impossible to deny the existence of evil in the world . . . In the records of witchcraft, or magic, or sorcery, as I have studied them throughout the continent of Europe, in Spain and Russia, in England and Italy, one finds oneself confronted, not once or twice, but literally as a whole, systematically and homogenously, with the same beliefs, the same extraordinary happenings, unexplained and (so far as we know today) inexplicable. The time has gone past when Science, so-called, can meet the phenomenon by a blank denial . . . these phenomena do occur . . . it is useless, it is unscientific, it is untheological, it is untrue to deny the fact.

In reading Frederick Kaigh's book, he said, 'I find myself continually paralleling what he relates with the pages of such writers as Heinrich Kramer', and he likened African dancing to the dancing at 'the great witch meeting at the haunted church of North Berwick'. In summary, Montie thought, 'Mr Kaigh's masterly study shows us something of what the witchcraft and magic of Africa can do, and is doing in our midst.' The next three chapters of this book show that belief like this in the reality of witchcraft still mattered in the early years of the twentieth century – and it matters now in the twenty-first. All over the world accusations of witchcraft could and can still lead to the trials of innocent people and to their deaths – in Africa, but also in Europe and North America.[16]

CHAPTER NINE

The Trial of John Blymyer:
Pow-Wow and Poverty in Pennsylvania

Sometimes the unlikeliest thing can spark a witch trial. In 1928, near York City, Pennsylvania, it was the building of a concrete road. In 1916 the American government passed a road-building law. Provided it cost the government under $10,000 per mile to grade and pour a concrete highway, communities could upgrade their dirt tracks into roads fit for automobiles. Farm trucks could reach market towns faster. Country dwellers could commute to urban factories. And, it transpired, people could more easily visit out-of-town witches. South of the small city of York, highway officials chose the Susquehanna Trail – the riverbank path named by the Iroquois-Lenape-Susquehannock people – for the construction of a concrete strip. The road was completed in 1923. And at dusk on 26 November 1928 a car quickly covered thirteen miles south of York on the smooth new Susquehanna highway. The driver was Clayton Hess, a sawmill manager. Beside him sat his wife Edna, tired from her shift at a wire screen factory. Crammed into the back were Clayt's eighteen-year-old brother Wilbert, thirty-two-year-old John Blymyer and fourteen-year-old John Curry. Clayt and Edna dropped their passengers near Hametown and the three left the concrete road, stumbling purposefully along the rutted dirt track to Rehmeyer's Hollow. They were going to visit, and ultimately murder, a 'witch'.[1]

Their target was Nelson Rehmeyer, an elderly farmer. In the days leading up to 26 November, John Blymyer had mulled over the prospect of hurting or killing Nelson because he suspected him of witchcraft, and he had brought the two boys Wilbert Hess and John Curry along to restrain the old man. John Blymyer believed the episodes of anxiety and depression he was suffering, his inability to eat, sleep or work, were caused by Nelson's curses. Nelson, he thought, had magical healing gifts but he could also use these powers to harm his enemies. John couldn't see how he'd crossed the old man, but he believed firmly Nelson had bewitched him. Yet later, at the trial of the three self-confessed murderers in January 1929, a further complication in John's thinking was revealed: not only was Nelson Rehmeyer murdered because he was a witch, but he, John Blymyer, was just as much of a witch himself. John believed he had magical powers too, and they were discussed at length in court, and so journalists described his murder trial as a 'witch trial'.

'Witch' was in some ways the wrong label, since John and Nelson both practised a magical art known as 'pow-wow', which comes from a Native American word. European colonists referred to Native American shamans as 'pow-wow magicians', a term appropriated from the Algonquian language. For Algonquian people pow-wow was a trance state used for divining or healing. In John and Nelson's case this American tradition was blended with the folk-magic of the 'Pennsylvania Deutsch', Germans who had settled York County. Their folk magicians were called 'hexenmeisters', witch-masters. Hexenmeister pow-wow magic repelled the harm witches were thought to do, turning back evil spells onto them by using spoken or written charms, prayers and protective signs: crosses, stars, circles. Those who practised the blended tradition believed the magic they performed was good, like that of Anny Sampson or Joan Wright. It divined, healed and blessed their clients, protecting them from 'black magic'. Yet no matter how good the pow-wowers' intent, their work depended on believing others were witches. That was how John and Nelson were bound together as rival pow-wowers, supposedly hurling spells at each other. In fact, John had stopped thinking of Nelson as a pow-wower and considered him merely a witch, one so dangerous he ought to be killed. In John's mind, the harmless German/Native American magical tradition of pow-wow had been weaponised by Nelson, and so he had to be murdered.

The journalists who attended John Blymyer's trial were outsiders to Pennsylvania Deutsch culture and some misrepresented all pow-wow as 'witchcraft', thinking it unchristian, pagan nonsense. But in fact, like Anny Sampson's prayers, it was profoundly shaped by Christianity and often took the form of a direct appeal to God or Christ. Pow-wowers saw it as their job to 'expose those who came to [them] for assistance to the glory of Almighty God and the many blessings that the Good Lord sends to all who sincerely ask for them'.[2] These distinctions between good and bad magic were too fine for most observers in 1929, however, and many were horrified that modern-day Americans believed in witchcraft at all. The New York novelist Theda Kenyon wrote with astonishment of Nelson's murder: it 'startled most of the country out of the complacent belief that witches were as dead as Macbeth, and left bankers and housewives and truck drivers shaking their heads in amazement'. The murder provided Theda with the message and title of her book *Witches Still Live*, but more importantly it showed that in the year Montie Summers republished Heinrich Kramer's *Malleus Maleficarum*, witch-hunting was still alive, and capable of killing people.[3]

Death crept towards Nelson slowly, accidentally, throughout the six years leading up to November 1928. Over those years, John Blymyer, fearing he was under a witch's curse, had knocked desperately on the door of one medical doctor or pow-wower after another, seeking advice about his illness and knowledge of who had bewitched him. Pow-wowers could be shopkeepers, salesmen or labourers, white or Black, male or female, and there were many in the Pennsylvania Deutsch areas. Many worked day jobs in the canning, machinery and cigar factories of Pennsylvania's small cities,

A cartoon showing Jean-Baptiste Girard and Marie-Catherine Cadière, one of a series of erotic prints produced in Holland in 1735.

Although there were fewer trials by the time Francisco Goya painted *Witches' Flight* in 1798, the supposed feats of witches were still rich material for artists and writers. One interpretation of the painting is that it satirises religious delusion and 'peasant' ignorance.

Jules Michelet, photographed by Nadar (Gaspard-Félix Tournachon) in the mid-1850s.

Marie-Catherine Cadière as she appears in an anonymous print from the 1730s.

St Mary's church, Bitton, from an engraving commissioned in the 1880s for a parish history by Henry Thomas Ellacombe, father of Montie Summers' boss Henry Nicholson Ellacombe.

Montie Summers in clerical dress in the mid-1920s, a photograph he used in publications of his literary essays.

Montie Summers' grave at Richmond cemetery, London. The headstone was designed and erected by admirers of his work and life in the 1980s, choosing a phrase he often used as a conversation starter.

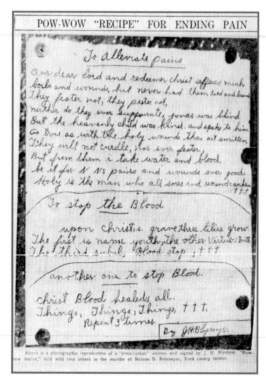

A photograph of some of John Blymyer's handwritten charms, obtained by police in 1928.

Nelson Rehmeyer's house, from a 'crime scene investigation' photograph taken for the *Philadelphia Inquirer* in December 1928.

The *Inquirer*'s coverage of Nelson Rehmeyer's murder was extensive: this page shows (left to right) his widow Alice and two daughters Gertrude and Florence, the three suspects John Blymyer, Wilbert G. Hess and John Curry, and Nelson himself.

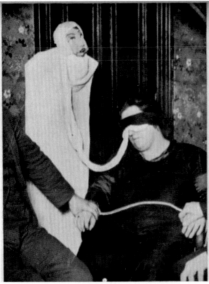

Photographs of Nellie's 'materialisations' at a Scottish séance in 1928, taken by Harvey Metcalfe. These were used in accounts of her mediumship that questioned its veracity, such as Harry Price's study, which concluded she faked ectoplasm.

As a young working mother, Nellie wore her hair in a fashionable, practical bob. Here she poses for a portrait before attempting her psychic tests in London in 1931.

Pursued by a *Daily Mirror* photographer, Nellie Duncan hides her face as she attends the Old Bailey court on the first day of her trial in March 1944.

Bereng Lerotholi at a horse-racing event in his district. He was named as his father's successor in this 1939 story by the *Illustrated London News* — only to be bitterly disappointed.

Queen-Regent 'Mantšebo on a visit to London in 1951.

The top four Basotho chiefs at an event in the 1940s, two wearing traditional mokorotlo straw hats and all four wearing the leopard skins that symbolised kingship. Gabashane is the first on the left and Bereng the third from left.

A protest in southern Nigeria in 2009, organised by children accused of witchcraft and their supporters.

In Rungani Nyoni's film *I Am Not a Witch* Shula attempts to run away from her accusers, but is caught and returned to a witch camp.

The women of Shula's witch camp, who are expected to entertain tourists with their scary magic, sing and chant.

Stormy Daniels speaks to the press in April 2018 outside a New York courthouse. Her then-lawyer Michael Avenatti stands beside her.

Rose McGowan addresses a #MeToo movement press conference in January 2020, on the first day of the trial of Harvey Weinstein.

A memorial to people executed for witchcraft in East Lothian, Scotland – including Anny Sampson and Gillie Duncan – designed by Andy Scott and erected in 2011. The woman's body is made of metal leaves and her book is intended to suggest dignity and power. In 2022 First Minister Nicola Sturgeon apologised to all the accused witches of Scotland.

From this nineteenth-century German engraving representing the medieval idea of the witches' Sabbath, witches have come a long way to these dancers celebrating the modern pagan Beltane festival in Scotland.

Nicole Kidman as the witch Isabel Bigelow, preparing to play the role of another witch – Samantha – in the 2005 film *Bewitched*. As with Andy Scott's memorial, her book confers authority as she reclaims the figure of the witch.

set amid crop-striped green and yellow fields. Knowing Nelson had a reputation for healing magic, John initially went to him for a pow-wow cure – maybe three times, John said later. He also helped Nelson dig up his potato harvest. But John did not get better. His quest went on. Four further practitioners, he said, were unable to tell him the name of his persecutor. Then at last a more skilful pow-wower, Emma Knopt, found the answer John wanted. She confirmed his growing suspicion that the witch was Nelson Rehmeyer himself.

To identify a witch, Emma asked her clients to bring a dollar bill with them, place it on their palm and think who might have cursed them. Perhaps a banknote was a good divining tool because it contained a portrait, like a photofit. It also declared 'in God we trust', like a holy document. And it ensured the consultation was paid for: Emma kept the money. When the client had looked at the bill and parted with it, she told them an image would appear in their hand – not the face of George Washington, but of the person who'd bewitched them. John Blymyer said that when he visited Emma in autumn 1928, he saw the face of Nelson Rehmeyer.[4] Emma advised John that to break the curse on him, he could steal Nelson's magic book, the hexenmeister manual *Pow-wows or the Long Lost Friend*. The Pennsylvania printer John George Hohman had written it a century before to share his collection of charms and medical remedies ('A Good Remedy for the Colic', 'To Make Chickens Lay Many Eggs', 'To Release Spell-Bound Persons'). Nelson ostensibly used his copy to combat witches, but Emma and John suspected he was using it to perform witchcraft. If John could get Nelson's book, Emma said, he should burn it. He might also cut off a lock of Nelson's hair and bury it eight feet deep. Both tasks would be difficult, but not impossible – and murder was not what Emma had in mind. She hoped the book or hair might be filched from Nelson somehow. As we know, John decided differently.

While all this intrigue was going on, a farmer called Milton J. Hess was being drawn into John Blymyer's fantastical world. The two met by chance one hot August day when Milt took a break at his workplace, the Pennsylvania Tool Manufacturing Company in York city, one of many factories and produce-processing plants that employed low-paid, moderately skilled labourers. As he stood in the alley behind the workshop, Milt saw a tall, thin young man standing in the backyard of a terraced house opposite, in North George Street. Milt said hi, and John Blymyer introduced himself using an alias, John Albright – we'll see later why he didn't use his real name. Milt asked where he worked, and John told him he was a cigar-roller in a nearby plant. Chatting with John, Milt said his family had a fourteen-acre farm on the Chanceford Pike, at Leader's Heights, south of town. Crop yields were down, he fretted; some of the farm's animals and people were sick, and chickens had escaped. In turn, John told Milt about his own illness: he was wasting away, couldn't sleep or eat. He was bewitched, he knew it. And then he wondered: maybe the Hess farm was hexed too? Perhaps they'd also been bewitched by Nelson Rehmeyer?[5]

If that was true, John said he could help Milt. He couldn't un-curse himself, it seemed, but would offer to help others by using his pow-wow skills if he was paid to do it. Some of the charms John Blymyer used are recorded:

> Our dear Lord and Redeemer, Christ,
> suffered much boils and wound
> but never had them tied and bound.
> They fester not, they pester not,
> neither do they ever suppurate.
> Jonas was blind, but the
> Heavenly Child was kind
> and spoke to him.
> As true as with the Holy wounds thou art smitten.
> They will not curdle, nor ever fester.
> But from them I take water and blood.
> Be it for N.N.'s pains and wounds ever good,
> holy is the man who all sores and wounds can heal +++.

The charm ends with three crosses to indicate the pow-wower should make the sign of the cross three times over the patient, N.N. (which meant 'whoever'). This charm sounds surprisingly similar to Anny Sampson's one, uttered back in the 1590s on the other side of the Atlantic, and there's a good chance Joan Wright and perhaps Tatabe would have recognised it too, circulating in American settler communities. Nelson Rehmeyer used related charms ('Bruise, thou shalt not heat; Bruise, thou shalt not sweat; Bruise, thou shalt not run, No-more than Virgin Mary shall bring forth another son. + + +'). It was a bitter irony that he and his killer John were in fact the same type of pow-wow healer – people who were trying to perform good magic.[6]

In a long, difficult life, Nelson had already suffered because of his pow-wowing. At sixty, he lived alone because he was separated from his wife Alice. She left him partly because of his devotion to his pow-wow clients. There were too many strangers coming to their house for consultations, Alice said – people like John Blymyer who were needy, odd and stayed all night. Nelson invited them for supper and spent hours divining and praying. His obsessive pow-wowing was impossible to live with, she concluded. He was interested in politics too, and put up posters for socialist candidates in the house. In York County, unionisation and strikes were regarded as evidence of Bolshevism, and with memories of the recent Russian Revolution still fresh, even mild socialism appeared subversive and atheistical to employers – just as it had appeared Satanic to Montie Summers. Alienated by Nelson's mysticism and radical political ideas, which she regarded as linked, Alice moved into a vacant house about a mile away from her husband, taking their two daughters with her. Nelson could keep in touch with her and the children but they would not live together at his old family home, Rehmeyer's Hollow.[7]

Years after his death, neighbours recalled how some people criticised Nelson's isolation as a 'funny way of living' for a married man. Everyone knew his mother had also lived apart from his father, to whom she was not married. As an illegitimate baby,

Nelson was already an anomaly when he was born into his conservative society, and now he was alone in his old age too. Half the people in the district's scattered farms were called Rehmeyer and were his cousins, but he had no family at home. That had practical as well as social consequences: family meant shared labour as well as religious conformity. Nelson had no one to help with his livestock, harvests or repairs, and he sought out pow-wow clients partly for company, partly to supplement his income and partly because some, like John, helped him with odd jobs in payment for his pow-wow skills. They were often frayed, furtive people, drifters seeking meaning in tough times. John fell into this category. And although Nelson did what he could for him, because John was a troubled man he came to suspect there was something sinister about Rehmeyer's Hollow and the lonely man who lived there.

Nelson's home was a slender, two-storey wooden house on Rehmeyer's Hollow Road, a track winding along the Codorus Creek. The house had no electricity or running water, although it did have a spring. Like many farmers' homes, it was surrounded by dilapidated animal sheds and useful junk. Nelson grew vegetables, kept chickens, a few cows, a mule and a pair of horses. But it was the house's isolation among woods and the dark, flaking paint protecting its planking that made it appear sinister. The woods were sweet enough in summer, with sunlight shivering on the broad leaves of saplings and deer skulking in grassy glades, but in winter the leaves fell early and so did the night. The trees stood bare through the long, dark months, snow fell in drifts and the little houses were bitterly chilly without a fire. That was why Nelson lit one for three young visitors on the late November night in 1928 when John Blymyer, John Curry (known as Curry) and Wilbert Hess (known as Hessy) came to see him. He remembered John Blymyer as an old pow-wow client and had no fear of him. In fact, John and Curry had been at his house the evening before, too. Now they'd brought another young man, Hessy. Nelson did not imagine they meant to take his *Pow-wows or the Long Lost Friend*, a lock of his hair – or anything else.[8]

When John and Curry had visited Nelson's home the day before the attack, at first they had not found him. They had gone over to Alice Rehmeyer's to ask where he was. Alice was angry with Nelson, according to John. He might be over at Gladfelter's farm, she supposedly sniffed, since 'he lays around there with Emma Gladfelter'. 'The old devilish cock!' John reports her adding, but all those sound like his words not hers. John left Alice's house and he and Curry walked back to Nelson's, to find he'd returned home. Curry said later that they talked with him about 'witchcraft' and personally he 'was afraid of the man'. John was suddenly struck by how big Nelson was, broad-shouldered and over six feet tall. It would be best, he decided, to come back the next day with another man: three would allow two to hold Nelson down while John cut his hair or seized his book or worse. He didn't reflect on why such violence was necessary; perhaps it was part of the established cure for bewitchment, or perhaps it was just how he had already decided to handle the witch. We don't know. As it was already late that night, Nelson unsuspectingly let his guests sleep in the living room by the stove.

The next night, as we know, John and Curry returned with Hessy. Once again, Nelson welcomed his visitors. He brought in logs, lit the fire and lamps, his back turned to his visitors as he coaxed the flames. And the three men leapt on him. John picked up a chair and smashed it over Nelson's body, beating him with a metal stove tool, while Curry and Hessy hit him with sticks of firewood and their fists. Nelson fought back, throwing them his money and, when he learned what they really wanted, shouting, 'Let me up and I will get the book.' But they carried on beating and kicking him until he lay still. Then they tied him with rope. A noose went round his neck, like the halters that once hanged witches. Horribly, the two younger men then realised he was dying or perhaps even dead – something they'd not intended. Later, it was determined the fatal attack had taken only a few minutes.

The three attackers panicked – but not so much that they forgot to search Nelson's bureau for a few coins. They didn't find

Pow-wows or the Long Lost Friend, and John decided now Nelson
was dead there was no need to cut off his hair and bury it eight
feet deep. Nelson's whole body would be buried soon enough, he
later said coldly. The killers washed places where they thought
their fingerprints might remain. They pulled a straw mattress over
their victim and set it alight with oil from the lamp and a match.
If the house burned down, the witch would be consumed by fire
and there would be no evidence of his murder. But as they hustled
out into the cold dark, something moved on the road: 'A shadow
of something,' said John. 'It started as though it backed out into
the road.' Terrified, the murderers raced into the woods, blundering
among the trees, hearts pounding, running and walking until they
reached the Hess farm nine miles away. They did not wait to see
if the fire spread – it didn't, and ample traces of their crime were
left unburned. Later the prosecution would use their failure to cut
Nelson's hair or take his book as evidence that the killers' motive
had been simple robbery.[9]

Was it? No, the motive was to overpower a dangerous witch,
not steal a few pennies. Did the murderers intend to kill Nelson?
Maybe John Blymyer did. After all, it would have been possible
for him to steal Nelson's *Pow-wows or the Long Lost Friend* and
even cut his hair while he slept. John had told Clayt Hess that he
intended only magical conflict with Nelson: 'I got to work on the
man's mind [by pow-wow]. I'll get him under my control.' But
once in the house he turned immediately to physical violence and
led the two boys in beating Nelson to death. When he was later
asked in court, 'Do you think it is right to kill a person that has
you bewitched?', he replied calmly, 'Why, I think it is right, yes.'
John did, however, deny a confession he'd made immediately after
he was arrested in which he'd confessed to the plan to control
Nelson, and that he had hit him with a chair and lit a match to
burn his body. His final story was that 'I didn't take no part in
killing him', and when he was then asked, 'Did you intend to kill
Rehmeyer?', he said firmly, 'No, sir.' But that contradicted his clear
statement that he believed it to be 'right' to kill his bewitcher, and

also many of his actions on the day of the murder. Was John a vicious, scheming killer? Or was he a hapless innocent, murdering Nelson by accident because he'd been brought up with a head full of witchcraft?[10]

John's early life provides conflicting evidence about his own 'witch' status and his attitude to Nelson's pow-wowing. He was born on Christmas Day 1895 at North Hopewell Township near York to Maggie and Emanuel Blymyer, basket-makers. The family had 'little to eat' and an observer later wrote that 'their clothes are shabby. Nothing ever happened, except a little bewitching now and then, to vary the monotony of their lives.' John was often ill as a child, and also suffered with a terrible fear of witches. His parents called in pow-wowers, to little avail, but began to believe their son had pow-wow gifts himself. As a young man, working in Eisenlohr's and Bobrow's cigar factories in the years after the First World War, John obsessed about defeating witches. It was a mind-numbing ten- to fourteen-hour day that earned only eleven dollars per thousand cigars rolled, and offered perhaps too much time to think. Outside of work, there was little joy in his life: he married, quarrelled with his wife, and two of his children died. In 1923 John's anxiety and depression got so bad he was committed to a mental hospital. Doctors there decided he was delusional. Here is a plausible picture of John as a malnourished, exploited, unwell victim of witch-belief, who acted in panic when he'd been failed by pow-wowers and told that his own magical skills had been overcome by a stronger 'witch'.

But there is a more troubling side to John's life story. After spending seven weeks in the mental hospital, he quietly walked out and disappeared. No one readmitted him for further treatment – they couldn't find him. This was because he was in jail. On his return home he'd attempted to murder his wife, Lillie Belle Alloway Blymyer. Lillie was the mother of his son Thomas (and the two other children, Richard and Josephine, who had died of pneumonia and measles). John was found to be armed with a gun and was charged with aggravated assault and battery. After three months imprisonment he agreed to plead guilty to common assault and battery, admitting he had often beaten Lillie. He was also accused of involvement in the sexually motivated murder of a young woman he knew, but nothing was proven. John was convicted of Lillie's assault but served just one further month in prison and, on his release, renamed himself John Albright – being his uncle's surname – so no one would find him, he later said. He then moved house frequently. When he met Milt Hess, he was living in North George Street, and at the time of his arrest for Nelson's murder he had moved to the corner of Chestnut and Pine Streets. He had also had eight or nine other addresses in the five years since his imprisonment. Lillie, meanwhile, had fled for her life and divorced him.[11] Here is a plausible picture of John as a dangerous schemer who was habitually, murderously violent and needed no magical excuse.

In 1929, when Nelson's murder came to trial, John had a sly strategy for avoiding blame, too. He changed his story, now incriminating his fourteen-year-old colleague and supposed friend John Curry. Curry had an equally unhappy home, but in his case it was not his own violence that caused it. His alcoholic stepfather beat him, he told police. Although Curry was a bright boy, he ran away and dropped out of school. He met John Blymyer when he went to work at Bobrow's cigar factory. There John heard him describe his plight at home and told him he was bewitched, and that it was Nelson Rehmeyer who was causing his stepfather to hate him. When John took him to see Nelson, he explained to Curry they were going to talk with the 'witch', perhaps tying him up to do so. Then he made up an alias – John Russell – for Curry, making him look suspicious. In court John Blymyer then alleged that 'Curry accidentally killed [Nelson]'. It was a convenient story, but although Curry confessed other aspects of the attack, he vehemently denied striking any fatal blow.

The third killer, Hessy, came from a more stable background. His parents Milt and Alice were vegetable farmers, godly and reasonably prosperous. They had a stall in York Market, where

Alice sold produce. But when misfortunes harmed their productivity, the Hess family blamed witches. When Hessy's father Milt met John Blymyer on that hot day outside the tool factory in York, Milt listened to John's suggestion that Nelson Rehmeyer was someone worthy of suspicion. He came to believe John's claims that his sister-in-law Ida Hess might have employed Nelson to hurt Milt's farm magically because Milt and Ida had fallen out in a boundary dispute. Milt then accepted John's offer to investigate more fully, using his pow-wow skills to confirm the witch's identity and defeat them.[12] Seeing all this developing, Hessy was worried for his parents. When questioned, he said consistently that he went along innocently with John and Curry to confront Nelson, speak with him and break his spells magically. Hessy hit him because the others did and was appalled when he realised Nelson was dead.

Nelson's badly burned body was found and identified on Thanksgiving Day 1928. Alice Hess told investigators about John and Curry's visit the day before the murder and they were arrested by York City Police, naming Hessy as an accomplice as they confessed. Hessy, too, admitted his guilt. But although the killers had confessed, they would still be tried formally: the sixth amendment to the United States Constitution conferred that right. First, on 5 December, came a preliminary examination by a magistrate. Lawyers were appointed for the defence and prosecution, as the sixth amendment also stipulated. Then, on 7 January 1929, the accused were driven to York County courthouse for their trial. Dressed in Sunday-best shirts and ill-fitting suits, they would have been intimidated by the elegant classical building and the trial preliminaries. A jury of twelve men – no women were allowed on juries – was nominated and the impartiality of each nominee challenged. One question probed whether any juror would refuse to recommend the death penalty. Conducting the challenge process were four legal teams. Two lawyers – Herbert B. Cohen (representing John) and Walter W. Van Baman (representing Curry) – had been appointed by the state, because the defendants could not afford legal fees. Hessy's family had raised money to employ well-known counsel Harvey A. Gross. District Attorney Amos W. Herrmann was the prosecuting counsel. It was late afternoon on the 7th before all four accepted twelve jurors and Judge Ray P. Sherwood could begin the hearing.

The prosecution first presented its case against John Blymyer. In the golden light of the yellow-shaded courtroom, Amos Herrmann stood to begin a near-impossible task. He wanted to prove that the motive for Nelson's murder was robbery and nothing more. Demonstrating that would let him argue the defendants were sane, capable of knowing right from wrong, and should be executed for their crime. It was a strategy that puzzled journalists: they'd already heard a different story from interviewees in town, a story about witchcraft. In some reporters' view, Amos's presentation of the case as a botched theft was not just a simplification, it was a ploy to spare York County embarrassment. No one wanted their community portrayed as witch-obsessed. But Amos's strategy was not framed solely to avoid scandal. The prosecution worried that mentioning witchcraft would affect jurors' perception of the severity of the murder. Might the charges – which were first- or second-degree murder, premeditated or at least malicious – then be rejected and the accused acquitted? Would jurors think belief in witchcraft was insanity, excusing murder? In particular, if John Blymyer believed he was a pow-wower – or 'witch' as the newspapers put it – was he therefore incapable of rationality? Journalists judged Amos 'harassed and over-worked' and predicted his chances of keeping the word 'witch' out of the trial record were slim. For them the murder trial was also a witch trial (and they were right).

Opposing Amos on John's behalf, defence attorney Herbert Cohen planned to argue exactly what Amos feared: that his client was insane and not responsible for his actions. Not only did he think Nelson was a witch, John thought he was a witch himself. What could be crazier? Anyone so deluded ought to be judged incapable of pre-planned or consciously wrongful murder, Herb would show. Instead of being sent to the electric chair, he would state that John should be hospitalised for life in hope of a cure.

But the rules of evidence prevented Herb introducing into court any theme not mentioned by the prosecution: he was there to rebut their claims, not add new material. He couldn't, therefore, mention witchcraft unless a prosecution witness did so first.[13] Across the first two days of the trial Amos and Herb examined all the witnesses, making their contrasting cases. Amos and the police officers Ralph Keech and W. C. Craver evasively stressed the robbery motive. Only one witness, Clayt Hess, Wilbert's brother, gave the defence counsel what he wanted. Clayt told the court that on the day after the murder John had said to him, 'I got the man.' But he added more: 'Shouldn't I say that word?' Clayt asked Amos nervously. Knowing what was coming and how it might damage his argument, the prosecutor had no choice: 'Spit it out,' he said irritably. 'Well,' said Clayt, 'he said, "I got the witch!"'

'State Unable to Evade Hex Angle' rejoiced the *Pittsburgh Post Gazette*. 'Witness Ruins Plan to Sidestep Mention of Witchcraft . . . Youth on Stand Blurts Out "He Said He Got Witch". Defence Elated'. Indeed they were. Once the word 'witch' had been spoken, Herb Cohen could begin to build his case for his client's insanity. On the morning of the trial's second day, he resumed questioning Clayt, who elaborated: John had told him he wanted to be driven to Nelson's house to 'get some of the man's hair' and 'put it eight feet in a hole'. On day three Herb summoned and questioned doctors who said John Blymyer suffered from 'psychoneurosis', with delusions that 'there was something or someone persecuting him' and 'hallucinations'. When he'd been committed to a mental hospital in 1923, John had told his carers, 'I am all unstrung, my nerves are all shot, I am unable to work, have no strength. I am unable to eat or sleep, and they are still after me.' This meant, summed up medical witness Oscar Altland, 'the witches are after him and they don't permit him to eat nor sleep'. John, he added, 'would run up along the wall to get away from them . . . shouting that the witches and the hex were after him'.

This discussion of his mental state led on to the question of John's own status as a witch or pow-wower. On which side of the demonological divide did he believe himself to fall? Wilbert's parents Milt and Alice Hess were called and explained that John had told the Hess family he was 'a pow-wow doctor', a good magician. Alice sobbed as she confirmed she had let Wilbert join the expedition to Rehmeyer's Hollow because John had described it in a magical way: he said one of the Hess family must be there 'to get rid of our trouble'. John, however, tried to deny he had presented himself to Milt and Alice as a pow-wower. Like all of our witchhunters so far, he preferred the narrative of himself as a victim of witches to being represented as a problem himself.

As 'trolley cars rumbled past, the exhausts of automobiles coughed and roared' on Market Street and 'a riveting hammer sounded on an adjacent steel structure', journalists listened with fascination as he discussed his witch-induced illness. 'I couldn't sleep or rest or eat,' he complained, and when asked, 'Do you know what was the cause of that?', replied simply, 'Yes, I was bewitched.' He described visits to different medical and pow-wow doctors 'ten or fifteen times', 'seven or eight times', and how he 'had a nervous disease, or mental disease, hypochondriacal melancholia'.[14]

When it came to describing the murder, John emphasised Curry's role, again deflecting blame. 'We threw [Nelson] down,' he said, 'and then Curry jumped in and helped to beat him . . . after I struck him with the chair, he got up. I hit him pretty often with my fist,' he continued, and then denied hitting him with the chair, contradicting himself. He said nothing about Nelson's death from a fractured skull and third-degree burns. Instead, he claimed that at the end of the attack, 'Curry gets the lamp off the table, takes off the top, takes off the burner and takes the oil and puts it this way alongside of Rehmeyer', miming sloshing oil. 'Then he said, "John, have you got a match?" I said, "I don't smoke, and I have no matches." Then Curry said, "Here, I have one."' This of course placed the blame for the fire firmly on Curry. When the blaze roared up, the killers fled to the Hess family home, John continued. They washed, divided up the pennies they'd stolen, lied to Clayt

Hess that they couldn't find Nelson, and were driven back to John's apartment in York. It was a sickening tale of callousness and Judge Ray Sherwood was convinced of John's guilt by the end of it. 'The man has made a full confession of the whole business,' he summed up as John's trial ended. With that judicial steer, the jury could hardly acquit him of murder, as Herb's closing statement asked them to do.[15]

Although journalists described Herb as 'a likeable young lawyer' who had made himself 'an over-night reputation', the defence claim that John was insane failed. On the evening of 9 January, at about 7.40pm, the jury found him guilty of first-degree murder, which meant they believed his crime was rational and premeditated. However, Herb had gained some traction: jurors had heard enough to decide John was not completely in control of himself. His responsibility for the murder was felt to be diminished and Amos's contention that robbery was the only aim of the murder was not universally accepted. The suggestion that both John and Nelson thought they were 'witches' was a major factor in saving John's life. 'Two fellows thought it was caused by hex,' reported the jury foreman years later, meaning that the murder was caused by a belief in witchcraft. Therefore, the foreman reported, fellow jurors had argued 'the jury should be lenient'. A single juror favoured acquittal. All the rest believed the right outcome was a first-degree murder conviction but, crucially, all recommended life imprisonment as the penalty, not death. John was sentenced to life in jail. He tensed as he heard the verdict, then yawned widely. It was as if he was at 'an uninteresting football game', one journalist wrote. His behaviour strengthened newspapermen's impression that he was both a 'witch' and 'a madman', and they described him that way.

The second defendant to be tried was Curry. The prosecution put their case on the morning of 10 January, and in the afternoon his lawyer Walter Van Baman began the defence. Although it was likely Curry would be found guilty of killing Nelson, as John had been, Walter made a plea for leniency, presenting his crime as unpremeditated. He pointed out that John Blymyer had supposedly told Clayt Hess during one conversation that 'I am to be blamed for it all . . . the other boys ain't supposed to be blamed'. He alleged Curry's confession was 'improperly obtained' by a promise from the district attorney – prosecutor Amos Herrmann – that 'you help me and I'll help you'. Amos candidly confirmed the confession had been encouraged with promises of a better outcome. Curry told the court how he 'wasn't welcome at home', where his step-father 'beat and cussed' him. He had gone with John expecting 'to see some of this witchcraft performed' by John, in defeating Nelson, and had not tried to stop the attack because 'I was afraid of getting killed myself . . . by Blymyer'. To some extent he gained the jury's sympathy, appearing scared and tearful, but the judge turned them against a manslaughter verdict in his summing up. Their verdict came before 2pm next day. Curry's trial had taken less than two days. Aged just fourteen, he was found guilty of first-degree murder with recommended life imprisonment.[16]

On 12 January, Hessy began his trial, with the advantage of a defence team hired by his family. His forceful attorney, Harvey Gross, was the only defender to examine the medical evidence in detail, proving the cause of death was unclear. Lax procedure in questioning suspects and recording evidence in the previous two trials as well as Hessy's was uncovered. Harvey identified Hessy's supposed weapon – a stick – showing it was not deadly, and used a stopwatch to dramatise his claim that the fatal fight lasted around one minute. He got Milt and Alice Hess to explain how it felt to be bewitched – 'as though my flesh was boiled continually', and 'so out and down that I couldn't do my own work . . . I didn't care if my children got anything to eat'. Finally, he presented Hessy as a dutiful son. 'I went for my father's and my mother's benefit,' Hessy explained. His mother told the jury how her son confessed, 'Mother, don't worry . . . I didn't want to go along down there . . . the man is dead . . . I hope youse will get better.' Harvey had also assembled seventy-seven character witnesses, and called four before the prosecution agreed to accept

Hessy had a good reputation. Because of these efforts, the jury found Hessy guilty only of second-degree murder, carrying a sentence of ten to twenty years imprisonment. In fact, Hessy (prisoner 5408) and Curry (5883) were both paroled in summer 1939.[17] John Blymyer remained in the Eastern State Penitentiary, Philadelphia, until 1953 as prisoner 5407, happier than he had ever been because he believed that 'if the spell is off of me, they can't put no spell on me no more'.[18]

The York County witch trial made headline news worldwide. Journalists as far away as India and New Zealand were astonished by a 'witchcraft trial' or 'voodoo trial' that made 'witchcraft . . . as much a reality as an electric light' in America. Inaccurately, though understandably, they called Nelson a 'practitioner of black magic' and John 'a rival worker in witchcraft'. Elsewhere John was referred to as a 'slim, small-skulled, self-styled sorcerer' in an attempt to link his poverty, supposed mental incapacity and witchcraft. Both men fitted with certain stereotypes of witches, the most notable exception being their sex. Nelson was suspected because of his lonely, subsistence-level life, association with adultery and illegitimacy, his subversive politics and his magico-medical skills, which drew on pagan Native American as well as Christian-German religiosity. John Blymyer was an equally typical witch: another isolated, poor man, divorced by his wife and suspected by his society as a misfit and possible sexual criminal – a man who knew the same culturally hybrid magic as Nelson and was a potentially dangerous 'madman'.

While many circumstances of twentieth-century life were different, in other ways little had changed since the witch trials of the medieval and early modern world. Nelson and John shared traits with Helena, Anny, Kari, Bess and the other earlier 'witches', and John also resembled Heinrich Kramer, Matthew Hopkins and the other witch-hunters in his fear of magical attack and his misogynistic violence. Some journalists linked Pennsylvania's Deutsch cultures to the 'backward' European past, but they also tied it to the African present, using anthropologists' term for African versions of pow-wow men: 'witch doctors'. According to one headline, the Pennsylvania state legislature declared its intention to 'prosecute Witch Doctors' in December 1928, because of 'the witchcraft practices brought to light by the murder of Nelson D. Rehmeyer'.[19] Like Montie, 1920s American journalists thought modern intercultural comparisons usefully contextualised witch trials for their readers.

Yet the murder and witch trial of 1928–9 make sense, not as a throwback to the sixteenth or seventeenth century, nor as a surprising echo of African practices in Pennsylvania, but as a sign of twentieth-century times right across the European and American world. Nineteen twenty-eight was the year of Montague Summers' edition of *Malleus Maleficarum*, one of a string of highly successful demonologies he published in the 1920s and 1930s in London and New York. People in the first half of the twentieth century wanted to know more about magic, and some wanted to practise it. Michelet-like experiments with non-Christian religion began to flourish in the form of Theosophy, Transcendentalism, 'new age' mysticism and Wicca. The end of the nineteenth century and the years after the First World War saw magical beliefs grow rather than receding, with a growing interest in diverse kinds of magic: charms and amulets, past-life visions, contacts with the dead.[20] The York County witch trial demonstrates not just the persistence but the modern vitality of magical beliefs and fears of witchcraft in Western societies, rather than their ebbing or their coming extinction. It was not just the old witchcraft beliefs of Europe that were on the rise. So too were beliefs in Eastern, indigenous and alternative Christian spiritualities, which also appealed to a deep human need for magic – and were also on trial.

CHAPTER TEN

The Trial of Nellie Duncan:
Witchcraft Acts and World War Two

The black and white film is grainy. We are far above the sea, looking down. A vessel lies on her side, a great hulk of a warship wallowing as she capsizes. As we watch, we see dots moving on that pale expanse of hull. They stream towards the stern, hesitating as they come to the cliff edge that's now hanging over the propeller and the boiling sea. The dots are men. They run over the hull, firm and careful, gauging their next move. Jump and they die. Slip and they die. Stay where they are, and they might live. Our hearts lift, we stop breathing – they're going to be okay. But suddenly, the ship explodes. Jets of black and white steam, smoke, fragments of iron, heavy projectiles roar upwards. A second explosion. The hollow, incurved ship becomes a spiky convex flower of destruction, blooming and falling. Most of the men disappear, vaporised or hurled into the sky. And as we watch the remainder running towards us, far below, across the sinking hull, the film ends.

The ship was HMS *Barham*, sunk in November 1941. Back in her home port of Portsmouth, on England's south coast, relatives of those lost heard rumours that their men were dead. And some, visitors to the séances of a spiritualist medium named Helen Duncan, apparently witnessed a miracle. Calling on her ability to connect with the dead, Helen spoke with the spirit of a recently deceased

Barham sailor and correctly announced the ship was lost. And she did so 'long before' the official announcement of the ship's sinking, a court was later told by Portsmouth's chief constable. How, the police questioned, did Helen know or guess these naval secrets? Was this a fraud, charging customers to hear nothing more than gossip? Had she 'foretold' the sinking, which a moment of ambiguity in the chief constable's statement suggested, or had she just pre-empted the announcement? And whatever her source of information, was it right to profit from speculation about those men running across the *Barham*'s hull?[1] As a woman claiming visionary knowledge, like Kari Edisdatter, Joan Wright or Marie-Catherine Cadière, Helen Duncan became part of the debate about whether and how occult forces existed. And the *Barham* story was brought up in evidence at the end of her eight-day trial under the British 1735 Witchcraft Act. Helen was not a witch in the old sense – and she was not accused of this under the Act – but the meaning of witchcraft in modern times included magical fraud in the form of pretended witchcraft, and so her trial was a witch trial.

Like her namesake Gillie Duncan, Helen Duncan was a Scot. She was born in the small town of Callander to Archibald and Isabella MacFarlane in 1897 as Victoria Helen, also known as Ellen and Nell; she called herself Nellie.[2] Nellie's respectable parents ran a building business and had nine children by the time she was thirteen. The family was Presbyterian, a puritanical Protestant sect enforcing piety, chastity and abstinence. Indeed, the MacFarlanes lived next to a no-alcohol hotel on Callander's Main Street. Nellie's religious upbringing shaped her. Initially it meant repression: her life was no cheerier than Abigail Williams's and Betty Parris's in seventeenth-century Salem. Most entertainment was banned. But Nellie was a lively, dreamy, tomboyish girl, struggling painfully with restriction. Frustration and inexperience were a toxic combination and, at sixteen, she was seduced or perhaps assaulted by someone she never identified. She became an unmarried mother in 1914, as the First World War broke out. Presbyterians loathed sexual 'sin', and the MacFarlanes banished their daughter. To support herself, she laboured in a jute mill in Dundee. Here fibres from the bark of the jute plant were woven into sacking on mechanised looms. Women and girls worked ten-hour shifts six days a week: dusty, lung-clogging work at dangerous machines. In 1915, Nellie applied to a wartime munitions factory instead. However, at seventeen, five-and-a-half feet tall, she weighed fifteen stone (210 pounds) and had tuberculosis. The munitions factory rejected her and hospitalised her for a compulsory cure. Afterwards, she found work at a bakery and married a cabinet-maker, Henry Duncan, in 1916. It was the best she could do to salvage her life and her child's prospects.[3]

Henry adopted Nellie's daughter Isabella and the Duncans had seven more children. But cabinet-makers relied on a thriving economy and the 1920s and 1930s did not provide it. Moreover, Nellie and Henry were constantly ill, Nellie with lung and kidney infections, Henry with a breakdown and heart attack. Tragedy haunted the family: Isabella lost an eye in an animal attack and another daughter, Henrietta, died as a toddler. Nellie suffered repeated pregnancy complications, but she had no access to information about reproductive health and contraception was seen as sinful. The family faltered into chronic sickness and debt.[4] Henry, wounded in the war, had an army pension of eight shillings a week plus a small family allowance, but there was no other income. There was hardly any welfare state, yet the children needed clothes and shoes, food and medicine. When Henry's business failed, they moved to a smaller house. Nellie took in washing and mending and worked in a bleaching plant, where linen was whitened. Each morning she woke in the dark, dressed with shivering fingers, huddled into a coat and shawl and trudged through the cobbled streets to work. Her shift started at five o'clock. At eight she went home to ready the children for school – sponging, combing, dressing and shovelling a meagre breakfast into them before rushing back to work. At two she came home to her second job as a laundress and seamstress. In the evening she made tea, lulled the children to sleep and went to bed bone-weary. Several hospitalisations followed, bills piled up and the Duncans feared eviction. But their family life was loving. Many poor people lived similarly and the Duncans were comforted by Nellie's faith in God. He loved them, she knew, and saw past her fear and anger, through her pain-wracked body to her shining soul.[5]

All her life, Nellie claimed personal contact with God. As a child she said she saw ghosts and dreamed prophecy. Many disbelieved her, but she found power in a visionary life that contrasted so starkly with her narrow reality. She began to experiment with séances (spirit 'sessions') in the 1920s. As she fell into an apparent trance the voices of spirits, the recently dead, would seem to speak through her lips. That meant she was a 'medium' for their communication with living people, attuned to spirit energies, like a shaman. Artefacts belonging to the dead would even materialise in her hands. She could explore the past and future through these objects by 'psychometry', divination through touch. Like Joan Wright, she could predict deaths, and see events as far away as Australia and America. Nellie also claimed that, like Anny Sampson, she could draw other people's sickness into herself and cure it. Magical intervention like this offered hope to families who could not afford a doctor. It was also comforting to think that apparently dead relatives were present in spirit. Messages that their loved one was happy in the afterlife reassured believers, who formed spiritualist churches that met in homes and community halls. Here they celebrated their belief in contact with the dead and conducted practical tests of connection. A mid-twentieth-century report showed that 35 per cent of British people thought such contact was possible and spiritualism spread to over forty nations worldwide by the 1950s.

The Duncans began attending a spiritualist church instead of a Presbyterian one. Spiritualists were and are Christians but hold distinct sectarian beliefs, separate from the main Protestant and Catholic Churches and recognised by neither. In the late nineteenth and twentieth centuries some spiritualist mediums claimed they could materialise the entire bodies of spirits, exuding a physical substance – a white gloop called 'ectoplasm' – to build up the form of the deceased. Female mediums were thought especially adept in this skill, which was after all a kind of miraculous birth.[6] Once she had seen how church mediums worked, Nellie aspired to experience the same manifestations. And a not unwelcome side effect would be that she could earn income from paying clients at private séances too. Soon she said she had a 'guide', Dr Williams, a powerful spirit who had contacted her to help her technique. He spoke through Nellie with a plummy accent, bringing upper-class masculine authority to her home séances. Dr Williams instructed Henry Duncan to curtain off part of the Duncans' parlour, set up a dim red lamp and make a metal cone as a speaking trumpet. From behind the curtain Nellie began to stage spectacular living-room séances, complete with ectoplasm.

To sceptics, ectoplasm looked awfully like muslin cloth. Photographs show hovering spectres beside Nellie that appear to be crude puppets trailing muslin gowns.[7] But clients affirmed that their dear mums and dads, their little brothers lost to war, had spoken through Nellie's mouth. Her séance business boomed – and its income was much needed in the Duncan household. While spirits swirled in her mind, Nellie's body weakened. By her early thirties she had borne eight children and had many miscarriages. Her last baby, Alexander, had died. Nellie chain-smoked, combined expensive opiate medication and alcohol to dull the pain, and soldiered on. However, when she became pregnant again, hospital staff were alarmed. She had suffered near-lethal fits during previous births. As the 1920s ended with economic depression and the Duncans' situation looked increasingly precarious, Nellie agreed to an abortion and sterilisation to save her life. Abortion was regarded as sinful – in that way 1920s Scotland was no different to 1730s Toulon – and sterilisation was dangerous: Nellie had her fallopian tubes 'tied' with steel clips.[8] She endured the loss of her baby, the metal invasion of her body and a debilitating recovery. Later a hysterectomy followed. Turning misery into opportunity, however, she said surgeons found evidence of ectoplasmic movements inside her body.[9]

For all its pain, Nellie's operation meant better health and steady work. She could gradually broaden her career as a medium, escaping back-breaking physical toil. Henry was keen that she do so, and one observer felt Nellie 'was greatly under the adverse influence of her husband', who was pushing her to build a reputation. In 1930 Nellie went to Edinburgh and London, making appointments with psychic investigators, who tested her to see if they could endorse her mediumship and grant her access to affiliated spiritualist churches. She was strip-searched, probed and X-rayed by midwives and doctors, tied up in a sack and expected to produce ectoplasm for flash-lit photography. Some observers confirmed her claims, but celebrity investigator Harry Price accused her of regurgitating muslin to fake materialisations, swallowing and storing it in her oesophagus. Later, accounts of her swearing and raging at doubters emerged: it was a gruelling time.[10] But Nellie's efforts paid off. Being accepted by the London Spiritualists' Alliance 'put me on the map', she said in 1933. Her fame and wealth grew. With this new income, the Duncans moved to a detached, four-bedroom bungalow in Edinburgh, with lilacs and a mountain view. They named it 'Albertine' after two spirit guides who had succeeded Dr Williams: Albert Stewart and Peggy Hazzeldine. Nellie wrote articles for the Dundee-based *People's Journal*, bought a fur coat and silk underwear.[11] She 'collected volumes from all parts of the world on séances of famous mediums' and became 'a voracious reader', her daughter recalled. She materialised more impressively, wrote letters from the dead and even materialised a fairy, according to witnesses. In late 1943, as Britain entered its fifth year of the Second World War, she was booked by Ernest and Elizabeth Homer to give materialisation séances at their spiritualist church in the naval city of Portsmouth, on England's south coast.

The Homers' church was called the 'Master's Temple Church of Spiritual Healing' or the 'Master Temple Psychic Centre', the 'Master' being Jesus Christ. It was a mid-terraced house at 301 Copnor Road, Portsmouth, with a ground-floor shop and a flat above. The shop was 'Homers Drug Stores', its window stuffed with jars, pill boxes and posters for Vaseline and Virol supplements. The Homers did not manufacture their own medicines – they were not qualified pharmacists – but they sold commercially available remedies. Arriving in December 1943, Nellie navigated their stacked shelves on her way to the back kitchen, overlooking a garden and garage. After tea and a cigarette, she went upstairs to the séance room. Here the bay window displayed a store-front sign advertising the church and a wooden cross. Looking skywards from queues for rationed sweets and fruit in adjacent shops, weary wartime housewives glimpsed a better afterlife.[12] Nellie had been to the Master Temple before. On séance days she walked from her lodgings at 6 Milton Road across the railway bridge and past the cemetery – a point of interest for people channelling the dead. To her right she saw St Cuthbert's Anglican Church, damaged by bombing in 1940 and 1941. Like many urban British buildings, it was glassless amid rubble. A wooden cross stood in the churchyard with a V (for Victory) nailed on. The city's mood was grim. Bombers targeting the naval dockyard dropped explosives in the Copnor and North End neighbourhoods. 'Parts of Portsmouth looked like old ruins' to visitors by 1941. People were frightened of death, injury, homelessness and invasion, and at times they could hear the guns across the Channel in France. Meanwhile 'the effect of air-raids on those in the immediate vicinity is one of tremendous psychological shock', wrote one observer. It amounted to a feeling of 'unreality' or 'mental blackout'.

During the war three-quarters of Portsmouth's citizens fled from air-raids, leaving the blacked-out city 'a tomb of darkness' where key workers huddled in underground shelters. Researchers working for the wartime government thought the mood worse even than blitzed London. Portsmouth's citizens became alienated from the authorities, who weren't seen as doing much to help. 'The [Anglican] church might show a bit of real feeling,' complained one: what about 'open doors and heating on for people who want to sleep there'? Others complained about the police standing armed guard over shattered shops. Everyone was edgy and suspicion abounded.

There was a 'spy scare' in 1941 – in which Nellie's naval knowledge and suspicions about HMS *Barham* would play a part – and campaigns urged citizens to 'take the offensive' against anti-social people like black-marketeers. Meanwhile, law-abiding shops like the Homers' pharmacy lost half to three-quarters of their pre-war income. 'If I had to rely on the shop alone,' said one retailer, 'I might as well close down at once.'[13]

The Homers owned two Portsmouth shops, as well as property in London and Birmingham, making about two hundred pounds a year. In 1940 they registered the Master Temple as a church business, charging for healing and séances. Church president Bessie Homer was a medium and psychic healer, curing by touch. During the 1914–18 war, she had performed in music-therapy concerts for troops, run by Lena Simson, wife of the queen's obstetrician. Music, Lena said, 'seems to break the spell that the horrors and the deafening noise of modern military warfare lays on the nerves . . . music has brought back memory . . . and speech'. Two decades later, Bessie was once again offering wartime healing, in her church and with a musical quartet. Although her husband Ernest, a 'pale, insignificant, bespectacled man', was notionally the patriarch, he was actually curate to his wife who was both a minister and a magical healer.

Bessie's gatherings, known as 'circles', had features of both a church service and a witches' Sabbath. There was a Christian sermon, prayers and hymns, but most officials were women and there was bodily contact with spirits, prophecy and visions.[14] Visiting mediums would preach on themes such as 'We should aspire to more spiritual things!' Then invisible spirits would speak psychometrically, when a medium 'read' objects belonging to attendees, relaying messages from people who had owned or touched the items. 'He says you can do great things,' Bessie Homer would tell clients, holding a cigarette-lighter or a lapel badge belonging to a friend or grandfather. Interspersed with ordinary 'circles' were materialisation séances, starring a medium in a curtained-off cabinet like Nellie's one at home. These séances were advertised in local newspapers. Ectoplasmic figures would speak, moving out of the cabinet into darkened rooms as ghostly white shapes. Yet Master Temple regulars saw all this as firmly Christian, if unusual.

Many spiritualist beliefs were, however, at odds with Anglican teaching. One believer summed this up: 'The orthodox [Anglican] church teaches us that by faith alone we are saved, whilst we, as Spiritualistic people, believe that the Word of God is still living, that God has not stopped talking, and he reveals himself to his people daily.' Séance attendees even reported animal materialisations, arguing 'animals have souls' – something that would be considered heretical by the Anglican Church. Although Britain had become far more religiously tolerant since the seventeenth century, as had been the case with the North Berwick or Manningtree 'witches', Bessie Homer's unusual approach to Christianity was still open to interpretation as wicked. One opponent described her comparison of ordinary human mediums with Jesus as outright 'blasphemy' when, as police broke up a séance, Bessie remarked, 'Never mind, friends; Jesus suffered like this.'[15]

Why were the police raiding spiritualist meetings? Because they classed materialisation séances as fraudulent money-making enterprises run by fake mystics. To non-believers, mediumship and psychic healing appeared to be a con-trick: the Portsmouth *Evening News* described the Master Temple group as 'charlatans'. Ordinary Master Temple services cost one shilling and sixpence, but materialisation séances cost twelve shillings and sixpence, around twenty-five pounds today. The Homers did some healing work for free and donated some profits to fundraisers – Aid to China, the Wireless Fund for the Blind, Wings for Victory, the National Savings fund. Later, when the Master Temple fell under police suspicion, these donations would be cited in court as evidence of good character. Less defensible in the 1940s was the fact that Ernest and Bessie had 'never been lawfully married'. Bessie had married another man in 1902 but they were separated. Ernest had adopted Bessie's daughter, Christine, who knew him as 'Daddy', as did the entire church community, and this evidence of benevolence and family feeling would later look good in court. Yet there were still questions about whether the Homers paid tax as a married couple or not.[16]

Nellie's family life was different: she did not donate her earnings because her workless husband and dependent children lived on them – but they lived very well. She earned at least eight pounds per séance. Thirteen Portsmouth séances raised today's equivalent of three and a half thousand pounds. Nellie had also held séances in London, Edinburgh, Glasgow, Durham, Manchester, York, Leeds, Bradford, Sheffield, Liverpool, Birmingham, Cardiff, Bristol, Gloucester, Taunton, Swindon, Torquay, Ventnor and elsewhere. Her operation was professional. In January 1944 she travelled to Portsmouth with her agent Frances Brown, forty-eight years old, a fellow medium and wife of a Sunderland colliery engineer. Frances and her family lived in 'Glenlaw', a three-bedroom bungalow in Newbottle, also on earnings from Nellie's work. The Portsmouth séances Frances booked between 12 and 19 January 1944 each had twenty to thirty attendees.[17] At each event Nellie materialised their mothers, fathers, sons, daughters, in-laws, friends and co-workers, and her spirit guides performed – Albert compering while Peggy sang and danced. She was a little Scottish girl, as Nellie had been, and police suspected 'Peggy' was actually Nellie, kneeling in the dark under a muslin sheet.

Do you believe Nellie could channel the spirits of the dead? Did *she* believe it? Those who doubted it thought her claims wicked. In one instance investigated by Portsmouth police, the mother of missing RAF navigator Freddie Nuttall visited Nellie's séance on 14 January 1944 and was told he had been shot. An enquiry by her friend on 18 January produced contradictory news: his aircraft's pilot, Pinky, had died but Freddie was 'living round about France and someone is caring for him'. Now, online RAF records show Frederick Nuttall, son of Sidney and Ellen, North End, Portsmouth, and Robert Pinkerton died when their plane exploded on 23 June 1943. Nellie was wrong. Another 'trembling' mother was told her son Cyril was dead, 'the upper part of the body being completely blown away'. For one mother of a missing son Nellie materialised a 'mutilated body . . . killed in an explosion out East'. Some people, 'full of grief', as one witness said, found closure in Nellie's stories. She herself had two sons in the RAF and Navy and lost a son-in-law fighting in Norway; perhaps she believed she comforted other mothers. But there are questions over what Nellie herself believed. When someone described her as 'an absolutely straight materialisation medium', she 'broke down and wept' – why? Relief her visions were verified? Guilt about their fakery? Many dismissed them as 'a lot of hooey', 'utter nonsense', 'a Punch and Judy show', 'out to make money from those who had probably lost somebody in the war'.[18]

Nellie's séance managers worked to deflect suspicion. Before séances her cabinet was inspected by attendees. Nellie was stripped by women, who – like examiners of the bodies of accused witches – would detect abnormalities. They searched for muslin secreted in underwear or upper body cavities, though few looked lower. Frances showed photographs of ectoplasm to new attendees. During sessions Nellie's spirits' abilities in French, Welsh, German, Gaelic and Gibraltarian Llanito were showcased.[19] But in January 1944, her luck ran out. Portsmouth police received a complaint from Stanley Worth, a twenty-nine-year-old lieutenant of the Royal Naval Volunteer Reserve at HMS *Excellent*. *Excellent* housed officers of a special branch providing training in gunnery, telegraphy, fire-fighting, damage repair, security and intelligence. Before the war Stanley was a haulage firm manager and volunteer part-time policeman. His wartime role is ambiguous. It's possible he was gathering information about threats to security and morale, but also that he worked on dull matters of logistics. Perhaps he cycled over to Copnor Road, as he claimed, because he was curious about spiritualism rather than official secrets. Later, however, rumours spread that Stanley was a government spy looking into Nellie's knowledge of HMS *Barham*. As the police investigation of the Master Temple turned into a trial, Nellie's lawyer Charles Loseby cross-examined him on the matter. Stanley protested he 'had not

been a spy, or anything in the nature of a spy, at Copnor Road',
and added, 'I was spying on my own account, if you prefer to call
it spying.'[20]

He first attended the Master Temple in 1943. But it wasn't until
a materialisation séance on 14 January 1944 that Stanley concluded
Nellie was a fake medium. During the séance Nellie's guide-spirit
Albert, speaking through her inside the cabinet, said, 'I have here
a lady who passed over with some trouble to the lower part of her
body.' Bessie prompted Stanley to ask, 'Is it for me?' 'That's the
voice,' confirmed Albert. Stanley invited the spirit out of the cabinet
and tested the white form that appeared in the darkened room:
'Are you my aunt?' All his aunts were living, but the spirit said
'yes', and accused him of behaving strangely before retreating. Then
came 'a gentleman who passed with some trouble to his chest',
whom Stanley asked, 'Are you my uncle?' Finally, Albert said, 'I
have here for the same gentleman his sister', and Stanley challenged
him: 'I have only one sister, who is alive.' 'Perhaps you don't
understand, but she was premature,' explained Albert. Stanley
retorted, 'There were no premature children in our family.' He said
he felt he 'had been defrauded' by muslin puppets speaking with
ventriloquised voices, and went to the police. They planned a raid
to catch Nellie 'red-handed', and at another materialisation séance
on the 19th, Stanley and a police constable, Thomas Cross, pounced.

Thomas leapt at Nellie, trying but failing to seize her ectoplasm.
She was arrested on suspicion of fraud, taken to Kingston Cross
police station and imprisoned in a white-tiled, metal-doored cell.
Detained overnight, she was remanded for five days in Holloway
prison where she said she was abused as 'a lazy and filthy woman',
'vile and wicked'. A female warder told her, Nellie wrote, that her
husband should divorce her and her sons disown her for her spiritualism. She was accused of nit infestation and doused in painfully
hot water. On 25 January, she was charged under the Vagrancy
Act, used to prosecute fraudulent travelling fortune-tellers. But on
8 February prosecutors substituted charges under the Witchcraft
Act of 1735, enabling more serious offences to be alleged. With

the use of the 1735 Act, Nellie was relabelled as a witch because her 'agency' was now presented as central to the pretended 'conjuration', the supposed act of raising and communicating with spirits as witches were thought to do.[21] As well as fraud and causing 'public mischief', the four co-defendants, Nellie, Frances, Bessie and Ernest, now faced accusations of conspiracy 'to pretend to exercise or use a kind of conjuration' – exactly as specified in the Act – so that 'through the agency of the said Helen Duncan spirits of deceased persons should appear to be present' and 'communicating with living persons'.[22] The mention of 'conspiracy' in the charges makes the group sound like a coven, and indeed the way they were portrayed in court and by the press shared many features with an imagined witch conspiracy.

Portsmouth magistrates passed the conduct of the trial to the Old Bailey court in London where nationally important cases were judged. John Maude KC would be prosecuting, assisted by Henry Elam. John, raised by actor-manager parents, was at ease in court. An aspiring Conservative politician, he had connections in the War Office. Nellie's supporters suggested he was employed by the state to frame her as a security risk because of her supernatural knowledge. But despite his counter-espionage experience, prosecuting her was just another job, albeit an unusual one. Simultaneously, John was defending a murder suspect in the adjoining courtroom. He and Henry Elam, a similarly high-flying junior counsel, were sure they could win their case, and were delighted by the defence team's approach.[23]

Nellie's defence was led by Charles Loseby, appointed by a spiritualist organisation. He was a passionate spiritualist and a stubborn fighter. Charles had served in British colonial and military regiments since 1906, joining both a South African and English cadet force. In 1917, he was promoted to captain in the Lancashire Fusiliers and awarded the Military Cross. Gassed in 1915 and wounded in 1917, by the war's end he was so ill with pain and 'neurosis' that he was prescribed electric shock therapy. In 1918 he was elected a member of Parliament for the National Democratic and Labour Party, a Liberal-facing splinter group, where he campaigned on behalf of veterans. When the party collapsed in 1922, he became a Conservative, but was not re-elected. Instead, he pursued a law career and chaired a psychic research society. A wealthy, educated man, Charles shared little with the defendants beyond spiritualism.[24] He was assisted in court by the urbane Tom Simpson-Pedler, about to marry a viscount's daughter.[25] But all Tom's suaveness could not improve the defence strategy.

The defence team might have argued their clients' beliefs were unusual but sincere. They might have said the four promised nothing definite to willing attendees at a performance of religious theatre. They could have argued about magical vocabulary: Nellie's séances contained nothing like 'conjuration', no chanted spells or rites, no demons raised. But they didn't. To be fair, the Witchcraft Act – which defined claiming any supernatural ability as 'pretence' – offered them limited wriggle room. So, Charles Loseby decided to argue that Nellie's abilities were not supernatural. They were natural and everything spiritualists asserted was true. There was no death; spirits lived on into another world. Nellie's materialisations were all real – no muslin, no ventriloquism. Charles produced over forty witnesses who described her work as completely authentic.[26] Perhaps he thought the jury would accept the dead were only 'dead – so called . . . not dead, but alive and vibrant with happiness and hope' because another version of this belief was central to Christianity. However, by 1944 many people were sceptical even of that. Among the Homers' congregation some doubted Nellie too and several Master Temple mediums were witnesses for the prosecution: Charles Burrell testified Nellie was a fraud and Taylor Ineson recounted teasing her, joking about her size and using the words 'bloody twisters'.[27]

Meanwhile, the defence team also treated Nellie with startling disrespect at the trial, which began on 23 March 1944. Charles said he saw all his clients as 'unimportant people', merely illustrations of spiritualist theories that he wanted to prove true. For him, Nellie was 'a kind of conduit-pipe' for spirits, 'a big fat woman', 'uninspired', 'a nobody', not 'an educated woman or a clever woman' and unable to 'speak in cultured English'. The jury should reject evidence of fraud because 'it involves deep thinking on the part of Mrs Duncan, which you may think is totally and absolutely ridiculous'.[28] This attempt to depict clients as too ignorant to be frauds appears misogynistic as well as snobbish. As an MP Charles did support feminist reforms like 'complete equal rights with men in industry'. But he opposed the extension of voting rights to all women over twenty-one in 1920 because 'there is an educational value attached to the vote'. Many women were too ignorant to make political decisions, he argued. The disapproving puzzlement of fellow MPs at this claim prefigured the way Charles's treatment of his female clients was received in court in 1944.

He did not invite Nellie or Bessie or Frances to speak in their own defence. The only defendant asked to speak was Ernest Homer. Charles decided he would only call Nellie if she was in a trance – her own voice would be silent, but a spirit guide like Albert would speak through her. He saw this as 'the acid test to which this woman ought to be willing to subject herself'. He hoped the courtroom could become a laboratory for testing Nellie's alleged 'witchcraft', if the judge allowed it – an idea that had been tempting lawyers since the eighteenth century. So, Charles asked the jury – seven people, as was the rule in wartime Britain – to pressure the judge, Sir Gerald Dodson, into accepting this unusual procedure. But both judge and jury declined, so instead Charles spoke for Nellie: 'I was a materialisation medium,' he said in his speeches to the jury. 'I was pilloried throughout the country as a fraud and an imposter and a cheat . . .' It was an act of ventriloquism as impressive as anything Nellie had been accused of. Utterly voiceless at their own trial, Nellie, Frances and Bessie could neither demonstrate their practices, nor speak about them. Later, a friend of Charles recalled regretfully that 'the method of proceeding in that case really did deprive [Nellie] of words that could be put in the defence'.[29]

During the trial it was also accidentally revealed that Nellie was a repeat offender – and Frances, too, had been previously convicted of shoplifting in 1929. The defence discussed events as far back as 1933 in their evidence, so the prosecution obtained permission also to reveal convictions at earlier dates, surely influencing the verdict. In 1933 Nellie had been convicted of fraudulent mediumship for representing the spirit Peggy with a vest masquerading as ectoplasm and attacking those who revealed the deception with a chair, 'foul and blasphemous language' and 'screamed curses'. Although Nellie supposedly shouted from the dock, 'I never did!', when on 31 March 1944 the prosecution and defence concluded their cases, the jury took just twenty-five minutes to find all four defendants guilty. Sobbing, 'I have done nothing. I have never done anything. Oh God! Is there a God? It's all lies!', Nellie was sent to prison for nine months, Frances for four. She served six of these, with Frances serving her full term. While the Homers were convicted, both were allowed to remain free because they had good reputations, and Bessie even continued to work as a faith healer, a 'demonstrator' of mediumship and a masseuse. Supporters unsuccessfully appealed the convictions of Nellie and Frances – but both remained in jail.[30]

As part of their campaign, her spiritualist backers sometimes labelled Nellie Britain's 'last witch' because they thought her the victim of a witch trial: certainly the magical language sometimes used to describe her ('conjuration', 'blasphemous', 'curses') recalled those trials. But, because of the changes in legal definitions and religious beliefs that we've seen, by 1944 the term 'witch trial' had usually come to mean something less magical: a 'miscarriage of justice, farce, conspiracy', as critics put it. In their opinion, the Portsmouth chief constable's reference to HMS *Barham* and government secrets during the court case was evidence that the state had begun to consider Nellie a security risk back in 1941 because she had revealed the ship's sinking before its official announcement. So, on a return visit to Portsmouth in 1944, they had framed her, plotting with Stanley Worth. It was a neat story, particularly because it linked Nellie's magical powers with shipwreck – just like the North Berwick and Vardø witches who'd also offended their governments – and it made Nellie look like a subversive threat to the state, a Michelet-style heroine.[31] However, evidence of state conspiracy to indict Nellie as a revolutionary witch is slim. HMS *Barham*'s loss took two months to be announced to the public, giving Nellie plenty of time to hear rumours of the sinking, so her knowledge of it was not supernatural.[32] And indeed, the prime minister, Winston Churchill, described the choice to hold a Witchcraft Act trial as 'obsolete tomfoolery'.

Yet a witch trial made sense for prosecutors in other ways. Although it was not directly motivated by HMS *Barham*'s sinking, it was driven by wartime concern about fake mysticism, seen in headlines such as 'Fake Seances to Cheat War-Bereaved'. The ancient date of the Act presented mediumship as a historical throwback, making Nellie 'appear to be a ridiculous person, a kind of witch – we all dislike witches', as Charles Loseby put it. Her rebranding as an occult threat did position her, Bessie, Frances and Ernest in a history of witch-hunting. And similar cases were to follow with another medium, Jane Yorke, convicted under the Witchcraft Act in September 1944.[33] Witches were, as we've seen, predominantly women regarded as politically subversive, religiously heretical, medically unqualified, socially disorderly and sexually immoral. All these describe the Portsmouth Four.

Nellie's reputation as a medium actually survived her trial. Like Marie-Catherine Cadière, outside the courtroom she was greeted by weeping 'disciples' with 'posies of flowers'. On her release, she recovered from 'that awful place' (HMP Holloway) and 'picked up wonderful'. She resumed séances as far from home as Plymouth, although a letter to *Psychic News* in 1945 suggests her increased reliance on morphine and alcohol made them disappointing. Allegations of fraud continued. Nellie died in 1956 while a Nottingham séance was under police investigation: Charles Loseby claimed: 'Helen Duncan was murdered.' In his view, the police had now executed their witch. From as far afield as New Zealand and South Africa, money trickled into a 'Helen Duncan Fund' to defend mediums. In 1951, Britain repealed the 1735 Witchcraft Act and replaced it with legislation explicitly targeting fraudulent mediums but not honest believers. The new legislation did not mention conjuration or other witch-like practices.[34]

Spiritualism was not witchcraft, but in many ways mediums were like witches. Whether it was the fifteenth or the twentieth century, women like Nellie were seen as ready conduits for supernatural forces. For witches these forces were demonic; for mediums they were ghostly or spiritual. In both cases the women were perceived as mere vessels: uneducated, overemotional and nowhere near as interesting as their supernatural visitors. Yet their visitors gave them unexpected cultural power. I suspect Nellie enjoyed impressing observers who would normally have sneered at or ignored her. She transformed her much-mocked plump body into a money-making generator of ectoplasmic magic. And she created a supportive community for herself: coven-like church leaders and congregations who were 'mostly women'. Whether we approve of her work or not, she was in some ways a pioneering female activist and professional. When she was put on trial, other pioneers defended her, even if some doubted her abilities, such as MPs Ellen Wilkinson and Eleanor Rathbone, and Eva Barrett of the National Council of Women. Women less in the public eye also protested, writing to government and newspapers: Mary Alice Hadwen, a market gardener's wife who assembled a petition; Dorothy Cope, an engineer's wife and mother of a missing soldier; Dora Paterson, a Manchester teacher, and others. These ordinary séance attendees all believed in Nellie's skill.[35]

Often, we think of such beliefs as belonging to a far-distant past. But they are actually endemic in cultures that describe themselves as 'rational' or 'scientific'. The survival of the spirit after death is a central pillar of Christianity today, so 1940s British spiritualism intersected neatly with mainstream belief – and in many ways it still would. Even if you don't believe in the pow-wow magic of Pennsylvania or in Nellie's spiritualism, have you ever prayed for a soul? Read a horoscope? Shivered at a ghost story? Thought an event was an omen? Such beliefs haven't lost their power any more than demonological thinking has. And such ideas are, of course, far wider than Western Christianity. Spiritualism drew on Eastern ideas of reincarnation as well as of the Christian heaven. Mid-twentieth-century mysticism appropriated ancient ideas from the Indian subcontinent, Egypt, the 'Middle' and 'Far' East – beliefs brought home by imperial adventurers. The Homers' Master Temple advertised 'Egyptian Séances', and many of its mediums claimed Indian, Chinese or Native American spirit guides. Nellie herself spent the evenings of her trial reading *The Teachings of Silver Birch*, written by the editor of the newspaper *Psychic News* with, supposedly, his Native American spirit guide.[36]

The belief that spiritual wisdom is to be found worldwide, especially among colonised peoples who are magically superior to their colonisers, is still potent. In the past, colonial powers had found that demonising the religious cultures of indigenous peoples as 'witchcraft' was a useful tool. But as with Nellie Duncan's spiritualism, some of these beliefs took on a life of their own in the cultures of their colonisers. Beliefs about witchcraft as a crime were exported by colonisers, but they came back as beliefs about witchcraft as empowerment. And in some of Europe's colonies, the idea of witchcraft continued to be used as a tool of repression and rebellion.

CHAPTER ELEVEN

The Trial of Bereng Lerotholi and Gabashane Masupha: Magical Murder at the End of European Empire

In a dusty red ravine just beyond the last huts of the village there's a steep-sided gully with a pool in the bottom. In the pool a body lies, face down, half-naked and muddied – a pitiful sight. It's the body of a young man with epilepsy, 'Meleke Ntai. Two days ago – 4 March 1948 – 'Meleke went to a funeral with his cousins, riding together on their bony horses through the heat of the day. It's autumn in Lesotho, and temperatures are beginning to fall at night towards the annual low in June, but the young men had no need to hurry home. The night would be mild enough for the blankets they wore to keep them warm. Yet some of 'Meleke's cousins galloped on ahead, leaving him behind. Then someone – many people – came for 'Meleke out of the dark, or so villagers told police as they clustered round the ravine, staring down at his body. They'd heard a car, horses, men on foot. Now 'Meleke lies dead, and when police turn his body over, they observe with a shudder that his lips are missing. Someone, or something, seems to have sliced into his face.

In the 1940s Lesotho was a British colony, known as Basutoland after its people, the Basotho, and British police ran the justice system as well as much of the country's government. These police categorised 'Meleke Ntai's death as a murder. To them, it looked like one of a series of murders committed throughout the decade, apparently so that the body parts of victims could be used in magical charms. Such killings did occur, and they were known as 'witchcraft murders', 'ritual murders' and, in local Sesotho language, 'liretlo murders'. Liretlo was a name for charms made of animal horns, containing the body parts of lions, bulls, birds and people that had been burned to ashes and mixed with fat. To British colonists, the charms were reminiscent of the magic they remembered as being practised by witches in their own countries in the past, and so they labelled liretlo users 'witches' or 'witch-doctors'.[1] 'Africa's most terrible form of witchcraft', shouted one newspaper report, 'is increasing in Basutoland . . . ritual murder in which men and women are disembowelled while still alive.' With this 'witchcraft of murder', the reporter added, indigenous Basotho leaders hoped to magically bolster their power against the colonial British authorities. The people who made and used the charms did indeed think this was possible – liretlo might enable them to resist the colonisers of their country. The British were in charge of policing, taxation, foreign affairs – all the levers of political power that Basotho leaders desired.

The labelling of Basutoland as the 'Land of Witchcraft' in the Western press was a misreading of Basotho culture, however. Basotho people did not believe that liretlo was evil, but rather understood it as part of a tradition of good magic performed by shaman-like healers called 'lingaka' (plural of 'ngaka'). Liretlo prepared by a ngaka could help win a court case or prepare for war, they thought. It was like pow-wow magic: helpful and positive. In Basotho culture malevolent witches were called 'baloi' and were imagined cursing and blighting their enemies – completely different to lingaka and their focus on helping people. However, the Christian missionaries who came to Africa in the nineteenth century felt much the same as Heinrich Kramer when it came to magic: for them it was all demonic. These missionaries brought to Africa a belief in devil-worship, like that described by Frederick Kaigh and Montague

Summers, which was quite alien to African ideas. When they welded this fear of Satanism onto concerns about the use of body parts in African lingaka's magic, it was easy for them to see the making of liretlo charms as demonic and the users of charms as 'witches'.[2]

Basotho lingaka did use human body parts in their magic. But the practice had a complex history. In the 1800s, the Basotho fought Zulu, British soldiers and South African settlers for their country, and their defence included liretlo charms made from the bodies of already dead enemies. Burning severed body parts and mixing them into ointment was believed to transfer opponents' strength to Basotho warriors.[3] When the colonial wars ended in the 1880s, in European imperial control, a new source of body parts had to be found. By the 1940s it was clear that ordinary Basotho villagers were sometimes being killed for liretlo ingredients, and the colonial authorities blamed Basutoland's indigenous leaders: lingaka certainly, but more importantly the district governors who employed them, whom they held responsible for commissioning liretlo charms. These governors were called 'marena' (headmen or kings). But beyond the district marena, the British even thought that Basutoland's queen-regent, 'Mantšebo Amelia 'Matšaba Seeiso, could be involved in liretlo murders. She was keen to curb British officials' power, so much so that they described her as disobeying 'orders' and engaging in 'active opposition', questioning their directives, which tried to cut her and her marena out of decision-making about their country.[4]

In May 1945, three years before 'Meleke Ntai's murder, the body of a man named Thulasizoe Stephen Thobeha had been found just two miles from Matsieng, 'Mantšebo's royal palace. It was a sensational, horrible discovery. The flesh of Thulasizoe's head and neck, jawbone, tongue, ears and eyes had been cut off and taken away.[5] That and the proximity of the body to the palace complex caused colonial officials to suspect 'Mantšebo. As queen-regent, governing on behalf of her toddler stepson, 'Mantšebo ruled Basutoland alongside British officials in an uneasy dual administration that left most power actually in British hands.[6] British officials knew she was insecure in her post. Perhaps, they reasoned, she had turned to liretlo to boost her power. However, it would be controversial to accuse Basutoland's queen of 'witchcraft murder'. Instead, the spotlight of the developing liretlo enquiry turned on lesser leaders – the marena governing Basutoland's districts and individual villages. Many of them were also suspected of other magically motivated killings as well.

Two of Basutoland's most powerful marena in the 1940s were Bereng Griffith Lerotholi and Gabashane David Masupha, combining the royal status of princes with the political power of cabinet ministers. They were both charismatic, forceful celebrities: Bereng quiet and decisive; Gabashane jovial, quick-witted and outgoing. They drove shiny Buicks and Cadillacs and wore traditional blankets and European trouser-suits with equal elegance. They drank fine French wines, hunted game with Italian rifles and read American literature. They were citizens of the world, who held court magnificently while subjects chanted praise poems. This glamour made them dangerous, both to 'Mantšebo and to British administrators.

Chief of these were the Basutoland resident commissioners Charles Arden-Clarke (from 1942 to 1946) and Aubrey Forsyth-Thompson (from 1946 to 1951) and the high commissioner for Southern Africa, Sir Evelyn Baring (from 1944 to 1951). They and their co-workers wrote fretful accounts of both men: virtues ('well-behaved . . . efficient . . . progressive' (Bereng); 'well educated . . . temperate . . . anxious to cooperate . . . charming . . . reads a good deal' (Gabashane)); and vices ('very reserved and shy . . . not easy to gain his confidence . . . stormy' (Bereng); and 'a potentate with almost absolute rights . . . precipitate . . . defiant . . . hostile . . . cruel' (Gabashane)) – all, of course, from their imperial point of view. Their descriptions were shaped by stereotypical expectations of Black men and their determination to keep the Basotho nation under colonial control.[7]

Bereng was the brother of 'Mantšebo's late husband, Seeiso. But when Seeiso died in 1940, Bereng had quarrelled with 'Mantšebo. Between 1941 and 1943 he argued that she should not take on Seeiso's royal role, both because she was female and because she had been married to Seeiso only through convention, not choice. It was the rule that a leader should marry his deceased brother's widow, and 'Mantšebo was taken on by Seeiso in that capacity. But instead of being disempowered by that forced marriage and abdicating the throne in favour of Bereng, 'Mantšebo had claimed her husband's nation for herself. Eventually, a British court agreed she had the right to do that on behalf of her heir, Seeiso's son. Bereng would likely never be king. He felt this defeat as a crippling blow to his dignity and influence. By the mid-1940s, Bereng was an embittered, saddened man who felt cheated out of the top job by his queen and by the British. He sought allies against 'Mantšebo.

Gabashane Masupha was not an obvious ally for Bereng. He'd been Seeiso's aide and had backed 'Mantšebo against Bereng – but since then he too had quarrelled with her. Described by racist white officials as 'obsessed with the colour-bar', in 1945 Gabashane had challenged a ticket-collector on a racially segregated South African train. When the collector interrupted the queen's meal, Gabashane shoved a handful of meat into the man's face, furiously exclaiming, 'Have some!' and embarrassing 'Mantšebo. Instead of being grateful, 'Mantšebo reprimanded Gabashane. She feared a diplomatic incident between Basutoland and the Union of South Africa – whose territory encircled the tiny Basotho kingdom. Then, when in 1946 Gabashane was tried for assaulting one of his subjects, his queen took the prosecutors' side. Gabashane narrowly avoided jail. He felt humiliated. Once he had been a bright, celebrated student at Fort Hare 'Native College', the South African university for Black pupils, where multiple friends and teachers called him progressive, distinguished and respected, a promising leader for his country's future. How dare 'Mantšebo snub him! Gabashane was governor of the important 'Mamathe's Ward, and with Bereng – governor of Phamong Ward – he created a strong anti-'Mantšebo faction. Both men were also critical of British policy and ran their districts with little reference to white officials. When challenged about holding 'secret' meetings or refusing to implement imperial laws, they shrugged and promised compliance. But they didn't comply.[8]

Under pressure from imperial governors and feeling sidelined by their queen, perhaps Bereng and Gabashane did seek magical power in liretlo charms. Certainly they turned to the Catholic Church – of which they were both members – for spiritual support against the British. The Bishop of Basutoland helped politically, protesting to the imperial government in London that in his view colonial administrators wanted 'to do away with the Native Government'. While some British officials wanted to strengthen marena's power, building towards Basotho self-rule, because they thought this ethically right, others belittled and threatened local leaders. This internal division within Basutoland worsened another threat: aggression by the Union of South Africa, where the 1948 election brought to power the National Party, expansionist imperialists and creators of apartheid. South African ambition to incorporate Basutoland grew as their government observed British–Basotho divisions, and a South African invasion would be cataclysmic. Many Basotho worked as miners in the Union and knew its openly racist laws, which had produced a segregated, murderous society. Queen 'Mantšebo even pleaded for the removal of South African workers from Basutoland's British administration: 'We are afraid of them,' she said simply.[9]

As colonial tensions increased, so did reports of killings: seventeen 'witchcraft murders' were reported in 1947 and twenty-five in 1948. They were attributed to various Basotho leaders, mostly the headmen of villages and district governors. Still nobody had been prosecuted for murdering Thulasizoe Thobeha, although 'Mantšebo was suspected of ordering the crime. But in March 1948, the discovery of 'Meleke Ntai's body ignited what became an international crisis. Viewing it, medical examiner Dr Robert Ogg concluded he had been murdered, as villagers alleged. But, he added, it was also possible 'Meleke had simply fallen into the pool where he was discovered, perhaps after an encounter with a crowd of revellers or an epileptic fit and accidentally drowned. There were no indisputable signs of violence on his body and crabs in the pool might have eaten his lips. This uncertainty would prove important, but for now the authorities were satisfied a murder had been committed.

Fusi Rakokoli, a ngaka, was initially blamed, then 'Meleke's cousin Moloi Ntai. Then a disturbing theory emerged: that Moloi had contracted with Bereng and Gabashane to murder 'Meleke, in order to provide liretlo ingredients for them. In this version of 'Meleke's death, Bereng and Gabashane stood accused of a monstrous crime: coveting the blood and lips of their innocent neighbour as magical trophies to promote their own political games. It would be a controversial step for the British authorities to detain two of Basutoland's senior marena on such shocking charges. But in July 1948 they did so. The Basotho community were stunned as their leaders were questioned, handcuffed, marched out of their sprawling mud-brick mansions and driven away to prison.

As that chill July ended, the British began to build a case against the two marena, conducting interviews and interrogations. They based the charges on the evidence of 'crown witnesses': some of 'Meleke's cousins, villagers living near the crime scene and officials working for Bereng and Gabashane. These crown witnesses were people who had identified themselves as accomplices in murdering 'Meleke and then incriminated others in return for clemency. It was hardly a transparent process, and it strongly recalled a witch trial, but it allowed the authorities to charge Bereng and Gabashane with 'Meleke's murder. Having gone that far, they also reconsidered their attitude to Basutoland's queen. Since they suspected her of involvement in least one similar murder, maybe they should act against her too?

By early August 1948, Bereng, Gabashane and several accomplices had all been charged with ordering and carrying out one liretlo murder, that of 'Meleke Ntai. Now 'Mantšebo was accused of another murder. There had been insufficient evidence and political will to charge her with complicity in Thulasizoe's killing in 1945, but, when in 1948 a herder, Borane Kali, also disappeared near her home, action was taken. Police told 'Mantšebo they had 'witnesses to prove she had murdered this boy for "medicine"' – meaning, to make a charm. 'I personally have been searched disgracefully,' 'Mantšebo wrote, 'my children . . . arrested.' When the lost man was, embarrassingly, found alive, the police backed off. But by then it appeared they had wanted to accuse all three Basotho leaders as murderous witches.[10] When Bereng and Gabashane were then accused of another liretlo murder dating back to 1946, the picture of a nation in crisis was complete.

Once they had been charged, Bereng and Gabashane were summoned to preliminary hearings about 'Meleke's murder, beginning on 3 August 1948. The Basutoland National Council Chamber – being used as a British courtroom – was 'packed to the doors' by spectators who'd walked along frost-hardened dirt roads to Basutoland's capital Maseru that winter morning. At this pre-trial hearing before a British district commissioner, two of Gabashane's half-brothers, Jonathan and Mapeshoane Masupha, accused him and Bereng of ordering 'Meleke's murder and drawing them in as accomplices. In particular, Mapeshoane told of a secret planning meeting, where Gabashane said 'he wanted something from a person who would be killed'.

The next day, Mapeshoane said, 'Meleke was captured and throttled into unconsciousness, and another accomplice cut off his lips while he was still alive. A further witness, Sepalami Mathibe, told the preliminary hearing that this mutilation was ordered by Bereng in person, but Bereng then rejected the liretlo flesh because 'Meleke did not bleed much from his wound. Bereng then told the group to throttle 'Meleke to death, Sepalami concluded, while Gabashane looked on. That would make both of them guilty of murder – ordering a killing was treated in the same way as actually carrying it out. The evidence looked bad for Bereng and Gabashane and Maseru's district commissioner E. C. Butler committed all the accused – the two marena and the accomplices – for trial. The crowd drifted away, excitedly debating.

*

Panic shuddered across southern Africa, inflamed by racist fears. 'Spiritual Danger in Basutoland', shrieked the Diocese of Bloemfontein in South Africa, warning witchcraft murder was rife, along with secret rites attempting 'to communicate with evil spirits . . . dancing, singing and feasting' – a misrepresentation of indigenous religion. Meanwhile, on 30 July, a new proclamation was issued by the British Basutoland government requiring lingaka to obtain a five-pound licence. It prohibited any ngaka from practising as 'a diviner . . . rain doctor or lightning doctor or the use of spells or charms', advising 'any person to bewitch or injure persons or property' or supplying any 'pretended means of witchcraft'. The liretlo crisis had blossomed into a witch-hunt, a wider crackdown on magical practitioners. It was different from a traditional witch-hunt in some ways – less violent, more bureaucratic and based on a series of verifiable, physical killings rather than supposed magical harm – but it was strikingly similar in its aim to show who was in charge. As in Norway and Massachusetts, in 1940s Basutoland a witch trial was being used to facilitate and showcase colonial power by putting indigenous people on trial.[11]

Between the preliminary hearing and the start of their trial on 2 November 1948, Bereng and Gabashane were held in Maseru jail, in a dismal complex of concrete cells. And on the 2nd they were driven to the capital's High Court, where a retired judge from the Supreme Court of South Africa, George Sutton, would preside over their trial with two 'Native' and two European 'assessors' – advisors and translators. There would be no jury. The Basutoland attorney general Arthur Thompson KC prosecuted, while N. J. Grobler KC of Bloemfontein defended his long-term client Bereng, and Israel Maisels KC of Johannesburg (who would one day defend Nelson Mandela) represented Gabashane. First, Arthur Thompson explained how murder could provide body parts for liretlo charms. There was ample evidence that since around 1900 some forty or fifty people had been killed for this purpose, their body parts sliced away both before and after they died. Medical reports showed how some of their wounds had been inflicted before death, how they had bled, and how severed limbs, heads and blood had been carried away for use in charms. 'Meleke's murder, Arthur said, was just another example of this abhorrent crime.

He may have been right. But Dr Robert Ogg, the medical examiner, was not so sure. As he stood in the witness box, sweating, Robert wavered over whether 'Meleke's death was murder or not. He had become more uncertain over time. Had 'Meleke simply drowned? Could crabs have eaten his lips after death? Robert and a second physician who had examined 'Meleke's body had found 'no signs of any assault', he explained, to a hushed courtroom. 'Meleke might be a victim of liretlo murder, or he might not. The two defence counsels seized on this uncertainty and cross-examined Robert at length. Eventually he was forced to concede: 'The injuries I found on the body . . . were caused by crabs.' Smiling, Israel Maisels and N. J. Grobler summed up, each for his own client: so, if 'Meleke had not definitely been assaulted, his lips not severed by a knife, and he had drowned – was this witchcraft murder at all? If not, how could Bereng and Gabashane be guilty?

Some of the prosecution evidence was less convenient for the defence. Could 'Meleke have fallen off his horse into the stream? It was far from his route home, so maybe not. Someone had unsaddled his horse and taken some of his clothing, so kidnapping seemed likely. Mapeshoane and another man who claimed to be an accomplice, Sothi Chela, reiterated their stories of the murder confidently. But as the first rains of spring fell on Maseru in mid-November, Gabashane took the witness stand. He attacked his accusers directly as 'bad characters', pointing to further flaws in their evidence. They had described how 'Meleke's lips were severed on the left-hand side, but the post-mortem showed the right side missing. They had alleged Gabashane's Buick was at the crime scene, but the car was being serviced at that time. Mapeshoane was caught lying: he claimed good relations with his wife, but she had left him after he threatened to stab her. Gabashane had taken Mapeshoane's knife away and punished him, giving Mapeshoane motive to incriminate him. It was a full rebuttal of the accusations against him, and the defence teams were jubilant.

But there was a growing cloud on the horizon: Gabashane's proof of inconsistencies and lies in the prosecution case did not appear in the local, white-run newspaper, the *Basutoland News*. Instead, a worryingly simple and consistent version of the accomplice evidence was publicised across southern Africa and the rest of the world. We don't know exactly how Gabashane phrased his rebuttal in court because his voice was being edited out of public coverage of his defence.[12] Perhaps, unsurprisingly, the British justice system and the British media were primed to disbelieve the two marena – as they would find out on the morning of 16 November. That morning, all the accused – the marena and at least ten accomplices – were herded into the dock for the verdict. Each man wore a metal sign around his neck, 'a big number plate to distinguish him', as one journalist wrote. It was a vile image, one Tatabe would have recognised from a slave auction, and although it was often the practice in mass trials of accused Black people in southern Africa, it was a shock after the apparent civility with which the trial of the respected marena had been conducted.

In stuffy, tense, unseasonal heat, these labelled Black men now faced their white judge. Accomplice witnesses had 'told a circumstantial and terrible story with a wealth of detail', Judge George Sutton announced. 'Mapeshoane was cross-examined in great detail,' he said, and 'his evidence was not shaken.' This was not wholly true; some of it had been badly shaken, indeed contradicted in court. And other inconsistencies were overlooked too: 'Sothi's evidence is, in many respects, at variance with that of Mapeshoane,' the judge admitted. But, he claimed, Sothi 'is an unintelligent man of weak character', which explained how he had come to make mistakes. Sepalami and Mapeshoane's evidence was 'substantially in agreement', and the judge was confident: 'I cannot believe that it was concocted,' he concluded, so 'the accused will be found guilty of murder.'

A murmur ran round the courtroom, followed by a stunned silence: these senior African leaders had been found guilty of witchcraft murder! Were they to be executed? That was the approved penalty. Grimly, the defence teams shuffled papers and whispered with their clients, who were each asked to make a statement. And that statement would have a set theme: it must be an argument explaining why the death penalty should not be chosen as punishment. Calmly, Bereng stood up and told the court, 'This matter is merely a lie.' The prosecution, he contended, had failed 'to establish as to how the deceased met his death'. He shrugged off the judge's attribution of guilt, just as he ignored the humiliating metal sign around his neck. 'I stand much higher than to condescend to such a thing,' Bereng declaimed. 'I am the second son of the late Paramount Chief Griffith . . . I am proud of my position.' No 'dead flesh', he sneered, could improve upon it. Bereng defied George Sutton: 'If you are satisfied with this evidence, do as you wish, but as for the case, it has been concocted.' Gabashane agreed flatly, unusually subdued. 'My senior brother has said all that is necessary,' he said, and sat down. Unmoved, George Sutton put on the black cap reserved for the moment of sentencing and he condemned both Bereng and Gabashane, plus two accomplices, to death.[13] Suddenly the whole trial looked like a foregone conclusion – a brief, unconvincing performance leading to a pre-scripted end.

Bereng and Gabashane were driven back to jail. Although they must have been stunned by the judgment, they rallied to plan a response with their defence teams. They would take their case to the Privy Council in London, they decided, the highest court for British imperial subjects. The Council was not an appeal court, but the lords who staffed it could intervene in the legal process and stop executions or reverse verdicts if they felt there had been 'infringement of the essential principles of justice'. The case would be heard in Britain's capital, and here Bereng and Gabashane would be represented by the lawyer Dingle Foot, a long-term critic of colonial law. They were not permitted to attend in person. The appeal case would take many months to prepare and Bereng and Gabashane would spend that period in Maseru jail, waiting to see whether or not they would be hanged. During that time, they spoke to their families, followers, interested anthropologists and journalists, preparing everyone for the worst but hoping for the best.

Their appeal case was heard in July 1949, in a cramped, wooden-panelled room in 9 Downing Street – the historic terraced townhouse next door to the British prime minister's official home. Around a table piled with law books, Dingle Foot fought for his clients' lives. Bereng and Gabashane's conviction was unjust, Dingle explained to the lords. The medical evidence was inconclusive, accomplice witnesses unreliable. Some of the witnesses had now also alleged they had been coerced into making accusations, he said; certainly they had been detained for months, hungry, cold and frightened. Some had claimed they were offered bribes and told to replicate each other's evidence. 'It was suggested to me,' 'Meleke's cousin Moloi Ntai had stated, 'that I should say the Chief [Gabashane] offered me money to kill the deceased . . . if I accepted this suggestion I should not be charged with murder.' Instead of sole reliance on such accomplice testimony, Dingle argued, corroborating proof of guilt should obviously have been found. Basutoland law required independent evidence to prove at least that the deceased had been murdered. Dingle argued that the medical examiners' opinion did not do that.

As Dingle concluded his arguments and left the room, he knew the lords would take several months to examine the case and announce their judgment. But he was hopeful of a good outcome for Bereng and Gabashane because the 1947 witchcraft murder appeal of Tumahole Bereng had provided him with a near-identical precedent for their case. Tumahole's conviction had been overturned by the lords very recently, in January 1949, because the medical evidence of murder was ambiguous, just as it was with Bereng and Gabashane. The lords had re-examined all the trial paperwork and decided that despite the original trial verdict, it was not clear Tumahole was guilty beyond all reasonable doubt. He was freed. But when the lords announced the outcome of Bereng and Gabashane's case, Dingle was crushed. The lords concluded 'Meleke Ntai had definitely been murdered. The motive, they stated, was the gathering of liretlo flesh, and Bereng and Gabashane had clearly ordered the killing. Therefore their conviction should be upheld.

In secret letters, colonial administrators cynically praised 'their Lordships' ingenuity in distinguishing this [case] from Tumahole'. But even they admitted the lords' reasoning was 'hardly convincing in logic'. Impartial observers were outraged by the injustice of the decision. In London the Reverend Michael Scott, an anti-colonial clergyman, led a campaign petitioning church and state officials for a reprieve for Bereng and Gabashane. A fat file of testimonials to their good characters, mostly letters from Gabashane's university teachers and white friends in Basutoland and Britain, was amassed. Compellingly, Michael Scott argued Britain was imitating the Union of South Africa in its injustice to two innocent Black Africans.

Meanwhile, in Basutoland, some of Bereng and Gabashane's followers took direct action. They attempted to rescue the men from Maseru jail on 28 July. A crowd of prisoners assembled in the dusty jail-yard and overpowered the gate guards; they dragged Bereng and Gabashane to the entrance, speeding them on their way with chanting and clapping. But Bereng and Gabashane refused to be saved. It was beneath their dignity to run from the jail as fugitives. Instead, both men turned away from the open road outside the gates and walked back in silence to their cells.[14]

Bereng, Gabashane and the two accomplice witnesses were hanged on 3 August 1949. The international press reported their deaths as punishment for 'using parts of [a] body for witchcraft', echoing the verdict of their witch trial. But in his last letter, published by the journal *Inkululeko*, Bereng wrote: 'It is untrue these cruel murders are committed by the chiefs. The Government has found a trick by which the chiefs can be taken by surprise and killed under the pretext of law.' He called this injustice 'genocide'. In the 1990s, Gabashane's widow, 'Mamathe, told historians that Bereng was justified in his outrage. 'Mamathe's view was that both Bereng and her husband were executed as witches by a government who hated 'enlightened' marena: 'The police had been instructed to find people who would claim they were present [at the murder] when in fact they were telling lies,' she said. 'It was such a heart-breaking lie.'

The accusations against Bereng and Gabashane were underpinned by deeply faulty colonial assumptions about witchcraft and race. Their convictions were widely seen as stamping down indigenous peoples' ambitions for self-rule in southern Africa, at a time when the wider British Empire was bankrupt and crumbling in the aftermath of the Second World War. While resistance was peaceful in Basutoland – taking the form of political argument rather than insurgency – in other places open warfare had broken out: Malaya, Palestine and India. In this context, Bereng and Gabashane's execution was described by Black-owned American newspapers simply as 'ironhand colonial rule'.[15] The men's judgment and condemnation ignored conflicting accomplice and medical evidence. Their appeal process was tainted by celebration of judicial 'ingenuity'.

And so, whatever the real story of the death of 'Meleke Ntai, Bereng and Gabashane's witch trial became part of anti-colonial African resistance. Critics were able to argue that the witchcraft murder trials of Lesotho were like the witch-hunts of old Europe: show trials of an imaginary crime designed to remove people who were thought to be enemies of the state. The witch trial was being utilised as it had been throughout history – to demonise and crush perceived opponents. In this particularly shocking and comparatively recent witch trial, the victims were the Black leaders of what would soon be independent African nations. Lesotho gained its independence in 1966, two years after 'Mantšebo's death as the stepmother of its new king. Bereng and Gabashane would have been part of its first government's administration, had they not been executed as murderous witches.[16]

Intermission: Witch Trials Today

Part Two has brought our story of witchcraft from the early eighteenth century to the mid-twentieth, explaining how the idea of the witch trial echoed through the history of those three centuries, changing over time. Witch trials became increasingly metaphorical, erupting into societies as a drama that played out anxiety about key issues: sexual boundaries and orientations, poverty and education, insanity, fraud and racial prejudice. Each trial was about wider issues, but also retained a demonological element of persecution and a magical element, which could be religious mysticism, Satanism, superstition, mediumship or a belief in charms.

Now, Part Three of the book broadens the scope of the witch trial stories it tells to think about the world we live in today. Witch trials continue, both metaphorically and in grim reality, and in both forms they demand our attention. The last two chapters focus that attention on two continents: Africa and North America. Each chapter focuses on a central trial but broadens out to include a wider discussion of the issues that have created the trial and explains how people have responded to it. The witch trials of Part Three are trials on film and TV, in novels and newscasts – trial by media as well as by judge and jury. They show the rise of new demonologies, transmitted through new communication technologies. Across the two continents, our last two witchcraft stories sum up the state of witch trials today.

PART THREE

Transformations

CHAPTER TWELVE

The Trial of 'Shula': Witchcraft in Africa

'When you sow sorghum, you harvest sorghum. When you sow maize, you harvest maize. But when you sow devil's thorns you cannot expect to harvest wheat!' With these words, Bennett Makalo Khaketla fictionalised the death of 'Meleke Ntai and Bereng and Gabashane's trial in a Sesotho-language novel published in 1951, just two years after the end of the trial. Bennett, a Basotho politician, had been a close observer of the events of 1949, and he wrote that *Mosali a Nkhola* (translated as *The Woman Has Betrayed Me*) was intended to make readers 'think carefully for themselves about liretlo murder, examine it on every side, and see how it could be brought to an end'.[1] He believed liretlo murder to be a common problem across southern Africa – under different names such as 'muti' (medicine) murder in areas where languages other than Sesotho were spoken. His novel suggested that if it was allowed to proliferate, the area's people would metaphorically reap 'devil's thorn', a spiny herb that lacerates anyone unlucky enough to touch it. How, asked Bennett, could southern African nations hope for independence when their people were being portrayed around the world as murderers and witches?

However, by 1951 some of Basutoland's anti-colonial activists claimed that no one there really believed in witchcraft or other kinds of magic anymore. Liretlo murder, they argued, did not exist except as a paranoid fantasy, and murder suspects were being persecuted for nothing at all. The evident injustices that sullied the trial of Bereng Griffith Lerotholi and Gabashane David Masupha appeared to support their argument. European history was also enlisted to contend that all trials revolving around ideas of witchcraft were self-evidently mistaken. In 1957, the Basutoland African Congress President, Ntsu Mokhehle, pointed to a double standard: Basutoland's British police had, he said, 'facilely accept[ed] that ritual murder is for using human flesh for magical compounds' because 'European belief readily welcomes the idea', and yet medieval European witchcraft accusations, he argued, were now thought to be 'fanciful charges'. While colonial administrators retorted that liretlo-related trials were for murder by violence, not by witchcraft, they could not duck the fact that suspects were being treated unjustly, similarly to the accused witches of the past. That made it hard for authorities to claim the moral high ground and act effectively, both against any liretlo murderers and also against people who wanted to harm those suspected of other types of witchcraft.[2]

Historians and anthropologists, Black and white, tell us that liretlo murders did and do occur in Lesotho and elsewhere. There is indeed good evidence that people are killed today in quite large numbers across southern Africa – sub-Saharan Africa, as it's sometimes known – so their body parts can be used in charms. Campaign groups such the Witchcraft and Human Rights Information Network and Amnesty International and international bodies such as the United Nations Human Rights Council all agree the issue is one of the most difficult facing countries such as Zambia, Malawi and Tanzania, where such murders are particularly well documented. Africans with albinism are at especial risk because their bodies are thought to be magical: 'They are being hunted for their bones and body parts, and the perpetrators are going unpunished,' reports Amnesty International. News stories such as journalist Annie Ikpa's campaign against magical child sacrifice in Uganda are troublingly common – 132 magical murders were reported there between 2019 and 2021.[3]

Meanwhile, thousands of people across southern Africa are still accused of a different kind of witchcraft – not physical murder for body parts, but the use of spells and curses to kill and harm neighbours magically. Violence against them is a daily event. In just four months in 2021, 324 witchcraft accusations were made in a single province in the Democratic Republic of Congo, with eight women reported murdered. In a neighbouring province, 114 people were accused, with five killed. Suspected witches are shot, hacked to death with axes and knives, beaten and burned. Some are simply set upon by accusers and killed immediately, while others are subjected to informal judgments delivered by secret hearings. Suspects live in terror. In 2020 Al Jazeera journalists spoke to four accused witches in the Central African Republic: Helene Ndenjia, Kamer Gabriel, Therese Yambissi and Martine Rengapou. All lived as virtual prisoners in their homes, abandoned by most of their family members. 'We are alone,' said Kamer wretchedly. 'I cannot even go outside of the house.'[4] The notion that a witch trial is an acceptable way of staging power and reasserting order continues across southern Africa, as does the accompanying belief that Christianity is an effective remedy against witchcraft.[5]

When Bennett Khaketla was writing his novel in Basutoland in the early 1950s, he believed that fictional representations of the problems both of witchcraft murders and of witch trials would reach a wider, more receptive audience than any trial record or official report. A factor that he found especially hard to raise in non-fiction was the role of Christian demonology in witchcraft belief. Accordingly, one of Bennett's characters – Pokane, a counsellor accused of witchcraft – is made to speak for Bennett in the novel. He laments:

The Church has failed in its mission. They didn't come here to win people's hearts by teaching them the ways of Christ, but to impress their senior supervisors abroad. They started off by terrifying everyone with hellfire and sulphur and burning eternally. They never made an effort to make people understand

exactly what God requires of His own children, to understand
that God is kind, loving and patient.[6]

Accordingly, he suggests, even good Christians fall into sin,
including the committing of liretlo murder and witchcraft accusation, because they are motivated by fear rather than love. The
suggested remedy is an attitudinal Christian change towards caution
in magical matters: 'education is the only answer . . . human life
is very important and should not be crushed as easily as breaking
a clay pot'.

It's striking that Pokane blames imported demonology for driving
witchcraft belief because Bennett was a committed Christian himself.
He opened his novel with a Biblical quotation and closed it with
a prayer. Yet the South African critic Toomy Selepe rightly summa-
rises the novel's argument as follows, 'if a foreign culture is imposed
on a people, it is bound to disrupt the social fabric of their lives,
thus causing mental dislocation, emotional displacement as well as
confusion of self-knowledge'. In the face of this confusion, *Mosali
a Nkhola* is an attempt to prompt conversation about witchcraft
within and beyond Africa, particularly in African churches, through
fictionalising real events.

Bennett's novel is an ancestor of an internationally award-winning
2017 film about an African witchcraft trial, *I Am Not a Witch*,
which also aimed to start conversations about southern African
witchcraft beliefs.[7] Directed by Rungano Nyoni, it's about a
Zambian child accused of witchcraft. Once upon a time, the film
begins, there was a little girl nicknamed Shula – meaning 'uprooted',
because no one knew her real name or where she was from. Shula,
played by Zambian child-actor Margaret Mulubwa, comes to an
equally nameless village, without any parents or relatives to look
after her, and is immediately suspected of being a witch. She is first
accused after staring at a woman carrying water from the well: the
woman stumbles, spilling her bucket. Soon Shula is being denounced
by the entire community who say they can no longer draw water
from their well because she has cursed it.

She is first tried by a police court, which holds a preliminary examination. A policewoman, Officer Josephine, presides over this court. Josephine questions the accusers about their stories. 'This child is a witch,' says one accuser. 'From the time that this child came into the village, lots of strange things have been happening, things that never used to happen.' Another accuser says Shula attacked him with an axe, cutting off his arm. Since he still has two arms, viewers are invited to laugh at him, and it's established that the axe attack happened in a dream. Officer Josephine is sceptical and refuses to record his testimony, but his evidence has had an effect and she is not sure how to proceed. Josephine only addresses Shula once directly, asking her name – a question to which she does not reply – and she does not feel able to dismiss the case because Shula is too overawed to confirm or deny her guilt.

Officer Josephine decides to consult a local politician, the government minister Mr Banda, about what to do. Unfortunately, Mr Banda – whose name recalls that of the then Zambian president, Rupiah Banda – is a greedy, corrupt man and spots an opportunity. If Shula is convicted, he will be able to employ her for free in his 'witch camp', a prison for witches exiled from their home villages. Here he will also be able to make money from her supposed magical skills. Mr Banda asks a nganga or witch doctor – the Zambian equivalent of a Basotho ngaka – to try Shula's case magically by killing a chicken and divining Shula's guilt from the manner of its death. If the chicken in its death throes staggers outside a chalk circle drawn on the floor, then she will be judged guilty. It's only a small circle, so of course the dying chicken flaps across the floor and leaves it: therefore, Shula is convicted. She is sent to the witch camp, a tented village in the dusty, pastel-shaded Zambian bush.

In the witch camp Shula lives with a group of women who have also been banished from their villages. Most of the convicted witches labour in the fields for local gang-masters, under Mr Banda's 'guardianship', as he puts it – in effect the politician holds the witches in a form of modern slavery, where they work for him for free. They are exhibited to gawping, camera-clicking tourists too, expected to act out spells and look scary for social media. But Mr Banda has realised he can earn even more money from presenting Shula as a diviner. She is dressed up in theatrical costumes, resplendent with ruffles and feathers, and her body is painted. She is driven to communities who need magical help and told to use her witchcraft power to identify a thief, make rain and entertain the audience of a TV chat show.

Corruption, misogyny and post-colonial economic strain shape Shula's and her fellow witches' lives: they are prisoners, commodities and spectacles. Surreally, they are prevented from flying away as far as the UK to kill people – a likely scenario according to the tourist guide – by being tethered to giant reels of fluttering white ribbon. The other prisoners are kind to Shula, but as the film goes on it is clear that her life is under threat, both from angry mobs and her 'guardian' Mr Banda. As she is driven from task to task by Mr Banda's henchmen, some people blame her for casting spells on them. The politician himself threatens her when she refuses to act out her role as a diviner – Shula is silent and passive for much of the film. The vulnerability of her position as a child witch becomes more and more worrying for viewers as we watch Shula's confused, despairing face, often blank with astonishment at the impossible tasks she is asked to perform. And sure enough, one day Shula is killed in unexplained circumstances and her tiny body dumped outside the witch camp.[8]

Shula's story is based on real witchcraft accusations and real witch camps that exist today in Zambia, Ghana and in southern Africa. Here hundreds of supposed witches, mostly women and some children, live in exile. Like the fictional Shula, many have been accused by people who dreamed that witches cursed them, and many have been tried by the chicken ritual. Speaking to Ghanaian journalist Justice Baidoo in 2019, convicted woman Wuriche Pinsuma explained she had been accused by one of her husband's other wives twenty years earlier and had lived in a witch camp ever since. Like Shula's prison, her camp is run by a powerful male governor whom inmates accuse of using them as 'cheap labour', 'just like slaves' and molesting them. Yet a witch camp still feels safer to some than home.

In another camp, Hawabu Issahaku recounted to a TV crew how her accusers back home beat her with a metal bar until 'my whole body was soaked in blood'. Like Shula, she was lucky to end her trial alive, but she remains traumatised by the way her community turned upon her, seeming not to care whether she died from her injuries or not. Convicted witches like Hawabu who are not banished to camps are often simply murdered, and their bodies dumped like Shula's is at the end of *I Am Not a Witch*.[9] Although this horrific persecution had been exposed before 2017 by documentary-makers like those who interviewed Hawabu, the fiction of *I Am Not a Witch* engaged new and wider audiences worldwide. The film won awards in the United States, South Africa, India, Canada, Britain, France, Sweden and Australia and, in conjunction with existing documentary-making and charity activism, prompted debate that spread beyond film review columns into newscasts and political action. In 2021 a United Nations resolution urged all states for the first time to 'condemn harmful practices related to accusations of witchcraft' and 'take all measures necessary' to end them.[10]

Like Bennett Khaketla's novel, Shula's story and its success in prompting debate shows how fictional representations of real events can make a difference to people's understanding of magic and witchcraft. In *I Am Not a Witch*, the focus is on raising awareness of the injustice of witch trials. Unfortunately, not all such fictions are equally thoughtful. Just as stories about witches can assist helpful change, so malign or less thoughtful ones can have real-life consequences. In particular, pastors, anthropologists and human rights activists have all suggested that Nigerian film and TV drama – known as Nollywood – is responsible for spreading real-life witchcraft accusations across Africa. Since 1991, Nollywood producers have developed a fantasy soap opera series of witch-themed dramas, which draw on Christian theology, world horror cinema and African folktale. They portray witchcraft as if it were a real threat, with witch-villains acting out a televisual demonology.

In 1992's *Living in Bondage*, Andy (Kenneth Okwonko) sacrifices his wife to a Satanic cult. In *End of the Wicked* (1999), written by real-life 'witch-hunter' Helen Ukpabio, witches including children like Shula are seen murdering and maiming victims, stealing a womb, one female witch even growing a penis before she is beaten to death. This film's opening titles demonstrably blur fiction with reality, claiming 'the powers of darkness' hampered its production. Although Nollywood was not well known outside Nigeria prior to 2003, that year the continent-wide AfricaMagic channel launched. After that, Nollywood films may have influenced accusations as far away as east Africa. Certainly, the Kenyan film-makers Mercy Murugi and Janet Kanini-Muiva criticised Nollywood's witch films in 2009 as setting a pernicious trend in Kenya, as well as neighbouring Tanzania and Zambia, Shula's home country. In 2021 Nigerian researchers summed up complaints from across the continent, concluding: 'The portrayal of witchcraft by Nollywood is promoting its existence.' They recommended film-makers assess whether audiences might turn demonology from TV fiction into real-life persecution. With Nollywood witch films now available on YouTube and Netflix, these platforms should also consider that and warn audiences worldwide about content.[11]

In 2021, Lagos film critic Bernard Dayo identified the inspiration of these Nigerian witch dramas as the same toxic combination of European and African influences described by Bennett Khaketla as operating seventy years before and 4,000 miles to the south. While Nigerian Yoruba cosmology had always contained witches who could do good or evil as healers and diviners, Bernard explained, 'the arrival of Christianity demonised these practices'. By the later years of the twentieth century this demonisation was getting worse because 'the Pentecostal churches that emerged in Nigeria in the twentieth century took supernatural evil much more seriously' than earlier sects. This – in a chicken-and-egg cycle – is partly because of ongoing Nollywood film-making, Chijioke Azuawusiefe suggested in 2020: 'By producing innumerable . . . movies that constantly reiterate the power and dangers of the occult as well as its anti-Christian values, Nollywood inadvertently makes the occult mainstream in popular religion.' 'Christian missionaries', he concluded, 'created a dualistic worldview of good and evil', and then Nollywood films adopted this demonology by portraying witches on TV.[12] Thus fiction bled into fact and good Christians today mistakenly accuse their neighbours of witchcraft in real life.

The flourishing of witch persecution across southern Africa today, like that dramatised in *I Am Not a Witch*, isn't surprising in the context of this witch trial history: throughout this book, we've seen what happens when the power of communicative media is added to a culture that prizes Christian demonology. The printed demonologies of the Reformation era transformed witchcraft beliefs into mass trials in fifteenth-century Europe; in the same way, Christianisation and the digital demonology it has shaped have changed modern Africa. Instead of books, demonology spreads today through TV streaming, social media, websites, blog posts. Africa is often portrayed as a place where witchcraft accusation 'survives', but the reality is that it held out longer than most other parts of the world against demonology. Unfortunately, the reality of witchcraft is now accepted, sometimes even by bodies trying to halt witchcraft-related violence. Like Officer Josephine, who tries to judge Shula fairly but fails, many authorities do not know what to do with the phenomenon of witchcraft accusation.

For example, in 1996 the South African government set up the Ralushai Commission in its Northern Province to report on ways to prevent further murders of suspected witches there. It was assumed the commission would begin its work by stating that witches could not actually harm anyone, so the murderers had no justification for their actions. But instead, the commission's report listed and endorsed reasons for belief in witchcraft: these included Biblical references to witches and claims such as 'Shakespeare would not have referred to witches if they did not exist' and 'all Africans historically believed in witchcraft'. The commission's members aimed sincerely to help end violence against accused witches, but they did not see how to do this without denying the existence of witchcraft – which they were unwilling to do.[13] As their reasoning shows, it's hard to untangle the cultural politics of witchcraft belief. Unhelpful fictions and reality reinforce each other, and European demonological ideas have become as influential as local ones, if not more so. As Christian missionaries built hospitals, churches and schools, trained midwives and ministers and introduced African students to Shakespeare, their insistence that the world was a binary battle between opposing forces spread. Unsurprisingly, some local congregations decided to hunt for wicked human followers of the devil.

It's certain, however, that witchcraft accusations occurred in Africa before Christianity was established. European Christians did not introduce witch trials to Africa – or other areas of colonial expansion – but, in conjunction with local people's choices, changed their nature and scale. Some trials are known from independent African kingdoms in the mid- to late nineteenth century, having been recorded by visiting Europeans. The trials they describe share common features, suggesting that a culture of witch prosecution was established before it was perceived by European observers. For example, in 1880 in Bulawayo – 800 miles north of Lesotho in Zimbabwe – the AmaNdebele king Lobengula Khumalo had his sister Mncengence and six others hanged for witchcraft. Mncengence was thought to have bewitched Lobengula's wife Xwalile, causing infertility. Lobengula was also said to have executed nine or ten other 'witches' monthly, indicating the practice was shockingly common at least under his rule.

Meanwhile, in the militantly anti-Christian Madagascan Merina kingdom, mass witch trials of rebellious districts were reported in the mid-nineteenth century. People were forced by royal officials to swallow a poison test. Those who died were pronounced guilty, those who survived innocent. In 1892, in the Xhosa kingdom of Mpondoland, settlers reported the torture of a suspected witch, Mamatiwane, stepmother of King Sigcau Kamqikela. Their intervention saved her. Other African rulers, such as the early nineteenth-century Zulu leader Shaka, were said to have had different attitudes. Shaka challenged 'witch-doctors' who smelled out witches – their favoured method of detection – and executed those he considered false diviners. Belief in witchcraft thus appears to have been widespread across nineteenth-century Africa, with regular trials. But witch-hunts on the scale we have seen in Europe and America appear limited.[14]

However, in the years during which Africa was most invasively colonised by European powers – roughly 1880 to 1960 – African societies and cultures were changing fast. The idea of witchcraft was reframed by Christian newcomers, and, to them, magic of any kind was unacceptable. Alongside this, scholars have recently suggested that the earlier trans-Atlantic trade in enslaved people was seen by its victims as a type of witchcraft. Just as they had previously imagined witches metaphorically consuming happiness, fertility and wealth, so some enslaved people described themselves as victims of witches who they thought would literally eat them in Barbados or Boston. Together with redefinition by incoming Christians, this new conception of witchcraft as slavery may have destabilised traditional beliefs. A study published in 2020 claims that in Africa, North and South America 'representatives of ethnic groups that were more severely raided during the Atlantic slave-trade era are more likely to believe in witchcraft today'.[15]

This hypothesis doesn't explain everything about contemporary African witchcraft trials, but it points to links between colonial violence and a legacy of social mistrust: an ideal incubator for witchcraft belief. Anthropologists who have studied trust also perceive interesting similarities between the African colonial period and medieval and early modern Europe. In both cases, religious, political and cultural conflict was endemic; authorities pursued enemies both imagined and real; neighbourly trust broke down as groups demonised each other; and traditional magics that once dealt with witchcraft suspicions through counter-spells were banned. This is a simplified picture, and most notably in Africa there was the added horror of race-based enslavement, but the parallels between the two continents and periods do cast an interesting light on the continuation of witchcraft today. It would be no wonder if people in such situations across any continent at any time accused each other of witchcraft, just as the Zambian villagers accuse Shula – a stranger who has come to their already poor and mistrustful community.[16]

But if this is true, and well-meaning Christians exported a medieval worldview to modern Africa, why did demonology not flourish there in the late nineteenth century? Ironically, after the end of the institutional slave trade in the mid-nineteenth century, European colonial administrators helped victims of witch accusations. Their scepticism about whether witches existed in practice – informed by cases such as Tatabe's and Marie-Catherine Cadière's – made formal witch trials impossible. Many administrators came to Africa with a gospel retaining the positive Christian message of love but ruling out 'medieval superstition'. They quickly rejected any witchcraft accusations brought to them, throwing accusers out of court with a confidence that Officer Josephine lacked in *I Am Not a Witch*.

By the mid-twentieth century the Witchcraft Suppression Acts of 1895 and 1957, suppressing witch trials rather than witchcraft itself, were in force across much of sub-Saharan, European-controlled Africa. Based on the British Witchcraft Act of 1735 and related European laws, they also, in a crucial point of difference, outlawed both accusations of witchcraft and 'pretending' to practise it. In some countries, however, laws were self-contradictory. In Zambia, Shula's home, a 1914 Witchcraft Act forbade making accusations, being a 'witch doctor or witch finder' or 'pretending' witchcraft. But, confusingly, it also appeared to confirm the existence of witchcraft, forbidding the use of 'any witchcraft or any non-natural means' to discover lost property or identify thieves and 'any other means, process or device adopted in the practice of witchcraft or sorcery'.[17] What African scholars have criticised as a 'lack of definition' meant that the act was hard to apply. No wonder Officer Josephine is confused.[18]

Late nineteenth- and twentieth-century European law-makers were also at times conflicted, however, not only by local beliefs but also by disagreement in their own communities. Missionary views often differed from those of administrators. While administrators liked quiet order – social control and economic productivity – missionaries often believed in the literal, disruptive presence of Satan among their congregations, which sometimes promoted conflict. There were troubling outcomes as European Christianity inspired new demonologies in African congregations. As early as the 1920s a witch-hunt in British-controlled Nigeria was begun by a 'Spirit Movement' containing elements of both African trance magic and Christian ecstasies that would have been recognisable by Abigail Williams or Marie-Catherine Cadière.

The Spirit Movement's worshippers believed they became 'possessed' by the Holy Spirit, which was thought to be able to detect witches. As the movement broke away from established religious organisations its practices became less and less subject to contemporary restrictions and witchcraft suspects were tortured and left to die, in part because no witch trials could be held under colonial law. While the church did not sanction this movement it became clear European missionaries could not force Christians to stop witch-hunting. Sadly, as the Spirit Movement gained traction, four 'witches' were murdered and thirty injured by people claiming divine inspiration. Three worshippers who participated in the killings were then executed by colonial authorities and the movement was shut down.[19]

In the mid-twentieth century, African Christianity grew further in influence and confidence in new nations, often splitting away from the European sects that had planted it across the continent. Then, in the 1960s to 1980s, a further wave of Christian missionaries, this time Pentecostal, arrived from the United States. Pentecostalists believe worshippers may be inspired directly by the Holy Spirit and, by speaking in tongues or prophesying, congregations may reveal hidden wisdom, including discovering witches. From the 1960s onward, such impulses were strengthened by a modern redefining of how witchcraft worked. The American prophet William Marion Branham taught Congolese followers that TV sets and phones may be demonic instruments, and his followers now believe that telecom workers may be witches, as well as educators and students using educational technologies – calculators, videos, the internet. Rather than being African in origin, these beliefs have been imported, and have affinities with those of modern American conspiracy theorists such as QAnon, who claim that politicians and tech company bosses are Satanists.[20] Some evangelical preachers have further dedicated themselves to 'delivering' or freeing victims of witchcraft, like Helen Ukpabio of Nigeria's Liberty Gospel Church, who also wrote the film *End of the Wicked*. Occasionally a supposedly secular leader today will also call for witches to be criminalised officially, as a Zambian magistrate did in 2016, to complement such church teachings. In this climate of opinion, unwanted or isolated children like Shula are in great danger of being accused of witchcraft.[21]

One of the consequences of tech-based demonology is that witch-accusers have specifically targeted children. The first documented accusations of children were in Cameroon, west Africa, in the 1970s. They were investigated by two anthropologists, the Australian Robert Brain and Dutchman Peter Geschiere.[22] Local people who explained the accusations to Robert Brain said that, in their view, the thinking around childhood was changing. Instead of being perceived as vulnerable, some children were reclassified as super-potent, understanding the modern world and its technologies far better than their elders.

Through exposure to the world beyond their villages, they'd supposedly been infected by the desire to become witches and possessed by evil spirits who caused them to do harm. The spirits also gave them special power as spell-casters and seers, people thought, like Shula, who is expected to act as a diviner. In Cameroon, community leaders decided the appropriate response to their children's special powers was to exorcise them, but the exorcism itself was traumatic. In African theology the exorcised person is both witch and victim, with a demonic spirit imagined as literally living inside the witch's body, so the boundaries are blurred, and the 'witch' must be attacked to drive out the 'spirit of witchcraft'. Instead of 'saving' the possessed person, exorcism can instead become trial and punishment.

As news of child witches spread across the continent through newspapers, TV and preaching, accusations, informal trials and exorcisms multiplied, reaching a new high in the 1990s and early twenty-first century as communicative technologies improved. They involved the torture, murder or banishment of children across Africa and the African diaspora. The United Nations Children's Fund UNICEF estimated in 2012 that around 20,000 'witch-children' were homeless in the Congolese capital, Kinshasa, even though accusing a child of witchcraft is illegal there.[23] Often a child's witch trial would have happened just like Shula's, with elders turning on a child when misfortune occurred. One teenager, Veronica, who spoke to Congolese journalist Mpoyo Gael in 2018, said she had been accused of witchcraft after a neighbour's child died shortly after she'd collected a mobile phone from him: 'I told him that I didn't know anything about it,' said Veronica, but 'he said he was going to bring a witchdoctor to the house, to find out whether it was me or not who cast a spell on his child.' At this illegal, informal trial, Veronica was convicted. She was exiled from her village, and in 2018 was living in an orphanage.

Other children have similar stories, many featuring Christian clergy. Merveille, a seven-year-old Congolese exile, said, 'We were in a prayer room when the pastor declared I am a witch . . . he then blindfolded me and started praying for me.' The minister accused the boy of killing his own mother, and Merveille's father agreed. It's easy to blame him for accusing and banishing his son, but anthropologist Jean La Fontaine – an expert in witchcraft beliefs – counsels understanding: framed by a post-colonial Christian worldview, it must feel to many African witch-accusers as if Satan is destroying their communities, she points out. The devil brings senseless violence, civil or international war, AIDS, collapsing social structures, chaotic migration, starvation, modern slavery. Communities in despair might well suspect the young as agents of change and globalisation. What is important is to end the global injustice that drives people into despair and stop the demonising, violence and cruelty that flows from it.[24]

Shula's story has brought the proliferation of southern African witch trials to broad global attention, and many other African and diasporic creatives, scholars and activists are also challenging their spread. But they face difficulties. Leo Igwe, founder of Advocacy for Alleged Witches, reports that he has been arrested and physically assaulted on a regular basis. In 2019 a conference on witchcraft beliefs at the University of Nigeria, Nsukka, organised by Professors Elizabeth Onogwu and Egodi Uchendu, was attacked by the Christian Association of Nigeria and Pentecostal Fellowship of Nigeria. Bishop Goddy Okafor called for 'aggressive prayers' to be directed against it, while Apostle Dr Joseph Ajujungwa called it an 'attempt to hand over the University of Nigeria Nsukka to the devil'. Some journalists misrepresented the event as a celebration of witchcraft by practising witches, the government-owned venue pulled out, and a keynote speaker resigned. Reflecting in 2021, Egodi Uchendu described 'both a misunderstanding of motive and ignorance of the theme and thrust of the conference'. At the time, she had been forced to state: 'We are not witches. We are professors and scholars who are intrigued by this phenomenon of witchcraft.'[25]

More hopefully, some Christian leaders supported her. Catholic Bishop Matthew Hassan Kukah argued that European Christians once 'took African religions to simply mean witchcraft and sorcery. However, with time, the Church has tried to dialogue with these beliefs', so this dialogue should continue, and universities should contribute. He pointed out that Africans themselves were best placed to discuss their own beliefs.[26] He's right. But non-African people shouldn't be silent either. Charities such as ActionAid work to help accused and convicted witches and to educate villagers in the hope of minimising accusation. The Witchcraft and Human Rights Information Network connects those concerned about witchcraft-related violence, including both liretlo-style killings and witchcraft trials, with the aim of developing solutions, training and resources, and at times staging targeted intervention. Children like Shula and women like her fellow inmates at the witch camp can be offered practical help: advocacy, transport, resettlement and financial aid to escape from accusers and exploiters and restart their lives. Those who work with accused witches can also offer them a renewed confidence – the respect and reassurance that comes from being heard. In many ways, they say, the most important thing is to believe them when they say, 'I am not a witch.'

CHAPTER THIRTEEN

The Trial of Stormy Daniels: Witchcraft in North America

It was a surprise to many people when the American president Donald Trump tweeted the words 'WITCH HUNT!' for the first time on 10 January 2017 – although it transpired that he had been using the term as a private citizen since at least 2011. He went on to tweet 'WITCH HUNT', usually in capitals, 379 times during his four-year presidency: at least one tweet per week, often two. The then president used the phrase to attack those who claimed he was deceitful, corrupt and anti-democratic, a sexual predator or agent of the Russian government, and those who wished to damage his allies, and put him or them on trial.[1] In some respects, Donald Trump wasn't unreasonable in using the term witch-hunt: claims that he was a criminal, abuser, charlatan, spy and insurrectionist recall the accusations levelled at Helena Scheuberin, Anny Sampson, Jean-Baptiste Girard, Montie Summers, John Blymyer, Nellie Duncan and the other 'witches' in this book.

However, that a supremely powerful white male world leader should claim the identity of a hunted witch has struck many people as disturbing – much as it would be if President Thomas Jefferson claimed to suffer as Joan Wright had, or King James VI suggested that it was he, rather than Anny Sampson, who was being demonised. In reality, the accusations made against Trump and his allies are based on written, film and audio evidence rather than intangible suspicions of magic. And, so far, his so-called witch trial has been repeatedly postponed despite various charges of misconduct having been made against him. That he's chosen to present himself as a witch, however, reveals how witchcraft continues to be potently symbolic, even in the supposedly rational world of democratic Western nations. Witchcraft still obsesses the USA and Canada, societies that in other ways consider themselves superlatively modern, and American media and political influence on other nations worldwide means that they too continue to be haunted by witches.

Donald Trump is not a witch, but he does share history with Americans who are. The most famous is Stormy Daniels, his long-term legal opponent, an actor in pornographic movies and allegedly the ex-president's former lover. In 2021 Stormy joined Donald in claiming that she too was being subjected to a 'witch trial'. In a Facebook post, she said accusations of witchcraft were being made against her because of her sex work, her other employment as a tarot-reader, ghost-hunter and medium, and also because she holds non-Christian religious beliefs, making her a pagan or, as she put it, a 'witch'. Stormy expressed her horror that her enemies would 'use my religious believes [sic] and profession to discriminate against me'. Her statement is the first time in this book that someone has proudly proclaimed they are a witch and referred to witchcraft as a 'religious belief'. So, what does Stormy mean when she uses the word 'witch'?

In today's North America the word 'witch' has come to describe a religious identity, which is one of the ways Stormy is using the word. Initially that usage might seem surprising: how could a word that once identified God's enemies, wicked heretics who were thought to worship the power of evil and Satan in person, possibly become a religious position today? But looked at from a different perspective, this is not such a shock. In fact, it looks like a self-fulfilling prophecy. Think about it this way: medieval demonologists and those who followed in their footsteps imagined witches as embodying their worst nightmares, which included expressions of female power, unfettered sexuality and subversive political intentions. In their time, these threats looked like the end of the world as they knew it. But in modern times, the fears of medieval clergymen have become freedoms prized by many people, including feminists, campaigners for sex- and gender-based rights, and critics of political systems they see as favouring wealthy white imperialists. The demonologists were right in one way: their world did end, and with it their definition of witchcraft.

Today, people who have redefined witchcraft and embraced the identity of 'witch' believe themselves to be liberated from the Christian worldview of the demonologists. Though not opposed to Christianity's focus on loving empathy, they do feel alienated by how some Christian teachings were interpreted as the church grew and gained power over the centuries. Like Helena Scheuberin, critics of this traditional church view are heretical – in the sense that they associate some Christian doctrines with misogyny, prejudice against sexuality, and a cultural conservatism that they perceive as repressive or corrupt. In the 1480s, Helena thought, heretically, that Heinrich Kramer embodied all these faults of the established Christian church of his time. Today, people who call themselves witches share her concerns. For them, the Heinrich Kramers of this world are the persecutory, prejudiced enemies of all virtue, and the Helena Scheuberins, those who were labelled as witches, represent a more humane, liberated and empowering good. In this way, Stormy Daniels follows in the footsteps of Helena Scheuberin and is a 'witch': though they're not identical, there are recognisable similarities with her and the other accused witches in this book, especially in dissenting from established religious tradition.

Stormy Daniels's reference to witchcraft as itself a religion has complicated roots in European and American history. The process of reversing the association of the word 'witch' with society's enemies and moving it towards an opposite association with campaigners for religious freedom was a lengthy one, beginning in the nineteenth century. In the years leading up to the publication of his history *La Sorcière* or *The Witch* in the 1860s, Jules Michelet and his wife Athénaïs redefined witches, drawing in part on their knowledge of the case of Marie-Catherine Cadière. Jules and Athénaïs's interest in feminism and alternative pantheist spirituality made them reimagine accused witches like Marie-Catherine as innocent victims who were persecuted by feudal lords and patriarchal churchmen. They attributed to these accused witches a strong commitment to charity and social justice and a feminine spiritual connection to the natural world. The Michelets' vague but potent definition of witches as social and religious rebels spread and was taken up across the Western world.

Then, in the 1890s, a distinctive North American twist was added to it. As part of her campaign to gain voting rights for women, New York suffragist Matilda Joslyn Gage wrote a history of witch trials into her book *Woman, Church and State*, published in 1893. Drawing on the Michelets' understanding of religious history, Gage argued that medieval witch trials were driven by churchmen's fear of women's independence and practical knowledge. That this worldview continued meant that women must now be given the vote – a right, she argued, that would ensure the power of modern-day Heinrich Kramers could be challenged, at least in the United States of America, a nation which she saw as a secular beacon of hope to oppressed women across the world.[2] She wasn't alone in thinking this. Her fellow campaigners, like the radical historian Charles Godfrey Leland, also linked the subversive witches of the past with suffragists: 'With every new rebellion . . . humanity and woman gain something, that is to say, their just dues or rights,' he celebrated in his book on witchcraft in medieval Europe.[3]

In the 1890s, the spiritual and political trajectories of witch trial history met and merged in the United States, creating an image of the witch as a very specific type of heretic and rebel. This reinvented witch was a secularist or religious reformer, a protestor taking action to assert her civil rights and permanently end religious discrimination against women. Matilda Gage believed women should be able to preach and act as ministers within the Christian

WITCHCRAFT

churches and also enter state political life as voters and candidates. Paradoxically, her demand for both religious and civic rights created a version of the revolutionary witch who the Michelets had mistakenly imagined existed in the medieval past.

Meanwhile in Britain, people dissatisfied with the cultural conservatism of the Anglican and Catholic Churches created their own version of the Michelet–Gage–Leland modern witch and built her into a new religion. They called their religious movement 'Wicca', a word deriving from the Anglo-Saxon 'wicce', meaning witch. Wiccans celebrated sexuality and humans' place in the natural world, casting aside what they saw as the Victorian constraints of Christian morality. Wiccan theology was developed by two rather surprising pagan missionaries: the civil servants Gerald Gardner and Doreen Valiente. Gerald had retired from colonial work in Malaya – now Malaysia – and Doreen was working for British intelligence when they became interested in developing a magical new religion in the 1950s. As part of designing their new church, both came to believe that the people tried as witches from the fifteenth to eighteenth centuries had in fact been pagans just like them, practising a surviving prehistoric religion. Gerald and Doreen thought that religion must have included dancing, singing, feasting and sexual rites designed to celebrate fertility. While this view was not historically accurate it has been highly influential in modern imaginings of the witch in North America through its association of witchcraft with the celebration of sexuality.[4]

All these ideas – the witch as religious rebel, campaigner for political rights and sexual activist – bring us back to Stormy Daniels, and all of them seem to be meaningful for her when she speaks about witchcraft or the accusations against her. Born in 1979 in Louisiana in the southern United States as Stephanie Gregory, Daniels adopted her professional name when she became a stripper and actor in adult films. By 2006, the year when she says she began an affair with Donald Trump, she was a successful performer and producer. Trump was then a reality TV personality who had made money in property development and gambling. His NBC show, *The Apprentice*, had gained millions of viewers through five seasons. Although he had recently married his third wife, Melania, and they had a small son, he was happy to nod along that year to the suggestion that he was a 'sexual predator' when he appeared on a radio show. The label was received as flattery, and it fitted into a growing history of stories from women and statements by Trump himself. Journalist Natasha Stoynoff said that in 2005 he had grabbed and kissed her, suggested they should have an affair and then lay in wait for her at an appointment. During the same period Trump was unwittingly recorded boasting: 'I just start kissing them . . . just kiss. I don't even wait. And when you're a star, they let you do it. You can do anything . . . grab 'em by the pussy.' His listener laughed. In 2016, shortly after the recording became public, sixty-two million American voters and 306 members of the Electoral College chose Donald Trump as their next president.[5]

Despite public acceptance, the president-to-be wanted to limit speculation about extramarital affairs and sexual assault. In 2016, Daniels reportedly accepted $130,000 as a gift from his lawyer Michael Cohen: a payment widely discussed as 'hush money' accompanying a non-disclosure agreement. Such an agreement would have banned her from revealing any sexual relationship with the president and the payment – which Michael Cohen has stated he gave to Daniels on Donald Trump's instructions – would also act as an inducement to silence. Daniels has also alleged she was subjected to personal intimidation, both at the time of signing the agreement and later on. It was the beginning of her belief that Donald Trump was witch-hunting her and that he and other powerful men would dearly like to subject her to a witch trial.

When Trump's legal team accused her of lying about the affair, Daniels fought back by initiating a libel suit. During the hearing of that case, she was arrested by vice squad detectives in Columbus, Ohio. She was accused of using her appearance at a strip club as a vehicle to touch women and men in the audience, which is banned under Ohio law. Suggesting that Daniels was directly exchanging sex for money would, of course, have been a useful technique of intimidation if it were to be connected to her libel suit. Remember how claims of promiscuity were used against Helena Scheuberin? Though the charges against Daniels were dismissed, and it was stated these crimes had not been committed, the allegations continued to swirl in political debate. Eventually, Daniels lost her claim for libel damages against Trump.[6]

As well as being attacked for her sexual activities, Daniels also found herself under fire for her magical reputation. She is a tarot-reader, medium and paranormal investigator, and so in 2020 she was accused in pre-trial court documents of being 'a "witch" who practises witchcraft'. Her accuser this time was her former lawyer Michael Avenatti, an ex-ally who had quarrelled with her over a book advance and was now being tried for defrauding her. In abusing her in the trial paperwork, Daniels saw him as aligning with the Trump team's attack on her. Avenatti's lawyers alleged Daniels's spiritual activities and involvement with *Spooky Babes*, a paranormal investigation TV show, meant that she believed 'fantastical' things that 'call into serious question her truthfulness, mental state, and ability to competently testify'. If Stormy thought she was a witch, the allegations implied, she must be too mad to recall truthfully her history with Michael Avenatti.

The court documents prepared by Avenatti's team suggested Daniels's experiences included many of the key features attributed to the witches in this book: spirit possession, a belief that she could use her psychic energy to affect electrical current and see through walls, the ability to exorcise spirits from paying clients, the possession of 'supernatural powers' and a belief that she could 'serve as a "medium" to the dead'. None of this evidence stopped Michael Avenatti from being convicted of defrauding Daniels and being sentenced to four years in jail. But, as she pointed out, the claims against her constituted 'literally a modern-day witch hunt'. 'It opens the door', she added, 'to attack and discrimination against every person that identifies as something other than Christian, reads tarot, is a medium and works in energy healing and paranormal in any capacity.' It was as she prepared for a court appearance in the Avenatti case in June 2021 that Daniels tweeted: 'What does one wear to a witch trial?'[7]

Ironically, then, claims of 'witch' identity have been made by different sides in current United States politics, as both defence and accusation. At first this seems bizarre, but it is not so surprising in the nation's historical context. The idea of witchcraft has haunted the United States throughout its history. In the 1690s the nation was primed by the Salem witch-hunt to see any future judicial trouble through the lens of a witch trial, especially if it involved politics and religion. Situations involving conflict, prejudice, injustice and compensation all also recall Salem, and so American culture has often turned to the image of the witch in polarised times, as now with Trump and Daniels. Most famously, Arthur Miller's 1953 play *The Crucible* reflected on the anti-communist agitation in the United States in the 1950s using the Salem trials as an analogy, setting the pattern for future uses of the terms 'witch-hunt' and 'witch trial'.

But witches often appeared in less serious American drama, films and TV too. In 1942, Veronica Lake starred in *I Married a Witch*; in 1957 Kim Novak played a witch in *Bell, Book and Candle*; the TV series *Bewitched*, with Elizabeth Montgomery as the witch Samantha, ran from 1964 to 1972. John Updike's Salem-inspired novel *The Witches of Eastwick* was filmed in 1987 and starred three top actors of its time: Michelle Pfeiffer, Cher and Susan Sarandon. The novel featured a – literally – steamy hot-tub orgy, a kind of Sabbath during which the witches were seduced by the devil, and Stormy Daniels reimagined this comically in 2005 in one of her adult movies, *The Witches of Breastwick*. This kind of filmic witch – an attractive woman with magical powers imagined for the purpose of entertainment – has become a symbol of the changes in the lives of Western women across the twentieth and twenty-first centuries. At first, plotlines insisted that witches abandon their magical powers after the wedding that ended each romantic comedy. But by the 1990s, some witches like the teen-witch character Willow in the series *Buffy the Vampire Slayer* (1997–2003) were allowed to hold down jobs, remain single and come out as gay. By 2005 the witch could be as frankly, frequently sexual as her creators wanted her to be.

The plotlines of these TV shows and films may seem unimportant when set against the deadly misogyny that prompted witch trials across the world throughout history, and that still instigates them in southern Africa, but North American comedies do reflect serious modern concerns in their reinvention of the witch. Like *Mosali a Nkhola* and *I Am Not a Witch*, these witchcraft fictions tell us truths about the societies that made them. During the twentieth century, witches on TV and film dramatised the gradual empowerment of Western women: women who had won the vote, the opportunity to work regularly outside their homes, entitlement to equal pay and to have their sexual and reproductive rights protected in law. Each version of the witch in popular culture reflected those new freedoms. Looking back at *Bewitched*, American reviewer Emily St James says: 'This [wa]s a show, no matter how goofy, about the growing power of women in both the home and society at large in the 1960s.' Similarly, viewers called the witch sisterhood drama *Charmed* (1998–2006) a fusion of 'witchcraft, feminism and fantasy'. This wasn't an accident: it was what the show's writers, producers and actors intended.[8]

Charmed's equation of witchcraft with feminism was drawn into the political spotlight when in 2018 Hollywood producer Harvey Weinstein was charged with sexual offences. Among his accusers was the actor Rose McGowan, most famous for embodying one of the witch family in *Charmed*, the character Paige, whom she played between 2001 and 2006.[9] Furiously angry at her treatment in the film industry, during the 2018 revelations about Harvey Weinstein Rose McGowan said that he had raped her in 1997. Denouncing not just him but also the wider landscape of misogyny and abuse in Hollywood, she claimed that some people who could have intervened more strongly had in effect tolerated sexual predation targeted against women. At the instigation of Rose McGowan's

Charmed co-star Alyssa Milano, many women began using the hashtag #MeToo on social media – a phrase pioneered by activist Tarana Burke – to express solidarity with Rose and her co-accusers and register their own experiences of sexual harassment.[10] Both *Charmed* actors promoted #MeToo activism as part of their existing commitment to raising awareness of women's rights.

Media commentators found the relationship between feminist activism and witchcraft irresistible when Alyssa Milano also attended the confirmation hearings for Donald Trump's nominee for Supreme Court justice, Brett Kavanaugh. He too was accused of sexually assaulting several women. Viewers watched the televised debate around his nomination with Alyssa glowering directly behind the would-be justice. 'I've never wished so hard that Alyssa Milano was a real witch,' commented one tweet. Yet, recalling Donald Trump's assertion that he was the victim of a witch-hunt, it was Brett Kavanaugh who was portrayed as the accused witch by right-wing media. The chat show host Tucker Carlson mocked the justice's accusers by playing footage of witchfinders from the 1996 film version of *The Crucible*. Meanwhile, the Republican National Committee also began to use the phrase 'witch-hunt' to defend its candidates and office-holders: it was effective. The idea of the witch-hunt as a baseless, trivial series of accusations made against a powerful governor or judge spread further into political culture.[11]

Judge Kavanaugh's nomination was accepted, and he joined the highest court in the American legal system; the accusations were not enough to halt his confirmation. Alyssa Milano called it 'an all-out attack by our government against women', predicting that with an increased conservative majority among its judges, the Supreme Court would soon rule abortion rights were not a constitutional entitlement. They did so on 24 June 2022, on the grounds that the eighteenth-century Constitution did not mention such a right, it was not essential to 'ordered liberty' and not part of 'the Nation's history and traditions'. It was noted that in its reliance on historical precedent the court's opinion – written by Judge

Samuel Alito – quoted Sir Matthew Hale, judge of an eastern English witch trial in 1664.

Nearly five hundred years ago, Judge Hale sentenced Amy Duny and Rose Cullender to death following their conviction by a jury. Shortly after their trial, he wrote a demonology, *A Collection of Modern Relations of Matters of Fact Concerning Witches and Witchcraft*. As well as quoting this seventeenth-century demonologist, Judge Alito's report also quoted Sir Edward Coke, a fellow legal authority who described witches as 'horrible and devilish offenders, which left the ever-living God, and sacrificed to the Devil'. He thought burning a better punishment than hanging.[12] In 2022 the words of witch trial judges were resurrected to bolster their counterparts in modern America. As witchcraft history repeated itself in the removal of women's legal rights, it was also deliberately inverted to portray the removers of those rights as victims. Meanwhile the women who accused such men of abuse were being subjected to trial by media and, in the case of Stormy Daniels, to a trial that involved claims of actual witch status because of her magical beliefs.

Accusing Stormy Daniels of witchcraft looked particularly odd in the context of the United States government's insistence on religious freedom as part of the nation's constitutional history. In theory, the American state accepts witchcraft as a respectable religion, its worship protected by law. In 2007 the witch or Wiccan pentangle symbol became a legally approved 'emblem of belief' for those serving in the United States military.[13] There are huge American Wiccan and witch communities on social media, gathering using hashtags like #witchesofinstagram and on WitchTok. Where once 'witch' was a shameful label, it is now celebrated publicly in jewellery, fashion and home décor. Online events such as 'Spellbound: A Magickal Bazaar with Tarot by Stormy Daniels' attract hundreds of attendees to shop with 'vendors specializing in all of your ceremonial, spell casting and healing needs; including altar tools, herbs, crystals, candles, oils, charms and more'. Most cities and many small towns have a 'magic shop' with in-person retail and events, like New York City's 'Enchantments', which supplies books, tarot cards, incense, resins, jewellery, talismans, cauldrons, chalices and wands.[14] By 2012 a survey suggested around 350,000 United States citizens out of 331 million defined themselves as Wiccan. The Canadian census records smaller numbers: 24,600 out of 38 million in 2021.[15] While an exact number of North American witches is difficult to determine, the religion has grown dramatically since the 1970s. As their numbers increased, witches and Wiccans have found public acceptance across the continent.

Canadian Wicca is especially well established, dominated by the Wiccan Church of Canada, founded in the 1970s. As its name suggests, the church has affinities with Christianity as well as witchcraft. Focusing on public visibility and respectability, it aims 'to bring to the non-Wiccan population an understanding that we are a positive, reputable and life-affirming religious and lifestyle alternative' and 'to achieve for Wiccans the same rights and freedoms enjoyed by other more mainstream religions'.[16] However, definitions of acceptable witchcraft practice remain a challenge in Canada. Until December 2018 Canadians could be prosecuted for pretended witchcraft under Section 365 of Canada's Criminal Code. In October and early December that year, Madeena Stevenson and Tiffany Butch, from Ontario, and Samantha Stevenson, from Toronto, Ontario, were charged with 'pretended witchcraft'. The women had been operating under a variety of labels: fortune-teller, psychic, spiritualist medium, clairvoyant – similar activities to the magical practices of Stormy Daniels south of the border.

The Canadian women's 'witchcraft' fitted their nation's Criminal Code's prohibitions just like Nellie Duncan's offences fitted the British 1735 Witchcraft Act, because the Code was based on that Act. Until 1982 Canada was tied legally to Britain, under its former Dominion status. The 1951 repeal of the Witchcraft Act in Britain did not cover Canada, however, so the Criminal Code retained its witchcraft-related definitions, including pretended witchcraft as fraud. It was illegal to 'pretend to exercise or use any kind of witchcraft, sorcery, enchantment or conjuration', tell fortunes or seek lost items magically. Penalties included a six-month jail term and/or $2,000 fine. The three women charged in 2018 were said to have defrauded clients separately of over $700,000 in total. However, the clustering of cases provoked criticism. In 2017, when the Canadian government announced its intention to overhaul the Criminal Code, the witchcraft section had featured in debate. 'It was the publicity over the fact that [the sections] were being removed that made police even remember that they were there,' suggested one critic.

The Canadian reform of witchcraft laws had been initiated by Prime Minister Justin Trudeau partly because of Canadian Wiccans' complaints that the law discriminated against them and against people whose cultural backgrounds included magical beliefs. Several of those prosecuted before 2018 were of Indian descent – not Native American, but subcontinental – or Hispanic. In 2009, Vishwantee Persaud was charged under Section 365 after a client paid her $27,000 to contact his dead sister. Charges were dropped when the defendant pleaded guilty to fraud. In 2017 astrologer and psychic Murali Muthyalu was prosecuted after being paid $100,000 to lift a curse. In 2012, Gustavo Valencia Gomez agreed to refund $14,000 that he had charged for the same service. Commenting on these cases, lawyer Omar Ha-Redeye suggested that Section 365's provisions 'reflect a primarily Christian mindset, where non-Christian traditions, including what we now may refer to as Wicca, totemism, or animism, or other traditions, were demonised as being evil'. He thought it 'no surprise' that 'these provisions are used primarily against women or against people who follow non-mainstream religious traditions'. Witch-hunting, he concluded, had retained the same targets throughout history.[17]

This is also evident in literal North American witchcraft accusations, ones that imagine witches demonologically as actual users of Satanic magic rather than – as in the accusations against Stormy Daniels – deluded pagans. In February 2022, in Nashville, Tennessee, Pastor Greg Locke accused six members of his Global Vision Bible

Church of being quite literally 'devil-worshipping Satanist witches', two of them in the ladies' Bible-study group. In a video shared on social media, he screamed accusations of 'pharmakeia' (witchcraft with drugs, poisons and remedies), burning sage (a Native American cleansing practice), being Freemasons and bewitching fellow worshippers. He has also made QAnon-inspired accusations that then House of Representatives speaker Nancy Pelosi was a 'demon baby-killing paedophile' and former Democrat secretary of state and first lady Hillary Clinton a 'high priestess in the Satanic church' – claims linked in their inspiration to the Capitol riot of 2021 and an attack on Nancy Pelosi's husband in 2022. The normalisation of the word 'witch' in political debate means opponents are sometimes accused of being literal witches. The first North American claims about witchcraft as Satan-worshipping paedophilia were made in the 1980s at a preschool in California. News coverage prompted other accusations, which spread to schools and day care centres. Many people were tried, but in 1990 the original defendant, Ray Buckley, was acquitted after the longest trial in United States history. Then the phenomenon was labelled a 'Satanic panic'. Now the targets of that panic are Democrats, particularly women. Demonology has been incorporated into threats to American democracy and the safety of government officials.[18]

Despite all the protections of American law, suspected witches are sometimes killed across the continent. In 1993 Celerino Galicia, a Mexican man living in Chicago, murdered his girlfriend Roberta Martinez because he thought her a witch. Like John Blymyer, Celerino stated he needed to kill her to remove a spell she had cast on him, and as in 1929, the judge refused to allow the 'witchcraft defence', preventing a psychology professor from testifying about magical beliefs. 'The witchcraft defence is not even medically acceptable,' one law professor summed up – a stance that holds true in most jurisdictions globally, although not all. It was not until 2017, for example, that in a landmark ruling the Zambian Supreme Court established that belief in witchcraft could not be considered an 'extenuating circumstance' in a murder case. The appellant in that case, Abedinego Kapeshi, had his conviction for murdering two suspected witches upheld. Similarly, seventeen years before Abedinego and sixty-four years after John Blymyer, Celerino Galicia was found guilty of first-degree murder.[19]

Embracing the identity 'witch' is seen by some modern pagans and feminists as a symbolic way of resisting such misogyny and violence. Since the 1970s, modern pagan witches have created 'reclaiming' movements, asserting their right to feel safe in public spaces, and have protested against threats to their safety, such as short sentences for rapists. Often these protests consist of reciting 'spells' at mass meetings or 'hexing' public figures. Some witches today describe this as an opportunity to 'do something' personally, a cathartic performance to express their anger and sadness. Others have a broader political aim: 'to reclaim the word Witch is to reclaim our right, as women, to be powerful'.[20] Stormy Daniels's adoption of witchcraft as a creed follows in the tradition of these women, part of a wider assertion of women's rights and freedoms. Sometimes it's ironic, comic or metaphorical; sometimes very serious. Like many of the witch-women in this book, Daniels has described herself as a survivor of sexual abuse and has told journalists that she receives ongoing hate mail, rape threats and death threats – sometimes delivered face-to-face in public places. She relates these unequivocally to her political activities and career choices. By 2018 she had become completely certain she would be killed, she says.

That was the year she gave a primetime TV interview about her claims against the then president, Donald Trump. In 2018, she says, she 'lived alone with the fear of being murdered to ensure my silence'. That's a shocking thought for a woman to have in a modern, democratic, civil society.[21] Although her fears have subsided somewhat since then, Daniels is still a controversial figure in American politics and culture. Her work as a witch is booming and she estimates she gave over three hundred tarot readings in 2022, costing up to $150 each. This makes her a hate-figure for some and results in abuse and mockery online every time she speaks or writes something new about her life. Yet, 'I'm not ashamed and I won't be bullied,' Stormy says – a phrase that has become something of a slogan in her interviews.

Women who advocate for nature-based, non-patriarchal belief systems are often mocked and reviled for their belief in supernatural powers, their earthy spirituality, their frank sexuality and their subversiveness. In the context of this book's history of witchcraft, it becomes more evident why that is: these are all traits long associated with witches; features seen as ignorant, wicked and shameful. Women with these traits have been demonised since the Middle Ages and across history, from Helena Scheuberin to Stormy Daniels.[22]

Epilogue: So, What is a Witch Now?

Witchcraft is still criminalised in multiple nations and quasi-states. In Guatemala, traditional healers have become targets for witch-hunters: several were killed in 2020 and 2021. When Indonesia's military dictator President Suharto resigned in 1998, suspected witches were hacked to death in the streets. In Nepal, during the civil war of 1996–2006, they were beaten or burned to death.[1] The Islamic State/Daesh beheads suspected witches, including for homeopathy and acupuncture, a practice also common in Saudi Arabia.[2] In Europe, children of African descent have been tragically killed by their own families and church congregations, often during exorcisms to expel the 'spirit of witchcraft'. In 2000 Victoria Climbié, who had come to Britain from the Côte d'Ivoire, was murdered in London, dying of hypothermia, malnutrition and organ failure after being tied up in a bath without food or water, beaten with hammers and chains, burned and cut.[3] In this global context, it is all the more repellent that Donald Trump would present himself as a witch, and frightening that his opponents, such as Stormy Daniels, Nancy Pelosi and Hillary Clinton, should be accused of witchcraft, both metaphorically and literally.

In our seven-century journey through the history of witch trials we've seen that people can most plausibly be accused of witchcraft if they are:

- female

or/and also:

- accused of sexual misconduct, as defined by their time and place,
- poor, either averagely or absolutely,
- an indigenous person, perceived to be in conflict with a colonial regime,
- disabled, vulnerable or unwell,
- claiming unsanctioned knowledge or power, especially religious or medical,
- perceived to be politically subversive.

Sometimes witch-hunters share characteristics of witches – being accused of sexual misconduct, claiming unsanctioned religious knowledge or being politically subversive themselves. Most witch-hunters are not uncomplicated villains, and, like the accused witch, the witch-hunter stands outside the social norm. But what is clear is that being a male, heterosexual, wealthy, white, able-bodied man at the pinnacle of state or church power is not the regular profile of a witch: that's a witch-hunter. A witch is more likely to be a migrant, a feminist activist, a pagan, an abused child, an unmarried mother living in poverty, a female politician, a sex worker.

This book's thirteen trials have shown us that the witch trial was a tool invented by demonologists to hurt and silence such perceived enemies, a literal labelling of marginalised groups as demonic for the purposes of persecuting them. Accused people symbolised their fears, and they attributed to them every evil quality imaginable. We have inherited this binary, demonological thinking to create a metaphorical demonisation today, working through prejudice, conspiracy theory and scapegoating. But demonology has also twisted and transformed over the course of history, until now it deliberately blurs the lines between witch and witch-hunter. These thirteen trials show you how to spot the difference.

What can you do? Find out about the work of organisations that advocate for and defend people accused of witchcraft around the world and consider supporting them. Watch documentaries about witch camps and child witches and talk about them. Read novels and plays about witchcraft and amplify the authors' voices. Notice when female politicians and activists are being called 'witch' – even as a joke, but especially as a slur – and think about why that's still happening. Do your best to sort fact from fiction and reject fake news.

If you're being encouraged to blame someone – attack, despise, persecute, banish, demonise them – think about whether they have any of the characteristics of the 'witch' as an innocent person wrongly accused. Do accusers' claims remind you of any made by witch-hunters? If so, how can you challenge their binary thinking, disentangle reality from fiction and stop witch-hunting – in politics, religion, wider society, even in the courts? For the fortunate, a witch-hunt is just a metaphor – but this history should make clear how many witches are truly still on trial.

Notes

Introduction:
What is a Witch?

1 Norman Cohn, *Europe's Inner Demons* (Brighton: Sussex University Press, 1975); R.I. Moore, *The Formation of a Persecuting Society* (Oxford: Blackwell, 1987).

2 Ronald Hutton, *The Witch* (New Haven and London: Yale University Press, 2017), 168–79; Stuart Clark, *Thinking with Demons* (Oxford: Clarendon Press, 1997); Michael Bailey, *Battling Demons* (Philadelphia: Penn State Press, 2002).

3 Lyndal Roper, *Oedipus and the Devil* (London: Routledge, 1994); Marion Gibson, *Reading Witches* (London: Routledge, 1999); Laura Kounine, *Imagining the Witch* (Oxford: Oxford University Press, 2018).

4 Marion Gibson, *Early Modern Witches* (London: Routledge, 2000); Malcolm Gaskill, *Witchfinders* (London: John Murray, 2006).

5 Keith Thomas, *Religion and the Decline of Magic* (London: Peregrine, 1971); Bengt Ankarloo and Gustav Henningsen, *Early Modern European Witchcraft* (Oxford: Clarendon Press, 1990); Jonathan Barry, Marianne Hester and Gareth Roberts, eds, *Witchcraft in Early Modern Europe* (Cambridge: Cambridge University Press, 1996); Diane Purkiss, *The Witch in History* (London: Routledge, 1996); Lyndal Roper, *Witch Craze* (New Haven: Yale University Press, 2006). Barbara Ehrenreich and Deirdre English, *Witches, Midwives and Nurses* (New York: Feminist Press CUNY, 1973) and Silvia Federici's *Caliban and the Witch* (Brooklyn: Autonomedia, 2004) overstate arguments, but their insights are interesting. For statistics, Julian Goodacre, *The European Witch-Hunt* (London: Routledge, 2016) 267–9.

6 Ian Bostridge, *Witchcraft and Its Transformations c.1650–c.1750* (Oxford: Oxford University Press, 1997); Joseph Crawford, *Gothic Fiction and the Invention of Terrorism* (London: Bloomsbury, 2013), 93–4, 107.

7   Important influences: Hallie Rubenhold, *The Five* (London: Doubleday, 2019); Marisa J. Fuentes, *Dispossessed Lives* (Philadelphia: University of Pennsylvania Press, 2016); Saidiya V. Hartman, *Scenes of Subjection* (Oxford: Oxford University Press, 1997); Hazel Carby, *Imperial Intimacies* (London and New York: Verso, 2019); Sonja Boon, *What the Oceans Remember* (Waterloo, ON: Wilfrid Laurier University Press, 2019) and 'Creative Histories: Vulnerability, Emotions and the Undoing of the Self' (2017) at https://storyingthepast.wordpress.com/2017/10/06/creative-histories-vulnerability-emotions-and-the-undoing-of-the-self-by-sonja-boon/

Chapter One
The Trial of Helena Scheuberin:
A Demonologist Hammers Witches

1   Hutton, *Witch*, 168–79; Bailey discusses Heinrich's debts to Johannes Nider in particular.
2   Heinrich Kramer, *Malleus Maleficarum*, ed. and trans. Christopher S. Mackay as *The Hammer of Witches* (Cambridge: Cambridge University Press, 2009), 277–8.
3   Christopher S. Mackay, *An Unusual Inquisition* (Leiden: Brill, 2020), 171; Kramer, 364.
4   Mackay, 204, 167; Hartmann Ammann, 'Der Innsbrucker Hexenprozess von 1485', *Zeitschrift des Ferdinandeums für Tirol und Vorarlberg* 3:34 (1890), 38.
5   Mackay, 166–70, 199; Ammann, 37.
6   Eric Wilson, 'Institoris at Innsbruck: Heinrich Institoris, the *Summis Desiderantes* and the Brixen Witch-Trial of 1485' in Bob Scribner and Trevor Johnson, eds, *Popular Religion in Germany and Central Europe 1400–1800* (Basingstoke: Macmillan, 1996), 92; Kramer, 361–2, 364; Ammann, 38.
7   Kramer, 361–2; Ammann, 5, 25; Manfred Tschaikner, 'Der Innsbrucker Hexenprozess von 1485 und die Gegner des Inquisitors Heinrich Kramer', *Tiroler Heimat* 82 (2018), 201–2, 214, 217.
8   Mackay, 197; Hans Peter Broedel, *The Malleus Maleficarum and the Construction of Witchcraft* (Manchester: Manchester University Press, 2004), 1–2.
9   Mackay, 197; Ammann, 40.
10 Mackay, 197–8, 172; Ammann, 35–6.
11 Kramer, 503; Mackay, 118–19, 136, 198; Ammann, 40.
12 Mackay, 197–9; Ammann, 20.
13 Broedel, 12–13.
14 Broedel, 11–12.
15 Mackay, 196; Ammann, 39.
16 Kramer, 164–7, 169.
17 Mackay, 197; Ammann, 39.
18 Kramer, 279; Mackay, 200; Ammann, 42.

19 Mackay, 150-1, 152-6, 161; Ammann, 11, 13, 15-16, 19-20, 23, 34, 43-52, 59-62.

20 Purkiss; Deborah Willis, *Malevolent Nurture* (Ithaca and London: Cornell University Press, 2005).

21 Mackay, 155-9, 170, 163, 145-6.

22 Mackay, 204; Ammann, 35.

23 Kramer, 517-21; Mackay, 204-5; Ammann, 66-7; Tschaikner, 207-9.

24 Mackay, 205-8; Ammann, 68-9.

25 Mackay, 208-9; Ammann, 69-70.

26 Mackay, 209-14; Ammann, 70-2.

27 Mackay, 216-21.

28 Sydney Anglo, 'Evident Authority and Authoritative Evidence: The *Malleus Maleficarum*' in Anglo, ed., *The Damned Art* (London: Routledge and Kegan Paul, 1977), 14-18; J.A. Sharpe, *Instruments of Darkness* (London: Hamish Hamilton, 1996), 21-2; *Formicarius* was written in the 1430s, *Daemonomanie* in the 1580s.

29 Kramer, 165-70, 385, 514, 530, 212, 366.

Chapter Two
The Trial of the North Berwick Witches: A King Delights in Demonology

1 Clark, 684-726.

2 Michael B. Young, 'James VI and I: Time for a Reconsideration?', *Journal of British Studies* 51:3 (2012), 540-67.

3 Louise Nyholm Kallestrup, *Agents of Witchcraft in Early Modern Italy and Denmark* (Basingstoke: Palgrave Macmillan, 2015), 35-6, 47.

4 Amy L. Juhala, 'The Household and Court of James VI of Scotland', thesis, University of Edinburgh, 2000, 52.

5 Louise Nyholm Kallestrup, 'Kind in Words and Deeds but False in Their Hearts: Fear of Evil Conspiracy in Late Sixteenth-Century Denmark' in Jonathan Barry, Owen Davies and Cornelie Usborne, eds, *Cultures of Witchcraft in Europe from the Middle Ages to the Present* (Basingstoke: Palgrave Macmillan, 2018), 137-53, 139-42.

6 *The True Lawe of Free Monarchies* (Edinburgh, 1598), B2v-B3, D-Dv; *Basilikon Doron* (Edinburgh, 1599), B3.

7 *True Lawe*, C2v, C3v; Anna Groundwater, 'The Chasm Between James VI and I's Vision of the Orderly "Middle Shires" and the "Wicket" Scottish Borderers Between 1587 and 1625', *Renaissance and Reformation* 30:4 (2007), 105-32, 122.

8 Julian Goodare, 'The Scottish Witchcraft Act', *Church History* 74:1 (2005), 39-67; P.G. Maxwell-Stuart, *Satan's Conspiracy: Magic and Witchcraft in Sixteenth-Century Scotland* (East Linton: Tuckwell Press, 2001), 57-60; 'Anentis Witchcraft' at https://statutes.org.uk/site/the-statutes/scottish-laws/1563-mary-c-73-anentis-witchcraft/

9 P. M'Neill, *Tranent and Its Surroundings* (Edinburgh, Glasgow, Tranent: John Menzies/Peter M'Neill, 1884), 3–4, 15, 104; Lawrence Normand and Gareth Roberts, eds, *Witchcraft in Early Modern Scotland* (Exeter: University of Exeter Press, 2000), 139, 152, 153, 243.

10 *Newes from Scotland* (London, 1591) in Normand and Roberts, eds 311.

11 Normand and Roberts, eds, 143, 145, 233–5; National Archives of Scotland PA2/38 f.181–97v.

12 Normand and Roberts, eds, 242.

13 Normand and Roberts, eds, 184, 136–7.

14 Normand and Roberts, eds, 87–103, 185; *Newes* in Normand and Roberts, eds, 315, 324.

15 Normand and Roberts, eds, 192.

16 Normand and Roberts, eds, 144, 152; *Newes* in Normand and Roberts, eds, 148, 316.

17 Normand and Roberts, eds, 145, 198, 174, 312, 314, 255–6.

18 Normand and Roberts, eds, 244; *Newes* in Normand and Robert, eds, 315.

19 Normand and Roberts, eds, 159, 173, 136, 267–77.

20 *Newes* in Normand and Roberts, eds, 249, 313; Normand and Roberts, eds, 187.

21 Bessie was also called Brown ('Brunn, her [Agnes's] daughter') and Bessie Thompson. Anny was also known as Thompson, a maiden name or previous marriage; Normand and Roberts, eds, 184, 199, 244, 224–30.

22 Normand and Roberts, eds, 197.

23 *Daemonologie* (Edinburgh, 1597), republished London, 1603.

24 *Newes* in Normand and Roberts, eds, 315.

Chapter Three
The Trial of the Vardø Witches:
Demonology at Europe's Colonial Edge

1 Liv Helene Willumsen, *Witches of the North* (Leiden and Boston: Brill, 2013), 223, 226; Rune Blix Hagen, 'Female Witches and Sámi Sorcerers in the Witch Trials of Arctic Norway (1593–1695)', *Arv Nordic Yearbook of Folklore* 62 (2006), 123–4.

2 Willumsen, *Witches*, 246.

3 Liv Helene Willumsen, 'Exporting the Devil Across the North Sea: John Cunningham and the Finnmark Witch-Hunt' in Julian Goodare, ed., *Scottish Witches and Witch-Hunters* (Basingstoke: Palgrave Macmillan, 2013), 50–2; Samuel Purchas, *Hakluytus Posthumus or Purchas His Pilgrimes* (Glasgow: James MacLehose and Sons, 1906), vol. XIV, 322–4, 326, 335, 347.

4 Liv Helene Willumsen, *Steilneset*, translated by Katjana Edwardsen (Varanger: Norwegian Public Roads Administration and Varanger Museum, 2011), 11–12.

5 Willumsen, 'Exporting', 55.

6 Christian Meriot, 'The Saami Peoples from the Time of the Voyage of Ottar to Thomas von Westen', *Arctic* 37:4 (1984), 373.

7 Willumsen, *Witches*, 304–15, 260; Ellen Alm, 'So What Is "Gand" Sorcery – Really?', *Gemini* (2018) at https://gemini.no/2018/02/hva-er-egentlig-gand/; Meriot, 374.

8 Liv Helene Willumsen, ed., *The Witchcraft Trials in Finnmark, Northern Norway*, trans. Katjana Edwardsen (Bergen: Skald, 2010), 11–12, 22–6; Per Einar Sparboe and Rune Blix Hagen, ed. and trans. Hans Hanssen Lilienskiold, *Trolldom og Ugudelighet* (Tromsø: Universitetbiblioteket, 1998), 68–73, 74–6.

9 Willumsen, ed., 22–6; Sparboe and Hagen, eds, 74–6.

10 Willumsen, ed., 26.

11 Anneli Jonsson, 'Sámi Goat Cheese' at fondazioneslowfood.com

12 Willumsen, ed., 31–3; Sparboe and Hagen, eds, 96–8, 90–2, 98–100.

13 Sparboe and Hagen, eds, 76–96; Knut Hansvold, 'The Northern Norwegian Boat Museum Takes You Back to the Region's Rustic Routes' at https://nordnorge.com/en/artikkel/the-northern-norwegian-boat-museum-takes-you-back-to-the-regions-rustic-routes/

14 Willumsen, 'Exporting', 64n.18; Sparboe and Hagen, eds, 74–5, 92–6.

15 Willumsen, ed., 27–9.

16 Willumsen, ed., 27–31.

17 Willumsen, 'Exporting', 59–60; Purchas, 318.

18 Willumsen, ed., 27–31; Sparboe and Hagen, eds, 90–2, 94.

19 Willumsen, ed., 54–5; Jens V. Johansen, 'To Beat a Glass Drum: The Transmission of Popular Notions of Demonology in Denmark and Germany' in Julian Goodare, Rita Voltmer and Liv Helene Willumsen, *Demonology and Witch-Hunting in Early Modern Europe* (London: Routledge, 2020), 233–42.

20 Rune Blix Hagen, 'Sámi Shamanism: The Arctic Dimension', *Magic, Ritual and Witchcraft* 1:2 (2006), 227–33; Willumsen, ed., 377–96.

Chapter Four
The Trial of Joan Wright:
Practical Magic and America's First Witch

1 E. Millicent Sowerby, *The Catalogue of the Library of Thomas Jefferson* (Washington: Library of Congress, 1952–1959), vol. 2, 352–3; MS 'Virginia General Court 1622–29, Cases, with Minutes', vol. 15, https://www.loc.gov/item/mtjbib026596/; Colonial Williamsburg Foundation, *A Study of Taverns of Virginia in the 18th Century* (Williamsburg, 1990); https://research.colonialwilliamsburg.org/DigitalLibrary/view/index.cfm?doc=ResearchReports%5CRR0164.xml#refn3; Jefferson, letters to John Daly Burke, 1 June 1805 and George Wythe, 16 January 1796, https://www.loc.gov/collections/thomas-jefferson-papers/articles-and-essays/virginia; https://www.monticello.org/site/research-and-collections/eyeglasses

2   Ruth Goodman, *How to Be a Tudor* (London: Penguin, 2015), 175–81.

3   Marion Gibson, *Witchcraft: The Basics* (London: Routledge, 2018), 26–7.

4   H.R. McIlwaine, ed., *Minutes of the Council and General Court of Colonial Virginia* (Richmond: Library of Virginia, 1924), 112.

5   McIlwaine, ed., 112; 'Virginia General Court', 288–9, 295; W.W., *A True and Just Recorde* (London, 1582), 2A7v, E3; Marion Gibson, *The Witches of St Osyth* (Cambridge: Cambridge University Press, 2022), 37, 151.

6   Nell Marion Nugent, *Cavaliers and Pioneers* (Richmond: Virginia Land Office, 1934), vol. 1: xxix, 53–4; Avery E. Kolb, 'Early Passengers to Virginia', *Virginia Magazine of History and Biography* 88:4 (1980), 413; W.G. Stanard, 'Abstracts of Virginia Land Patents', *Virginia Historical Magazine* 1:1 to 8:2 (1893–1900), 1:4 441, 5:1 94.

7   Jacob Heffelfinger, *Kecoughtan Old and New* (Hampton, VA: Houston, 1910), 4–7.

8   John Camden Hotten, *The Original Lists of Persons of Quality* (London, 1874), 183, 261; Stanard, 1:4 441; 1:3 311; Martha McCartney, *Documentary History of Jamestown Island*, vol. 3 (Williamsburg, VA: National Park Service, 2000), 51, 406.

9   Hotten, 261–2; Stanard, vol. 2, 79; McIlwaine, ed., 22–4, 82, 101; A.W. Welch, 'Law and the Making of Slavery in Colonial Virginia', *Ethnic Studies Review* 27:1 (2004), 1–22, 2.

10   Hotten, 209; McIlwaine, ed., 14, 19, 44, 61–3, 85, 93. Jane is defended by Isabella Perry in General Court testimony; later Isabella accused Joan, 23 May 1625 ('Virginia General Court', 147; McIlwaine, ed., 62); McCartney, 406.

11   McIlwaine, ed., 104–5, 114, 119; McCartney, 200.

12   1 James 1 c.12 at https://statutes.org.uk/site/the-statutes/seventeenth-century/1604-1-james-1-c-12-an-act-against-witchcraft/

13   Stanard, 1:2 191, 450–1; McCartney, 200; McIlwaine, ed., 58.

14   Stanard, 2:1 70–1; 7:2 193.

15   Stanard, 2:3 181–2; 4:4 423, 426; 7:1 70; McCartney, 135; McIlwaine, ed., 81, 96.

16   Stanard, 3:4 402; William Armstrong Crozier, *Virginia County Records* vol. 6 part 1 (March 1909), 31.

17   Stanard, 1:3 310; 6:2 185; McCartney, 279; McIlwaine, ed., 76.

18   Hotten, 232, 270; McCartney, 17, 35, 131; Stanard, 451–2; McCartney, 129–31, 259; McIlwaine, ed., 113.

19   Stanard, 1:1 84–6, 88–9; 1:4 450; Hotten, 157–8; McCartney, 104, 287–9, 387–8, 411–15.

20   James Sharpe, *The Bewitching of Anne Gunter* (London: Profile, 1999).

21   McIlwaine, ed., 113–14, 4–5, 78, 93, 15–17, 142; Renée Celeste, 'Forty Lashes: The Comparison of Court Punishments in Early Modern England and Colonial Virginia', thesis, Texas Tech University, 2014, 101–2, 113–14.

22   McCartney, 138 (Study Unit 3, Tract E), 341, 406.

Chapter Five
The Trial of Bess Clarke: Disability and
Demonic Families in the English Civil War

1 Essex Record Office D/P 343/1/1; D/DA T212, T218; Gaskill, *Witchfinders*, 9–27; Frances Timbers, 'Witches' Sect or Prayer Meeting? Matthew Hopkins Revisited', *Women's History Review* 17:1 (2008), 21–37; Peter Elmer, 'East Anglia and the Hopkins Trials 1645–1647' at https://practitioners.exeter. ac.uk/wp-content/uploads/2014/11/Eastanglianwitchtrialappendix2.pdf 27; Helen Barrell, 'Mistley and the Witchfinder' (2015) and 'The Witchfinder General' (2017) at https://essexandsuffolksurnames.co.uk/mistley-and-the-witchfinder/ and https://www.freeukgenealogy.org.uk/news/2017/10/25/ halloween-special-guest-post/; Philip Cunningham, 'The Witch Finder's Step Sister' at www.manningtree-museum.org.uk

2 ERO D/P 343/1/1, D/DA T218, D/DA T223, D/DHw Q1, D/DHw M72; Gaskill, *Witchfinders*, 41.

3 ERO D/P 343/1/1; Gaskill, *Witchfinders*, 38, 41; John Stearne, *A Confirmation and Discovery of Witch-Craft* (London, 1648), 14–15; Malcolm Gaskill, ed., *The Matthew Hopkins Trials* (London: Pickering and Chatto, 2003).

4 H.F., *A True and Exact Relation* (London, 1645) in Gaskill, ed., 11; ERO D/P 343/1/1; National Archives ASSI 35/62/1–35/86/1 (6 March 1620–17 July 1645).

5 Michael Sachs, Jörg Bojunga and Albrecht Encke, 'Historical Evolution of Limb Amputation', *World Journal of Surgery* 23 (1999), 1088–93; Eric Gruber von Arni and Andrew Hopper, 'Battle-Scarred: Surgery, Medicine and Military Welfare During the British Civil Wars' at http:// www.nationalcivilwarcentre.com/media/civilwarcentre/Battle-scarred%20 NCWC%; Alanna Skuse, *Surgery and Selfhood in Early Modern England* (Cambridge: Cambridge University Press, 2021), 5, 87–93, 108.

6 Ronald Holmes, *Witchcraft in British History* (London: Frederick Muller, 1974), 134; Sharpe, *Instruments*, 128; ERO D/P 343/1/1, D/P 173/1/1; H.F., 16.

7 Matthew Hopkins, *The Discovery of Witches* (London, 1645), 2, 4, 6; H.F., 11–13; Stearne, 322.

8 ERO D/DCm T99, D/DHw T59, D/DHw M73; Stearne, 17–18; Hopkins, 3, 5, 6; H.F., 2–3.

9 Stearne, 'To the Reader', 13–15; H.F., 2–3, 13; Elmer, 28; Hopkins, 5.

10 H.F., 2; Stearne, 15.

11 Stearne, 15, 322, 353; H.F., 2–3, 12, 13, 16; ERO D/DHw M72, D/DHw M66.

12 George Gifford, *A Dialogue Concerning Witches and Witchcrafts* (London, 1593), iv; ERO D/DHw T55, D/DHw M29; Stearne, 38–9.

13 Gaskill, *Witchfinders*, 37–8; ASSI 35/81/1, 35/82/2.

14 Timbers; H.F., 12, 17, 20–1; Stearne, 39.

15 H.F., 19; ERO D/DHw T120, D/DHw M72, D/DQs 4.
16 H.F., 20.
17 H.F., 24–5.
18 NA ASSI 35/86/1; Gaskill, *Witchfinders*, 123–7; Gibson, *St Osyth*, chapter six.
19 ERO D/Hw M72, D/DHw M29.
20 NA ASSI 35/86/1; Elmer, 'East Anglia'; Stearne, 11.
21 Hopkins, 1, 6.
22 Hopkins, 3, 10; ERO D/DRc B10; John Gaule, *Select Cases of Conscience Touching Witches and Witchcraft* (London, 1646), A3–A4; Stearne, 60–1.

Chapter Six
The Trial of Tatabe: Slavery and
Survival on the Salem Frontier

1   Elaine G. Breslaw, *Tituba, Reluctant Witch of Salem* (New York: New York University Press, 1997), 12–14, 24–5; Chadwick Hansen, 'The Metamorphosis of Tituba', *New England Quarterly* 47:1 (1974), 3–12; *Salem Witchcraft Trials* at https://salem.lib.virginia.edu/home.html: Essex County Court Archives ECCA1163, Massachusetts Archives, 135:20, 31, Judicial Archives Boston, Superior Court of Judicature, 7–8.
2   Andrés Reséndez, *The Other Slavery* (2016; New York: Mariner, 2017); 'An American Secret' (20 November 2017) at https://www.npr.org/2017/11/20/565410514/an-american-secret-the-untold-story-of-native-american-enslavement; Breslaw, 13–14; Bernard Rosenthal, *Salem Story* (Cambridge: Cambridge University Press, 1993), 13.
3   Breslaw, 6–8, 13–18.
4   Larry Gragg, *A Quest for Security* (New York and Westport: Greenwood, 1990), 68; Breslaw, 3–8.
5   William Rawlin, *The Laws of Barbados* (London, 1699), 155.
6   Jacob Eliezer Pomerantz, 'Building the Bridge: Labour and Governance in Seventeenth-Century Bridgetown, Barbados', thesis, University of Pittsburgh, 2021, 22–3, 56, 142; Fuentes, 19–26, 30–3, 37–41.
7   Sue Appleby, *The Cornish in the Caribbean* (Market Harborough: Troubador, 2019), 134; Breslaw, 21–3, 54.
8   Gragg, 2–9, 13–16, 72–3; Breslaw, 58–61; Richard Ford, 'A New Map of the Island of Barbadoes' (c.1675–1680), John Carter Brown Library, 8189–32 at https://jcb.lunaimaging.com/luna/servlet/detail/JCBMAPS~1~1~1133~100880001:A-New-Map-of-the-Island-of-Barbadoe.
9   https://salem.lib.virginia.edu/home.html: New York Public Library NYPL04B; Gragg, 32, 34, 46–9, 50–1; Emerson Baker, *A Storm of Witchcraft* (Oxford: Oxford University Press, 2015), 43, 53–5; Richard B. Trask, *The Devil Hath Been Raised* (Danvers: Yeoman, 1992), 111.
10 Danvers Library, Salem Church Records: https://www.danverslibrary.org/archive/wp-content/uploads/2015/09/ChurchRecords_020.jpg; Breslaw, 78–87; Baker, 87–9.

11 Mary Beth Norton, *In the Devil's Snare* (New York: Alfred A. Knopf, 2002), 5, 21, 48–50, 86–111; https://salem.lib.virginia.edu/home.html: NYPL03A-B.

12 Danvers Library, Salem Church Records: https://www.danverslibrary. org/archive/wp-content/uploads/2015/09/ChurchRecords_020.jpg; https://www.danverslibrary.org/archive/wp-content/uploads/2015/09/ ChurchRecords_021.jpg; John Hale, *A Modest Enquiry into the Nature of Witchcraft* (Boston, 1702), 23–4; Rosenthal, 25–7.

13 https://salem.lib.virginia.edu/home.html: NYPL03B; Norton, 21–7, 56–7.

14 https://salem.lib.virginia.edu/home.html: Massachusetts Historical Society, 16b, 23b, 37a; Norton, 58–9; Rosenthal, 13.

15 https://salem.lib.virginia.edu/home.html: ECCA1033, 1034, 2131; some accounts contain standard English; this one (by Jonathan Corwin) appears to record *verbatim*.

16 https://salem.lib.virginia.edu/home.html: ECCA1033, 1034, 2131, 1016.

17 https://salem.lib.virginia.edu/home.html: ECCA1015, 1016, 1017, 1018, 1021.

18 https://salem.lib.virginia.edu/home.html: ECCA1013, 1029; NYPL03A-B. Hathorne says the search post-dated her examination, but it has already occurred in NYPL03B.

19 https://salem.lib.virginia.edu/home.html: ECCA1034, 1032, 1007; NYPL05.

20 https://salem.lib.virginia.edu/home.html: NYPL04B.

21 https://salem.lib.virginia.edu/home.html: Massachusetts Supreme Judicial Court Archives: Suffolk, 31–2:2760.

22 https://salem.lib.virginia.edu/home.html: ECCA1008, 2130, 1013, Massachusetts Archives, 135:24, Massachusetts Archives Judicial, J01–4.

23 https://salem.lib.virginia.edu/home.html: Massachusetts Supreme Judicial Court Archives: Suffolk, 31–2:2760.

24 Danvers Library, Salem Church Records: https://www.danverslibrary. org/archive/wp-content/uploads/2015/09/ChurchRecords_025.jpg; https://www.danverslibrary.org/archive/wp-content/uploads/2015/09/ ChurchRecords_026.jpg; https://www.danverslibrary.org/archive/ wp-content/uploads/2015/09/ChurchRecords_041.jpg; Baker, 9, 229–32, 255; Norton, 290–2.

25 https://salem.lib.virginia.edu/home.html: Massachusetts Historical Society undated 'Restitution Document'; Norton, 408.

26 https://salem.lib.virginia.edu/home.html: ECCA2140, 2141, 2143.

Intermission:
From Demonology to Doubt

1 Increase Mather, *Cases of Conscience Concerning Evil Spirits* (Boston, 1692); Balthazar Bekker, *De Betoverde Weereld* (*The World Bewitched*) (Amsterdam, 1691); Joseph Glanvill, *Saducismus Triumphatus* (London, 1682); Thomas; Bostridge.

2 Owen Davies, *Witchcraft, Magic and Culture 1736–1951* (Manchester: Manchester University Press, 1999) and *America Bewitched* (Oxford: Oxford University Press, 2013).

3 Massimo Introvigne, *Satanism: A Social History* (Leiden: Brill, 2016), 35–43.

4 Brian Levack, 'King Louis XIV of France: The Decriminalisation of French Witchcraft' in Levack, ed., *The Witchcraft Sourcebook* (London: Routledge, 2015), 181–3.

5 9 George 2 c.5 at https://statutes.org.uk/site/the-statutes/eighteenth-century/1735-9-george-2-c-5-the-witchcraft-act/

Chapter Seven
The Trial of Marie-Catherine Cadière:
Witches Reimagined and a French Revolution

1 http://www.toulon.maville.com (2010); Jason T. Kuznicki, 'Sorcery and Publicity: The Cadière-Girard Scandal of 1730–1731', *French History* 21:3 (2007), 294–5.

2 *A Compleat Translation of the Whole Case of Mary Catherine Cadière* (London, 1732), 17–19; Mita Choudhury, *The Wanton Jesuit and the Wayward Saint* (University Park: Pennsylvania State University Press, 2015), 16–19.

3 Cyrille Roumagnac, *L'Arsenal de Toulon* (Stroud: Allan Sutton, 2001); David Hannay, 'Toulon', *Encyclopaedia Britannica* (Cambridge: Cambridge University Press 1911), 98–9; Michel Vergé-Franceschi, *Toulon* (Paris: Tallandier, 2002).

4 Choudhury, 22–5; Jules Michelet, *La Sorcière*, trans. A.R. Allinson as *Satanism and Witchcraft* (London: Tandem, 1965), 170–1.

5 Choudhury, 21, 32, 37.

6 *Compleat Translation*, 52; Choudhury, 38; Kuznicki, 295.

7 Choudhury, 39–40.

8 *Compleat Translation*, 26–8, 41, 165; *A Compleat Translation of the Sequel* (London, 1732), 50–1; Choudhury, 39–43, 25; Kuznicki, 296–7.

9 *Compleat Translation*, 48, 31, 35–9, 128, 37, 144–6; Choudhury, 49–56, 63–4, 70–1; *Memoirs of Miss Mary-Catherine Cadière* (London, 1731), 10.

10 *Compleat Translation*, 22, 47, 19, 25, 30, 58–9; Mark 5:1–20, Matthew 8.28–34, Luke 8:26–39; Choudhury, 53, 71; Kuznicki, 297–8.

11 Kuznicki, 301–4; Choudhury, 53, 56–7, 59–61, 4, 108–9; Colin Haydon, 'Anti-Catholicism and Obscene Literature: *The Case of Mrs. Mary Catharine Cadière* and Its Context', *Studies in Church History* 48 (2012), 202–18; *A Defence of F. John Baptist Girard*, parts 1–3 (London, 1731).

12 *Compleat Translation*, 43, 155–6; Choudhury, 75–7, 110.

13 *Compleat Translation*, 60–1, 65–9, 75; Choudhury, 78–81; *The Tryal of Father John-Baptist Girard* (London, 1732), 39.

14 *Compleat Translation*, 66–7, 73, 98–135; *Tryal*, 34; Choudhury, 90–5, 97–8.

15 Choudhury, 110, 115 – *sorcier/ère* means 'sorcerer' and 'witch'.

16 *Compleat Translation*, 115, 128; *Tryal*, 40; *Sequel*, 14; Choudhury, 115–21.

17 *Compleat Translation*, 214; *Tryal*, 47; Choudhury, 113–69; Kuznicki, 304, 307, 311. Some accounts purport to be by Marie-Catherine but reiterate already-published material.

18 Michelet, 173, 179; Jennifer Airey, 'Cult: The Case of Marie-Catherine Cadière', *Studies in Eighteenth-Century Literature* 48 (2019), 257–8.

19 J-K. Huysmans, *Là-Bas*, trans. Terry Hale (London: Penguin, 2001), 18; Linda Orr, 'A Sort of History: Michelet's *La Sorcière*', *Yale French Studies* 59 (1980), 128–9.

Chapter Eight
The Trial of Montague Summers:
Satanism, Sex and Demonology Reborn

1 *Kelly's Directory of Clergy* (London, 1909), 1: 990; Parish Register, St Michael, Two Mile Hill 1881, 1891 census at Ancestry.com; Parish Register, Emmanuel, Clifton, Bristol Archives P.EC/R/2/a; Montague Summers, *Antinous*, ed. Timothy D'Arch Smith and Edwin Pouncey (1907; London: Cecil Woolf, 1995), 11.

2 Montague Summers, *The Galanty Show* (London: Cecil Woolf, 1980), 81–5, 33, 59–61, 21; Joseph Jerome (Brocard Sewell), *Montague Summers* (London: Cecil Woolf, 1965), 2, 30, 88.

3 Joseph Foster, *Oxford Men and Their Colleges 1880–1892* (Oxford, 1893), 2:583; Summers, *Galanty*, 60–1, 47, 52, 57; Jerome, 5; Victoria Bates, *Sexual Forensics in Victorian and Edwardian England* (Basingstoke: Palgrave Macmillan, 2016), 13; Cambridge University Library GBR/0012/MS Add.9813/C1/108.

4 Summers, *Antinous*, 15, 19, 33–4, 36–7, 73–4.

5 Introvigne, 145–150.

6 Huysmans, 224–8 and *Là-Bas*, ed. Montague Summers (London: Fortune Press, 1946), 5–10; Simon Heffer, ed., *Chips Channon: The Diaries 1918–38* (London: Hutchinson, 2021), vol. 1, 12 January 1928.

7 Gloucestershire Heritage Hub PS/SO/M1/1 and 2, D5009 1908–1910 and D2430 1908–1915, Q/SIb7.

8 Bates, 12, 180–1; Arthur Hill, ed., *Henry Nicholson Ellacombe* (London: Country Life/Newnes, 1916), 43–5, 198–215, 53.

9 1911 Census and London Street Directory 1920, NW3, at Ancestry.com; Jerome, 19, 24, 25, 44, 58.

10 Heffer, ed., vol. 1: 14 and 24 February, 8, 12, 23 and 30 March 1928.

11 Jerome, xviii, 28, 17.

12 Jerome, xiii, 70–1, 22; 1939 Register; 1891 Census at Ancestry.com

13 Montague Summers, *The History of Witchcraft* (1926; London: Mystic Press, 1988), xiv, 32, 6–7, xvi, 1; some translations were by E.A. Ashwin.

14 Summers, *History*, 10, 17, 22, 26; Heffer, ed., 12 January 1928.

15 Sybil Thorndike, 'Foreword' in Jerome, ix, xv.

16 Andrews Newspaper Index Cards, 1790–1976, 11 April 1950 at Ancestry. com; Gerard P. O'Sullivan, 'The Manuscripts of Montague Summers', *Antigonish Review* 159 (2009), 111–31; Frederick Kaigh, *Witchcraft and Magic of Africa* (London: Lesley, 1947), 153 and Montague Summers, 'Foreword', viii, x–xii.

Chapter Nine
The Trial of John Blymyer:
Pow-Wow and Poverty in Pennsylvania

1 Richard F. Weingroff, 'From 1916 to 1939: The Federal–State Partnership at Work', *Public Roads* 60:1 (1996) at https://highways.dot.gov/public-roads/ summer-1996/1916-1939-federal-state-partnership-work; Stephen H. Smith. 'The Susquehanna Trail as a Ribbon of Concrete', *YorksPast* (7 November 2014) at https://yorkblog.com/yorkspast/the-susquehanna-trail-as-a-ribbon-of-concrete/; Arthur H. Lewis, *Hex* (New York: Trident, 1969), 78–9.

2 Karl Herr, *Hex and Spellwork* (York Beach, ME: Red Wheel/Weiser, 2002), 3.

3 Theda Kenyon, *Witches Still Live* (1929; London: Rider, 1931), 13.

4 J. Ross McGinnis, *Trials of Hex* (np: Davis/Trinity, 2000), 214, 205; Lewis, 42–4, 47, 55–7.

5 McGinnis, 6–8, 23–4, 191–2, 213, 402; 1910, 1920 United States Federal Census at Ancestry.com; John George Hohman/Hoffman, *Pow-wows or the Long Lost Friend* (USA, 1820) at https://www.sacred-texts.com/ame/ pow/index.htm; Lewis, 26–9, 62–8.

6 McGinnis, 4; Hohman, 'To Remove Bruises and Pains'.

7 Patricia A. Cooper, *Once a Cigar Maker* (Urbana: University of Illinois Press, 1987), 288.

8 1870, 1880, 1890, 1900, 1910, 1920 United States Federal Census at Ancestry.com; McGinnis, 317, 25; Lewis, 53–4.

9 McGinnis, 215–20, 226, 104, 252, 282–3, 286; Lewis, 71–82, 84–5.

10 Lewis, 69; McGinnis, 228–30, 234.

11 Cooper, 205–9; Lewis, 20, 23–5, 35, 38–9, 48–50; McGinnis, 155–7, 165, 204, 186; 1900, 1910, 1920 United States Federal Census, 'Emanuel Blymire Dies Suddenly at Home near East Prospect', US World War II Draft Registration Card, Pennsylvania Death Certificates 1906–1963 at Ancestry.com; in the documentary *Hex Hollow*, made with the Blymyer/ Blymire and Rehmeyer families, his relatives believe him guilty (dir. Shane Free, Freestyle Media, 2015).

12 Lewis, 58–66; McGinnis, 221, 277, 3–21.

13 McGinnis, 65–70, 75–83, 222; Lewis, 96–103.

14 Lewis, 104–5, 120; McGinnis, 93, 95, 105, 173, 181–2, 235–6, 193–6, 208–16.

15 McGinnis, 214–19, 226–9; Lewis, 120–63; Pennsylvania Death Certificates at Ancestry.com

16 McGinnis, 222–3, 236, 240–3, 259, 277, 292–6, 301–2; Lewis, 164–71; 'District Attorney Misled "Hex" Slayer, Is Plea for New Trial', *Daily News* (15 April 1929), np; 'Curry Found Guilty; Life Term Is Asked', *Gettysburg Times* (11 January 1929), 1 at Ancestry.com

17 Lewis, 176–83; Pennsylvania, US Prison, Reformatory and Workhouse Records 1829–1971, ESP, Bertillion Handbooks; 1940, 1950 United States Federal Census at Ancestry.com; 'Boy Sentenced to Life in Hex Death Paroled', *Daily News* (13 July 1939); 'Youth in Hex Case Paroled', *Gettysburg Times* (21 June 1939), 4; FindAGrave.com; McGinnis, 363, 375, 377, 399, 404.

18 McGinnis, 220; Pennsylvania, US, Prison . . . Records 5407; 1930 United States Federal Census, US World War II Draft Registration Card 3352, at Ancestry.com; 'John Blymyer, "Hex" Slaying Defendant, 76', *Philadelphia Inquirer* (13 May 1972), 6.

19 'Witchcraft Trial in America', *Civil and Military Gazette* (Lahore) (5 January 1929), 14; *Aberdeen Press and Journal* (14 January 1929), 7; 'Black Magic', *Evening Star* (Dunedin) (26 January 1929), 5; McGinnis, 160, 274, *Philadelphia Record* (11 January 1929), np; 'Will Prosecute Witch Doctors', *Charleroi Mail* (15 December 1928), 5 at Ancestry.com

20 Owen Davies, *A Supernatural War* (Oxford: Oxford University Press, 2019); Hutton, *Triumph*, 171–201, 205–52.

Chapter Ten
The Trial of Nellie Duncan:
Witchcraft Acts and World War Two

1 C.E. Bechhofer Roberts, *The Trial of Mrs Duncan* (London: Jarrolds, 1945), 337; Malcolm Gaskill, *Hellish Nell* (London: Fourth Estate, 2001), 230; Gena Brealey, *The Two Worlds of Helen Duncan* (London: Regency, 1985), 116.

2 1901, 1911 census at ScotlandsPeople.gov.uk

3 Brealey, 18–19, 24–6, 32–9; Gaskill, *Hellish*, 31–47, 62–3; Marriages, District of Saint Giles, Edinburgh at ScotlandsPeople.gov.uk

4 Kenneth Macauley, 'Birth Control Knowledge in Scotland 1900–1975', thesis, University of Glasgow, 2015, 68, 71, 89–90.

5 Brealey, 42–8; Gaskill, *Hellish*, 64–7, 73.

6 Alex Owen, *The Darkened Room* (Chicago: University of Chicago Press, 1989), 10, 93, 146–7.

7 Brealey, 20–2, 40–2, 48–68; Victoria Duncan, 'Secrets of My Second Sight', and 'My Clairvoyante Secrets', *People's Journal* (7 October, 21 October, 25 November 1933), 24, 24, 22; Gaskill, *Hellish*, 34–9, 72, 154; NA DPP 2/1204; *Parliamentary Debates* 481:24 (London: HMSO, 1 December 1950), 1464.

8 Macauley, 82; Gaskill, *Hellish*, 330, 332.

9 Brealey; Bechhofer Roberts, 37; Gaskill, *Hellish*, 114; K.M. Goldney, 'Mrs

Helen Duncan' (9 May 1957), CUL GBR/0012/MS/SPR/Mediums Duncan, Mrs. Helen; Victoria Duncan, 'Secrets of My Second Sight' (18 November 1933), 24.

10 Bechhofer Roberts, 37, 133; Gaskill, *Hellish*, 126–38; Harry Price, *Regurgitation and the Duncan Mediumship* (London: National Laboratory of Psychical Research, 1931); CUL GBR/0012/MS/SPR/Mediums Duncan; Manfred Cassirer, *Medium on Trial* (Stansted: PN Publishing, 1996), 16–48.

11 Victoria Duncan, 'My Second-Sight Secrets', *People's Journal* (9 September 1933), 6–7; (16 September 1933), 6; 'Secrets of My Second Sight' (7 October 1933), 24; (14 October 1933), 25; 'My Second-Sight Secrets' (21 October 1933), 24; (28 October 1933), 25; (4 November 1933), 25; (11 November 1933), 25; 'Secrets of My Second Sight' (18 November 1933), 24; 'My Clairvoyante Secrets' (25 November 1933), 22; 'Saved Man from Committing Terrible Crime' (2 December 1933), 23; 'My Second-Sight Secrets' (9 December 1933), 25; 'Mending Broken Hearts' (16 December 1933).

12 1939 Register EBCQ County Borough of Portsmouth 90/1 at Ancestry.com; Bechhofer Roberts, 51; NA DPP 2/1204, CRIM 1/1581, HO 144/22172; CUL GBR/0012/MS/SPR/Mediums Duncan; 'Humbug – Pest', *Daily Mirror* (1 April 1944), np; Phyllis Davies, 'A Maid Saw Through Mrs Duncan's Claim to Be a Medium', *Daily Mail* (4 April 1944), np.

13 Mass Observation, 'Portsmouth 1941' File Report 850; 'Portsmouth', Report 606 (March 1941); 'Portsmouth Shops and Shopping', Report 876 (September 1941); 'Notes on Air Raids in Portsmouth', Report 271 (June 1940); 'Public Opinion', Report 1147–8 (March 1942); 'I'm Getting Fed Up with Spies', Report 1035 (January 1942) and Diary 5049; 'Channel Roar', *Hampshire Telegraph and Post* (14 April 1944), 13.

14 Lucinda Moore, 'Music and Morale – Lena Ashwell and the Healing Power of Concerts at the Front', *Picturing the Great War*, 18 July 2014 at blog. maryevans.com; Bechhofer Roberts, 18, 337, 141, 153, 159, 208; *Evening News* (4 September 1943), 5.

15 Bechhofer Roberts, 36, 109, 232, 238, 280; NA HO 144/22172.

16 1939 Register at Ancestry.com; NA DPP 2/1204, CRIM 1/1581; CUL GBR/0012/MS/SPR/36 Charles Loseby; Bechhofer Roberts, 93, 49–50, 132, 140; '"Group of Charlatans"' Says Counsel', *Evening News* (15 January, 29 February 1944, 1 May 1943), 5, 4, 5.

17 Bechhofer Roberts, 50, 57, 123, 190, 214, 223–4, 234, 250, 260, 277, 282, 293, 303; Brealey, 124, 130; 1939 Register at Ancestry.com

18 Bechhofer Roberts, 44, 79, 82, 92, 151, 283; NA DPP 2/1204; Royal Air Force Commands, Halifax II BB324 at http://www.rafcommands.com/database/serials/details.php?uniq=BB324; NA HO 144/22172; Brealey, 113; Gaskill, *Hellish*, 176; CUL GBR/0012/MS/SPR/36 Charles Loseby.

19 Bechhofer Roberts, 169, 173, 267, 274; Gaskill, *Hellish*, 243; 'Mrs Duncan Breaks Down at the Old Bailey', *Portsmouth Evening News* (29 and 30 March 1944), 4, 5.

20 UK Navy Lists 1942–1945 at Ancestry.com; Bechhofer Roberts, 53; NA DPP 2/1204, HO 144/22172, CRIM 1/1581.

21 Bechhofer Roberts, 14–15, 53, 64, 127; NA HO 144/22172; George Orwell, 'Clink' (1932) in *Decline of the English Murder* (London: Penguin, 2009), 1–14.

22 Bechhofer Roberts, 4; NA DPP 2/1204; Gaskill, *Hellish*, 198; CUL GBR/0012/MS/SPR/36 Charles Loseby and Mediums Duncan.

23 NA CRIM 2/256 (6 March), DPP 2/1204; James Morton, 'Extraordinary Judgement', *Law Gazette* (27 October 2014); Peter Cotes, 'Obituary: Judge Henry Elam', *Independent* (27 August 1993), 23; Bechhofer Roberts, 264; Gaskill, *Hellish*, 200–1, 294–5.

24 NA WO 339/14142; *London Gazette* supplement (6 September 1915), 8830; Gaskill, *Hellish*, 196–7.

25 *Burke's Peerage* volume 3, 3540 at https://www.burkespeerage.com/

26 Bechhofer Roberts, 54–5; B. Abdy Collins, *Mrs Duncan's Trial* (London: Psychic Press, 1945).

27 Bechhofer Roberts, 43, 114–15.

28 Bechhofer Roberts, 306, 98–9, 311.

29 Hansard, 9 April, 19 July, 20, 27 November 1919, 4, 11, 19, 27 February 1920 at http://www.theyworkforyou.com; Fiona Reid, 'The Ex-Services Welfare Society and Mentally Wounded Veterans After the Great War', *War in History* 14:3 (2007), 347–71; Bechhofer Roberts, 18, 114–15, 119, 121; CUL GBR/0012/MS/SPR/36; Charles Loseby, *Parliamentary Debates* at https://api.parliament.uk/historic-hansard/people/captain-charles-loseby/1920

30 Bechhofer Roberts, 340, 261, 287, 337; Gaskill, *Hellish*, 154–6; NA DPP 2/1204, HO 144/22172, 'Medium Sentenced for Fraud', *The Times* (4 April 1944); '"Fake Séances to Cheat War-Bereaved" Charge' (1 March 1944); 'Nine Months' Imprisonment for Medium', *Portsmouth Evening News* (1 April 1944), np; 'Medium Weeps and Shouts at Verdict', *News Chronicle* (1 April 1944), np.

31 CUL GBR/0012/NS/SPR/36 Charles Loseby and Mediums Duncan.

32 G.H. Bennett, 'Women and the Battle of the Atlantic 1939–45' in Angela K. Smith, *Gender and Warfare in the Twentieth Century* (Manchester: Manchester University Press, 2004), 111–31.

33 Bechhofer Roberts, 23–4, 337; NA HO 144/22172, CRIM 1/1581, 4/1709, DPP 2/1204; Brealey, 118; Gaskill, *Hellish*, 188, 323–4; CUL GBR/0012/MS/SPR/36 Charles Loseby and Mediums Duncan; 1939 Register at Ancestry.com; Gaskill, *Hellish*, 282. Another security story concerns HMS *Hood*.

34 Brealey, 133–4, 143, 148; Gaskill, *Hellish*, 340; NA HO 144/22172; W.A.E. Jones, 'Helen Duncan's Wealth from Seances', *Daily Herald* (4 April 1944); CUL GBR/0012/MS/SPR/Mediums Duncan; *Parliamentary Debates*; 'Helen Duncan was Murdered', *Two Worlds* (26 January 1957), 1.

35 NA HO 144/22172; Gaskill, *Hellish*, 199, 258–60; CUL GBR/0012/MS/SPR/Mediums Duncan.

36 NA HO 144/22172; *Evening News* (26 August 1943), 5; Maurice Barbanell,

'Behind the Scenes in the Helen Duncan Case', *Psychic News* (8 April 1944), 7.

Chapter Eleven
The Trial of Bereng Lerotholi and Gabashane Masupha: Magical Murder at the End of European Empire

1   Colin Murray and Peter Sanders, *Medicine Murder in Colonial Lesotho* (Edinburgh: Edinburgh University Press, 2005), 57, 88, 94; 'Ritual Murder in Basutoland', *Manchester Guardian* (27 August 1948), 5; 'Witchcraft Murder', *Daily Telegraph* (17 November 1948), 5; 'Mr. Jones Takes On the Witch Doctors', *Daily Mail* (18 July 1949), 2; Frederic D. Ellenberger, *History of the Basuto* (London: Caxton, 1912), 231–3.

2   Ellenberger, *History*, 249, 259–60, 267: Elizabeth A. Eldredge, 'Land, Politics and Censorship: The Historiography of Nineteenth-Century Lesotho', *History in Africa* 15 (1988), 191–209; Hugh Ashton, 'Ritual Murder in Basutoland' in NA DO 119/1377.

3   NA DO 35/1177; 'Woman Chief to Die for "Witch" Murder', *Daily Mirror*, 8 and 'Mr Jones', *Daily Mail* (27 August 1948), 2; Lord Wemyss, 'Life in the Land of Witchcraft', *Dundee Courier* (12 October 1949), np; 'Death Law in Colonies', *Daily Telegraph* (5 April 1947), 5; Peter Sanders, *Throwing Down White Man* (Pontypool: Merlin, 2011), 11.

4   'Seeiso Amelia 'Matsaba Mantšebo', *Dictionary of African Biography*, ed. Henry Louis Gates, Emmanual Akyeampong and Steven J. Niven (Oxford: Oxford University Press, 2011), 320; Elizabeth Eldredge, *Power in Colonial Africa* (Madison: University of Wisconsin Press, 2007), 191, 202–4, 211–12; Murray and Sanders, 337–9, 35–6, 95; NA DO 119/1376, DO 35/1177; L.B.B.J. Machobane, *Government and Change in Lesotho 1800–1966* (Basingstoke: Palgrave Macmillan, 1990), 252.

5   Murray and Sanders, 37. 'Basutoland' designates the colonial administrative unit; 'Basotho' and 'Lesotho' the people and modern nation.

6   'Queen Dies for Ritual Murder', *Aberdeen Journal* (9 June 1949), np; Scott Rosenberg and Richard F. Weisfelder, *Historical Dictionary of Lesotho* (Lanham, MD: Scarecrow Press, 2013), 302; Peter Sanders, *Last of the Queen's Men* (Johannesburg: Witwatersrand University Press, Morija Museum and Archives, 2000), 131; http://members.iinet.net.au/~royalty/states/africa/lesotho.html; G.I. Jones, 'Chiefly Succession in Basutoland' in Jack Goody, ed., *Succession to High Office* (Cambridge: Cambridge University Press, 1966), 57, 69–70; Sanders, *Throwing*, 18.

7   NA FCO 1168 S197, CUL PS/MED/D/5.2; Murray and Sanders, 32–3, 103–5; Rosenberg and Weisfelder, 163; Sanders, *Last*, 136–44.

8   Rosenberg and Weisfelder, 76–7; Murray and Sanders, 30–3, 440, n.24; NA DO35/1177; 'Personalities of the Week: At Home and Abroad', *Illustrated London News* (29 July 1939), 198; Marc Epprecht, *This Matter of Women*

Is Getting Very Bad (Pietermaritzburg: University of Natal Press, 2000), 108, 110; CUL PS/MED/D/4; NA DO119/1373.

9   NA DO 35/1177; Murray and Sanders, 48; Machobane, 231–33; 'Basuto Appeal to the King', *Manchester Guardian* (10 November 1949), 6; Sanders, 48–52.

10 CUL PS/MED/D/5.2, Murray and Sanders, 101, 108–9, 92, 244; G.I. Jones, *Basutoland Medicine Murder* (London: HMSO, 1951), 97; NA DO 119/1378, DO 35/4155, 4154; Epprecht, 114; J.A. Gray, 'The Land of Moshesh', *South Africa* (November 1948), 33–4.

11 'Ritual Murder Allegation', *Basutoland News* (3 and 10 August 1948), 2, 1; 'Spiritual Danger', 'Maseru Murmurings', (10 August 1948), 2, 'Native Medicine Men May Practice – But Not Witch Doctors' (17 August 1948), 1; Sanders, *Last*, 25.

12 Murray and Sanders, 100–8, 110–11, 114; the full court record remains undiscovered: Lesotho National Archives are inaccessible, but extracts are in CUL PS/MED/D/5.1 and other files quoted; J.R. Crawford, 'The History and Nature of the Judicial System of Botswana, Lesotho and Swaziland – Introduction and the Superior Courts', *South African Law Journal* 86:4 (1969), 478, 87:1 (1970), 77–8; NA DO 119/1372.

13 Murray and Sanders, 101; 'Maseru Murmurings', 'Ritual Murder Trials', *Basutoland News* (17, 24, 31 August 1948), 2, 1, 1, (7 September 1948), 1, 4; 'Ritual Murder Charge', 'Ritual Murder Case Continued', 'Ritual Murder Case' (9, 16, 23 November 1948), 1–2, 1, 1; Lesotho National Archives, box 58 in Murray and Sanders, 99–103, 107, 464–5 and NA DO 119/1372, 1374, 1377; Gray, 34.

14 Tumahole Bereng and Others v the King (13 January 1949) at https://www.casemine.com/judgement/in/56b4961e607dba348f016d3b; 'Bereng Griffith Lerotholi and Others v the King', NA DO 119/1374; 'Our London Correspondence: Basutos' Appeal' and 'Basutos' Appeal Dismissed', *Manchester Guardian* (22, 26 July 1949), 6, 8; 'Ritual Murder', *Times* (8 February 1949), 3, untitled (16 February 1949); 'Allegation of Ritual Murder', *Basutoland News* (19, 26 October, 1948), 2, 1; DO 119/1376, 1377, 1379, 1383, 4102; Crawford, 'History', 80; Murray and Sanders, 109, 248, 264–5; Lambeth Palace Library, Fisher Papers 1949.64.

15 *Afro-American* (3 August 1949), 5; *New York Age* (13 August 1949), 25.

16 *Inkululeko* (19 November 1949) in CUL PS/MED/D/8; *Afro-American* (3 August 1949), 5; NA DO 119/1379; Jones, *Basutoland*, v, 34; DO 199/1377, 1378, 35/4154, 1177; Eldredge, *Power*, 202–3; PS/MED/D/3, Murray and Sanders, 126; NA CAB 129/45/17.

Chapter Twelve
The Trial of 'Shula': Witchcraft in Africa

1   B.M. Khaketla, *Mosali a Nkhola*, trans. Johannes Malefetsane Lenake as *She's to Blame* (Cape Town: Oxford University Press, 2019), 2, 285; PS

MED/D/9; Murray and Sanders, 176, 180–2; Nhlanhla Maake, 'Murder They Cried: Revisiting Medicine Murders in Literature', University of the Witwatersrand Institute for Advanced Social Research (1996) at wiredspace. wits.ac.za

2   N.M. Tlale, 'Ritual Murders in Basutoland', *African World* (February, 1949), 11–12; 'President Speaks on "Liretlo' Murders"', *Mohlabani* (May, 1957), 14, (June, 1957) 12, (November, 1957), 16–18.

3   'The Ritual Murders of People with Albinism in Malawi' (2 February 2017) at https://www.amnesty.org.uk/ritual-murders-people-albinism-malawi; Decca Aitkenhead, 'I Used to Work on Love Island: Now I Fight Against Child Sacrifice' (22 January 2023) at https://www.thetimes.co.uk/article/ fceoof56-9353-11ed-a195-2b5c5dce7b9b?shareToken=99e3374a255db7 662399e001926737d1; Jones, *Basutoland*, v; David Pratten, *The Man-Leopard Murders* (Edinburgh: Edinburgh University Press, 2007), 11–18, 223, 227, 236–8, 271, 299; 'Ritual Murders', *Western Morning News* (4 August 1949), 7; Richard Rathbone, *Murder and Politics in Colonial Ghana* (New Haven: Yale University Press, 1993); Jeremy Evans, "Where Can We Get a Beast Without Hair?": Medicine Murder in Swaziland from 1970 to 1988', *African Studies* 52:1 (1993), 27–42; Roger Gocking, 'A Chieftaincy Dispute and Ritual Murder in Elmina, Ghana, 1945–6', *Journal of African History* 41:2 (2000), 197–219; Gerard Labuschagne, 'Features and Investigative Implications of Muti Murder in South Africa', *Journal of Investigative Psychology and Offender Profiling* 1:3 (2004), 191–206; Jacques Mathee, 'Indigenous Beliefs and Customs, the South African Criminal Law and Human Rights: Identifying the Issues', *Legal Pluralism and Critical Social Analysis* 53:3 (2021), 522–44; Murray and Sanders, 117, 133, 135, 92; 291; DO 35/4010, 35/1177, 1376, 1378, 35/4155.

4   'Witch-Hunt Murders Surge in Democratic Republic of Congo', *Guardian* (28 September 2021) at https://www.theguardian.com/world/2021/sep/28/ witch-hunt-murders-surge-democratic-republic-congo-women-south-kivu-province; Marco Simoncelli and Davide Lemmi, 'In Pictures: The Witch Hunts of Bangui', *Al Jazeera* (24 March 2020) at https://www.aljazeera. com/gallery/2020/3/24/in-pictures-the-witch-hunts-of-bangui; B.L. Meel, 'Witchcraft in Transkei Region of South Africa', *African Health Sciences* 9:1 (2009), 61–4 at https://www.ncbi.nlm.nih.gov/pmc/articles/PMC2932523/

5   'Ritual Murder', *Basutoland News* (2 August 1949), 4; 'Christianity as Weapon Against Ritual Murder', *The Star* (Johannesburg, 31 May 1949), np; DO 119/1377, 1378; 'Basutoland Murders', *Basutoland News* (7 September 1948), 3; PS/MED/D/5.2; Adam Kuper, 'Like Cutting a Cow', *London Review of Books* 28:13 (6 July 2006), np; DO 119/1378; Murray and Sanders, 126, 143–4, 159, 289.

6   Khaketla, *Mosali*, 270–1, 280, 289.

7   T. Selepe, 'Deculturation: An Afrocentric Critique of B.M. Khaketla's *Mosali a Nkhola*', *Literator* 30:3 (2009) at thefreelibrary.com

8　*I Am Not a Witch*, dir. Rungano Nyoni, Clandestine, BFI, Ffilm Cymru/ Channel Four, 2017, also starring Henry B.J. Phiri and Nancy Mulilo.

9　*Camps of Bondage*, dir. Justice Baidoo, JoyNews/ActionAid, 2019; *The Witches of Gambaga*, dir. Yaba Badoe, AWDF, 2011.

10　UN Resolution 47/8 (12 July 2021) at https://documents-dds-ny.un.org/ doc/UNDOC/GEN/G21/191/99/PDF/G2119199.pdf?OpenElement

11　*Living in Bondage*, dir. Chris Obi Rapu, NEK, 1992–3; *End of the Wicked*, dir. Teco Benson, Liberty Films, 1999; Mark Oppenheimer, 'A Nigerian Witch-Hunter Defends Herself', *New York Times* (21 May 2010), np; Samuel Waje Kunhiyop, 'The Role of Nollywood in Witchcraft Belief and Confession' (2 February 2016) at https://henrycenter.tiu.edu/2016/02/ the-role-of-nollywood-in-witchcraft-belief-and-confessions/; Gary Foxcroft, *Witchcraft Accusations and Persecution: Muti Murders and Human Sacrifice* (WHRIN, 2017), 18–19 at http://www.whrin.org/whrin-releases-latest-un-report/; Adedeji Arijeniwa, Emeke Precious Nwaoboli, Uyinmwen C. Oviasuyi and Ugo A. Tiekuro, 'Perception of the Portrayal of Witchcraft in Nollywood Movies Among Benin Residents' (June 2021) at https://www. researchgate.net/publication/352056511; Benjamin Njoku, 'Nollywood Celebrates Witchcraft, Voodoo, Say Kenyan Filmmakers', *Vanguard* (24 October 2009) at https://www.vanguardngr.com/2009/10/nollywood-celebrates-witchcraft-voodoo-say-kenyan-film-makers/; 'Nollywood and AfricaMagic', *Modern Ghana* (2 December 2009) at https://www. modernghana.com/nollywood/6004/nollywood-and-africamagic-pushing-the-nigerian-motion-pictu.html

12　Bernard Dayo, 'Nigeria's Cinematic Witches Were Rooted in Horrifying Reality', *Foreign Policy* (31 October 2021) at https://foreignpolicy. com/2021/10/31/nigeria-witches-nollywood-horror-cinema-yoruba/; Chijioke Azuawusiefe, 'Nollywood and Pentecostalism: Preaching Salvation, Propagating the Supernatural', *CrossCurrents* 70:3 (2020), 207, 217.

13　Hutton, *Witch*, 28–41; N.V. Ralushai, 'Witchcraft and Ritual Murders' (1996) at http://policyresearch.limpopo.gov.za/handle/123456789/406

14　Marieke Faber Clarke and Pathisa Nyathi, *Lozikeyi Dlodlo* (Bulawayo: Amagugu, 2010), 36–48; Jennifer Weir, 'King Shaka, the Diviners and Colonialism' in Peter Limb, ed., *Orb and Sceptre* (Clayton, VIC: Monash University Press, 2008), 1–18; Stephen Ellis, 'Witch-Hunting in Central Madagascar 1828–1861', *Past and Present* 175:1 (2002), 90–123; Simeon Mesaki, 'The Evolution and Essence of Witchcraft in Pre-Colonial African Societies', *TransAfrican Journal of History* 24 (1995), 162–77; Hutton, *Witch*, 28; Andrew Kettler, 'Smelling Out Anachronism: Embodiment and Hegemony in the Medicine Murder Cases of Basutoland', *Australian Feminist Law Journal* 45:1 (2019), 159–77.

15　Boris Gershman, 'Witchcraft Beliefs as a Cultural Legacy of the Atlantic Slave Trade: Evidence from Two Continents', *European Economic Review* 122 (2020), 2, 5–8; Rosalind Shaw, 'The Production of Witchcraft/ Witchcraft as Production: Memory, Modernity and the Slave Trade in

Sierra Leone', *American Ethnologist* 24:4 (1997), 856–76 and *Memories of the Slave Trade: Ritual and the Historical Imagination in Sierra Leone* (Chicago: University of Chicago Press, 2002); Wyatt MacGaffey, 'The West in Congolese Experience' in Philip D. Curtin, ed., *Africa and the West* (Madison: University of Wisconsin Press, 1972), 49–74.

16 Peter Geschiere, *Witchcraft, Intimacy and Trust* (Chicago: University of Chicago Press, 2013).

17 'Witchcraft Suppression Act 3 of 1957' at https://www.justice.gov.za/legislation/acts/1957-003.pdf, The Witchcraft Act at parliament.gov.zm

18 Yaiman Bande, 'Witches Get Stitches: Analyzing the Legal Framework of the Witchcraft Act cap. 90 of the Laws of Zambia' (12 August 2022) at https://www.linkedin.com/pulse/witches-get-stitches-analyzing-legal-framework-witchcraft-bande; Onesimus K. Mutungi, 'Witchcraft and the Criminal Law in East Africa', *Valparaiso University Law Review* 5:3 (1971), 524–55; Katherine Luongo, *Witchcraft and Colonial Rule in Kenya 1900–1955* (Cambridge: Cambridge University Press, 2011).

19 Pratten, 106–7, 111.

20 Paul P. Murphy, 'Born on the Dark Fringes of the Internet, QAnon Is Now Infiltrating Mainstream American Life and Politics' (3 July 2020) at https://edition.cnn.com/2020/07/03/us/what-is-qanon-trnd/index.html

21 Katrien Pype, 'Branhamist Kindoki: Ethnographic Notes on Connectivity, Technology and Urban Witchcraft in Contemporary Kinshasa', Koen Stroeken, 'Witchcraft Simplex: Experiences of Globalized Pentecostalism in Central and Northwestern Tanzania' in Knut Rio, Michelle MacCarthy and Ruy Blaines, eds, *Pentecostalism and Witchcraft* (Basingstoke: Palgrave Macmillan, 2017), 115–43, 257–79; 'Witchcraft Is Real in Zambia: Amend the Act to Deal with Perpetrators – Magistrate Shanduba', *Lusaka Times* (28 February 2016) at lusakatimes.com; Leo Igwe, 'Ukpabio's Witch Hunting Mission Must Stop', *News Ghana* (15 September 2017) at https://newsghana.com.gh/ukpabios-witch-hunting-mission-must-stop/. See Chapter Thirteen.

22 Robert Brain, 'Child Witches' in Mary Douglas, ed., *Witchcraft Confessions and Accusations* (London: Tavistock Press, 1970), 161–82; Peter Geschiere, 'Child Witches Against the Authority of their Elders' in R. Schefold, J.W. Schoorl and J. Tennekes, eds, *Man, Meaning and History* (Den Haag: Instituut voor Taal, Land en Volkenkunde, 1980), 268–99.

23 Angus Crawford, 'Witnessing "Child Witch" Exorcism in the DR Congo', *BBC News* (2nd March 2012) at https://wwrn.org/articles/36966/

24 Mpoyo Gael, 'The Agony of Congo's "Child Witches"', *AfricaNews* 16 March 2018 at https://www.africanews.com/2018/03/16/the-agony-of-congo-s-child-witches//; Jean La Fontaine, *Witches and Demons* (New York: Berghahn, 2016), 75–80, 96, 46, 81; Ørbulf Gulbrandsen, 'The Discourse of Ritual Murder: Popular Reaction to Political Leaders in Botswana' in Bruce Kapferer, ed., *Beyond Rationalism* (New York: Berghahn, 2002), 215–31.

25 https://twitter.com/leoigwe?lang=en; Egodi Uchendu, https://www.researchgate.net/publication/334114165; Cletus Ukpong, 'How Nigeria Can Gain from "Witchcraft" Conference – Organisers', *Premium Times* (26 November 2019) at https://www.premiumtimesng.com/news/more-news/365343-how-nigeria-can-gain-from-witchcraft-conference-organisers.html; 'The Sad Lessons I Learned from My Witchcraft Conference in 2019 – Prof Egodi', *The Authority* (22 January 2021) at https://authorityngr.com/2021/01/22/the-sad-lessons-i-learnt-from-my-witchcraft-conference-in-2019-prof-egodi/; 'UNN's Professor Uchendu: How "Witchcraft" Can Help Pastors!', *The News* (26 November 2019) at https://thenewsnigeria.com.ng/2019/11/26/unns-professor-uchendu-how-witchcraft-can-help-pastors/; Akeem Alaq, 'UNN: Nothing Stops the Conference on Witchcraft from Holding – Prof Egodi' (2019) at http://edugist.org/unn-nothing-stops-the-conference-on-witchcraft-from-holding-prof-egodi/; Chinedu Adonu, 'CAN Warns UNN Against Witchcraft Conference, Declares Prayer' (21 November 2019) at https://www.vanguardngr.com/2019/11/can-warns-unn-against-witchcraft-conference-declares-prayer/

26 'African Prelate Says Development, Not Denunciation, Is the Way to Fight Witchcraft', *Crux* (6 December 2019) at https://cruxnow.com/church-in-africa/2019/12/african-prelate-says-development-not-denunciation-way-to-fight-witchcraft; Ochereome Nnanna, 'Fr Kukah's Witness to Justice', *Vanguard* (6 November 2014) at https://www.vanguardngr.com/2014/11/fr-kukahs-witness-justice/

Chapter Thirteen
The Trial of Stormy Daniels:
Witchcraft in North America

1   https://www.thetrumparchive.com/

2   Matilda Joslyn Gage, *Woman, Church and State* (1893; Watertown, MA: Persephone Press, 1980), 105.

3   Charles Godfrey Leland, *Aradia* (London: David Nutt, 1899), 113.

4   Ronald Hutton, *The Triumph of the Moon* (Oxford: Oxford University Press, 1995), 205–52.

5   Tierney McAfee, 'A New Wife, Baby and Two Alleged Mistresses: Inside Donald Trump's World in 2006', *People* (7 March 2018) at https://people.com/politics/donald-trump-life-2006-stormy-daniels-affair/; Ben Schreckinger, 'When Trump Met Stormy Daniels: The Strange Story of Four Wild Days in Tahoe', *GQ* (22 March 2018) at https://www.gq.com/story/donald-trump-stormy-daniels-karen-mcdougal-tahoe-weekend; Natasha Stoynoff, 'Physically Attacked by Donald Trump – a PEOPLE Writer's Own Harrowing Story', *People* (12 October 2016) at https://people.com/politics/donald-trump-attacked-people-writer/

6   Samantha Schmidt and Lindsey Bever, 'Stormy Daniels Was Arrested and Accused of Touching Strip-Club Patrons. The Charges Were Dismissed',

Washington Post (12 July 2018) at https://www.washingtonpost.com/news/
morning-mix/wp/2018/07/12/stormy-daniels-is-arrested-at-an-ohio-strip-
club-michael avenatti-says/; Toby Luckhurst, 'Why the Stormy Daniels
– Donald Trump Story Matters', *BBC News* (3 May 2018) at https://www.
bbc.co.uk/news/world-us-canada-43334326

7   Heather Greene, 'Stormy Daniels' Religious Beliefs Under Scrutiny as
    Federal Trial Against Avenatti Begins', *Religion News Service* (24 January
    2022) at https://religionnews.com/2022/01/24/stormy-daniels-defends-
    her-religious-beliefs-as-federal-trial-against-avenatti-begins/; Thumper
    Forge, 'Stormy Justice (and Justice for Stormy)', *Fivefold Law* (21
    June 2021) at https://www.patheos.com/blogs/fivefoldlaw/2021/06/21/
    stormy-justice-and-justice-for-stormy/; Meghann M. Cuniff, '"I Am
    Truly Sorry": Michael Avenatti Asks for 3-Year Sentence in Stormy
    Daniels Fraud', *The Recorder* (20 May 2022) at https://www.law.com/
    therecorder/2022/05/20/i-am-truly-sorry-michael-avenatti-asks-for-3-
    year-sentence-in-stormy-daniels-fraud/?slreturn=20220701093526; Kara
    Scannell, 'Michael Avenatti Sentenced to 4 Years for Stealing Nearly $300K
    from Stormy Daniels', *CNN Politics* (2 June 2022) at https://edition.cnn.
    com/2022/06/02/politics/michael-avenatti-stormy-daniels-sentencing/index.
    html; Stormy Daniels tweet 7.21pm, 19 July 2021 at https://twitter.com/
    stormydaniels/status/1406316322611417089

8   Emily St James, '*Bewitched* Tweaked '60s Gender Roles and Became One
    of the First Feminist Sitcoms', *AV Club* (24 September 2012) at https://
    www.avclub.com/bewitched-tweaked-60s-gender-roles-and-became-one-
    of-t-1798233613; Sophie Moss, 'Culture Throwback: Thinking Back on
    How *Charmed* Captured Feminism', *LunaLuna* (23 November 2015) at
    http://www.lunalunamagazine.com/blog/culture-throwback-thinking-back-
    on-how-charmed-captured-contemporary-feminism

9   Cara Buckley and Melena Ryzik, 'Rose McGowan Attacks Ben Affleck
    Over Harvey Weinstein: "You Lie"', *New York Times* (10 October 2017)
    at https://www.nytimes.com/2017/10/10/movies/rose-mcgowan-ben-affleck-
    matt-damon-weinstein.html

10 Sandra E. Garcia, 'The Woman Who Created #MeToo Long Before
    Hashtags', *New York Times* (20 October 2017) at https://www.nytimes.
    com/2017/10/20/us/me-too-movement-tarana-burke.html

11 AP, 'Stormy Daniels Strips near White House as Trump Reveals Brett
    Kavanaugh as Pick for Supreme Court' (10 July 2018) at https://
    eu.usatoday.com/story/news/nation/2018/07/10/stormy-daniels-strips-
    nearby-trump-reveals-kavanaugh-court-pick/770535002/; Meredith B.
    Kile tweet (27 September 2018) at https://twitter.com/em_bee_kay/
    status/1045432500296634368; 'Tucker Carlson Likens Sexual Assault
    Survivors to an Unruly Mob Complaining About Demonic Possession
    in *The Crucible*' (25 September 2018) at https://www.mediamatters.org/
    tucker-carlson/tucker-carlson-likens-sexual-assault-survivors-unruly-mob-
    complaining-about-demonic

12 Alyssa Milano, 'Alyssa Milano on Witnessing the Kavanaugh Hearings and
    Our Government's War on Women', *Refinery29* (22 October 2018) at https:
    //www.refinery29.com/en-us/2018/10/214647/alyssa-milano-kavanaugh-
    supreme-court-abortion-laws-essay; Samuel Alito, '1st Draft, Supreme
    Court of the United States No. 19–1392' (Dobbs vs Jackson Women's
    Health Organization et al., 10 February 2022), 9–17, 24, 67; Deanna
    Pan, 'Who Was Matthew Hale, the 17th Century Jurist Alito Invokes in
    His Draft Overturning Roe?', *Boston Globe* (6 May 2022) at https://www.
    bostonglobe.com/2022/05/06/metro/who-was-matthew-hale-17th-century-
    jurist-alito-invokes-his-draft-overturning-roe/; Gilbert Geis and Ivan Bunn,
    A Trial of Witches (London: Routledge, 1997); Edward Coke, *The Third
    Part of the Institutes of the Laws of England* (1644; London, 1669), 44;
    Edmund Heward, *Matthew Hale* (London: Robert Hale, 1972), 71–87.

13 'Burials and Memorials', Department of Veterans' Affairs (25 April 2007)
    at https://www.cem.va.gov/hmm/emblems.asp

14 https://www.facebook.com/events/the-goat-new-orleans/spellbound-a-
    magickal-bazaar-w-tarot-by-stormy-daniels/178128680679827/; https://
    enchantments.nyc/

15 American Religious Identification Survey About ARIS – ARIS (trincoll.
    edu); Sean McShee, 'Estimating Growing Number of US Pagans' (9 January
    2019) at https://wildhunt.org/2019/01/estimating-growing-number-of-us-
    pagans.html; 'Religion by Visible Minority and Generation Status: Canada,
    Provinces and Territories . . .' at https://www150.statcan.gc.ca/t1/tbl1/en/
    tv.action?pid=9810034201

16 'About the Wiccan Church of Canada' at http://www.wiccanada.ca/about.
    html

17 Robin Levinson-King, 'Canada's Last Witch Trials: Women Accused
    of Fake Witchcraft' (30 October 2018) at https://www.bbc.co.uk/news/
    world-us-canada-45983540; Gabby Bess, 'Double, Double Trudeau and
    Trouble: Canada Legalizes Witchcraft', *Vice* (15 June 2017) at https://
    www.vice.com/en/article/xw8m8n/double-double-trudeau-and-trouble-
    canada-legalizes-witchcraft; Kristine Phillips, 'Canada Decriminalized Fake
    Witchcraft: But It Was Too Late for the "White Witch of the North"',
    National Post (20 December 2018) at https://nationalpost.com/news/canada/
    canada-decriminalized-fake-witchcraft-but-it-was-too-late-for-the-white-
    witch-of-the-north

18 Ewan Palmer, 'Pastor Greg Locke Threatens to Expose "Witches" in His Church
    in Viral Video' (15 February 2022) at https://www.newsweek.com/pastor-greg-
    locke-threatens-expose-witches-church-viral-video-1679331; Sarah Hughes,
    American Tabloid Media and the Satanic Panic 1970–2000 (London: Palgrave
    Macmillan, 2021); https://www.youtube.com/watch?v=Mp1Mm43pYzA;
    https://twitter.com/rightwingwatch/status/1441033387062571014; CNN,
    'Alleged Paul Pelosi Attacker Posted Multiple Conspiracy Theories' (28
    October 2022) at https://edition.cnn.com/2022/10/28/politics/pelosi-attack-
    suspect-conspiracy-theories-invs/index.html

19 Adrienne Drell, 'Witchcraft Murder Defence Fails', *ABA Journal* 79:5 (1993), 40; L.O. Aremu, 'Criminal Responsibility for Homicide in Nigeria and Supernatural Beliefs', *International and Comparative Law Quarterly* 29:1 (1980), 112–31; https://scholarship.law.cornell.edu/scr/vol3/iss1/10/

20 Naomi Blacklock, 'Conjuring Alterity', thesis, Queensland University of Technology, 2019, 25–6; Starhawk, *The Spiral Dance* (1979; San Francisco: HarperSanFrancisco, 1999), 31.

21 Allan Smith, 'Stormy Daniels Felt Her Life Was In Danger After Her "60 Minutes" Interview and Had Her Friend Record a Video of Her Final Will and Testament', *Business Insider* (1 October 2018) at https://www.businessinsider.com/stormy-daniels-book-full-disclosure-60-minutes-interview-2018-10?r=US&IR=T

22 Coco Khan, '"It Was My Most Terrifying Experience – and I've Seen Trump Naked!": Stormy Daniels on StandUp, Tarot and Reality TV', *Guardian* (27 January 2023) at https://www.theguardian.com/tv-and-radio/2023/jan/27/it-was-my-most-terrifying-experience-and-ive-seen-trump-naked-stormy-daniels-on-standup-tarot-and-reality-tv?CMP=Share_iOSApp_Other; https://twitter.com/StormyDaniels/status/1620921748727431169

Epilogue:
So, What is a Witch Now?

1 Conner Yearsley, 'The Murder of Guatemalan Maya Spiritual Guide Jesús Choc Yat', *HerbalGram*, 130, 39; James Siegel, *Naming the Witch* (Bloomington, Indiana: Stanford University Press, 2005); *Witchcraft Accusations and Persecution in Nepal* (WHRIN, 2014) at http://www.whrin.org/wp-content/uploads/2014/04/2480903_nepal_report_FINAL.pdf.

2 Kareem Shaheen, 'Isis Militants Behead Two Syrian Women for Witchcraft', *Guardian* (30 June 2015), 7; Colin Freeman, 'Inside Islamic State's New Stronghold in Libya', *Daily Telegraph* (18 January 2016), 4; 'Al-Qaeda in Yemen Claims Killing of Men over Witchcraft' (10 October 2015) at Aljazeera.com/news; 'Saudi Man Executed for "Witchcraft and Sorcery" (19 June 2012) at https://www.bbc.co.uk/news/world-middle-east-18503550.

3 Lord Laming, *The Victoria Climbié Inquiry* (2003) at https://www.gov.uk/government/publications/the-victoria-climbie-inquiry-report-of-an-inquiry-by-lord-laming 37.

Index

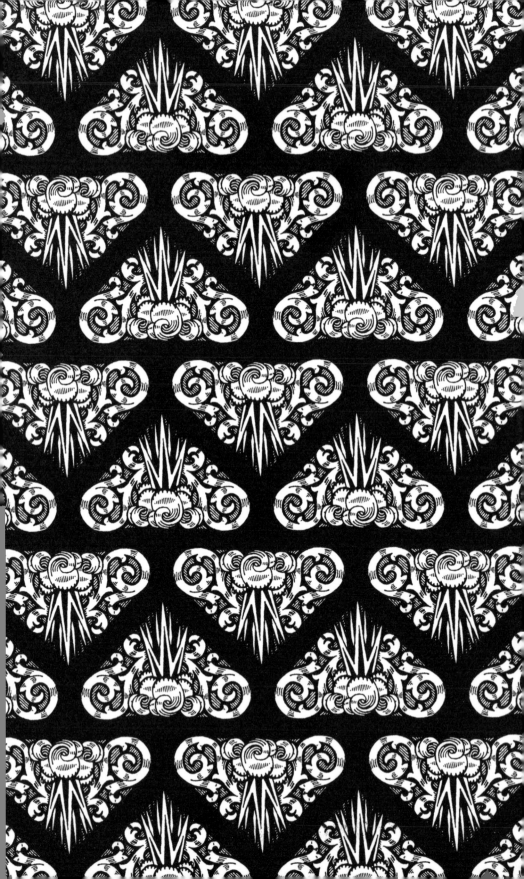